07883

Mercier Vega, Luis
Guerrilas in Latin America

Date Due

Guerrillas in
Latin America

Guerrillas in Latin America

The Technique of the Counter-State

LUIS MERCIER VEGA

Translated by
DANIEL WEISSBORT

FREDERICK A. PRAEGER, *Publishers*
New York · Washington · London

Frederick A. Praeger, Publishers
111 Fourth Avenue, New York, N.Y. 10003, U.S.A.

5 Cromwell Place, London SW7, England

Published in the United States of America in 1969
by Frederick A. Praeger, Inc., Publishers

ENGLISH TRANSLATION © 1969 IN LONDON,
ENGLAND, BY PALL MALL PRESS

Originally published by Editions Pierre Belfond,
Paris, as Technique du Contre-Etat

LIBRARY OF CONGRESS CATALOG CARD NUMBER: 70–83394

Printed in Great Britain

Contents

Contents

List of Abbreviations

AD   *Acción Democrática:* Democratic Action (Venezuela)

AD-COPEI Combination of AD and COPEI (Venezuela)

ALN   *Alianza de Liberación Nacional:* National Liberation Alliance (Peru)

APRA   *Alianza Popular Revolucionaria Americana:* Popular Revolutionary American Alliance (Peru)

CP   Communist Party

COPEI   *Comite de Organización Política Electoral Independiente:* Social Christian Party (Venezuela)

CPSU   Communist Party of the Soviet Union

CTV   *Confederación de Trabajadores de Venezuela:* Venezuelan Trades Union

ELN   *Ejército de Liberación Nacional:* National Liberation Army (Colombia)

FALN   *Fuerzas Armadas de Liberación Nacional:* Armed Forces of National Liberation (Venezuela)

FAR   *Fuerzas Armadas Revolucionarias:* Revolutionary Armed Forces (Guatemala)

FARC   *Fuerzas Armadas Revolucionarias de Colombia:* Colombian Revolutionary Armed Forces

FIR   *Frente Izquierda Revolucionaria:* Leftist Revolutionary Front (Peru)

FLN   *Frente de Liberación Nacional:* National Liberation Front (Peru and Venezuela)

FLN-FALN Combination of FLN, FALN, MIR, PCV and other groups (Venezuela)

FND   *Frente Nacional Democrático:* National Democratic Front (Venezuela)

GC   Peruvian political police

MIR   *Movimiento de la Izquierda Revolucionaria:* Leftist Revolutionary Movement (Peru and Venezuela)

Abbreviations

MNR	*Movimiento Nacional Revolucionario:* National Revolutionary Movement (Bolivia)
MOPOCO	*Movimiento Popular Colorado:* Colorado Popular Movement (dissident faction of Colorado Party (Paraguay))
MR 13	*Movimiento Revolucionario 13 de Noviembre:* Revolutionary Movement of 13 November (Guatemala)
OAS	Secret Army Organisation or Organisation of American States
OLAS	(Havana-inspired) Organisation of Latin American Solidarity
ORI	*Organizaciones Revolucionarias Integradas:* Integrated Revolutionary Organisations
PC	*Partido Comunista*
PCB	*Partido Comunista de Bolivia:* Bolivian Communist Party
PCC	*Partido Comunista de Chile/Colombia/Cuba:* Chilean/Colombian/Cuban Communist Party
PCP	*Partido Comunista del Paraguay:* Paraguayan Communist Party
PCV	*Partido Comunista de Venezuela:* Venezuelan Communist Party
PGT	*Partido Guatemalteco del Trabajo:* Guatemalan (Communist) Party of Labour
PIP	Peruvian political police
POR	*Partido Obrero Revolucionario:* (Trotskyist) Revolutionary Workers' Party (Bolivia)
URD	*Unión Democratica Republicana:* Democratic Republican Union (Venezuela)
YPFB	*Yacimientos Petrolíferos Fiscales Bolivianos:* Bolivian National Petroleum Co.

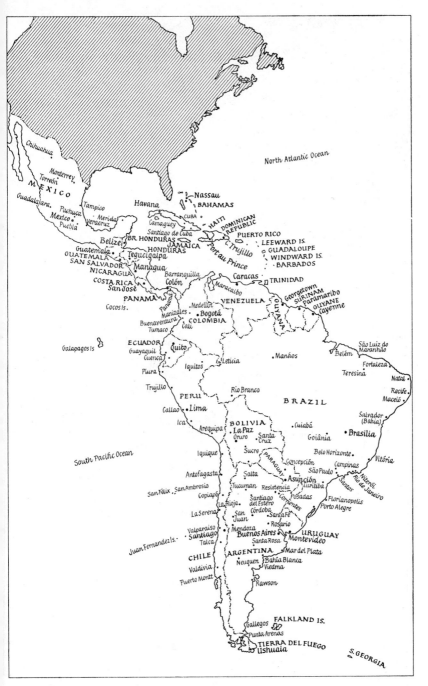

1. Political map of Central and South America

North Atlantic Ocean

Tropic of Cancer

Gulf of California

Gulf of Mexico

WEST

INDIES

Caribbean Sea

Lake Nicaragua

North Pacific Ocean

Magdalena

Llanos

Orinoco

Meta

Guaviare

Guiana Highlands

Putumayo

Negro

Equator

Japurá

Marañón

Javari

Juruá

Purús

Madeira

Tapajós

Xingu

Amazon

Araguaia

Tocantins

São Francisco

Sertão

10°

Lake Titicaca

Mato Grosso Plateau

Brazil Plateau

South Pacific Ocean

Pantanal

Gran

Chaco

Parnaíba

Paraguay

Entre Rios

Uruguay

Paraná

20°

Tropic of Capricorn

Salado

Plate

South Atlantic Ocean

Patagonia

Colorado

30°

Cape Horn

Land over 6,000 feet

40°   110°   100°   90°   80°   70°   60°   50°   40°   30°   20°

40°

30°

20°

10°

10°

20°

30°

2. Physical map of Central and South America

Introduction

THE WORD GUERRILLA signifies a type of warfare that is expressive both of a people's natural hostility to the state and its representatives, and the inability of that people to confront the state openly. The 'small war' reflects an incompatibility between rulers and ruled, a basic refusal of an important section at least of the inhabitants of a region to accept a position of subordination to a *de facto* authority. As this natural antagonism is denied either verbal or physical outlet in the everyday relations between those compelled to obey and the forces of coercion, it takes the form of brief and violent clashes wherever and whenever the usually powerless subject is able, however limitedly, to act. The more wholly his action expresses the profound feelings of a large majority of the population, the more identifiable, positive and significant it becomes.

History is rich in examples of guerrilla wars. It is not our intention here to differentiate between the various types, or to attempt a classification. Nevertheless, it should be pointed out that the term itself is used to describe phenomena resulting from extremely variable and frequently dissimilar circumstances and struggles. A strong national government wishing to integrate a particular region within its state system might encounter a local desire for autonomy and a will to resist. An army forced to abandon national territories might retain strong links with groups of partisans that have remained on the spot. On the other hand, in a period of conquest, an invading army might look for support among local groups representing a wide range of popular interests. The latter takes the opportunity of

I

opposing the imperialist or colonial power and acts, consciously or unconsciously, as the vanguard of the invasion forces. Malaysian rebels, Serbian or Greek maquis-fighters, Transvaal Boers, Philippine Huks, anti-Russian or anti-German Ukrainians, Kurds of Iran or Iraq, all stubbornly resisting great centralising thrusts, in spite of the bloody repressions that are the very condition for the survival of empires, provide one with innumerable fascinating examples, tragic enough to make one doubt the validity of the internationalist ethic, the inevitability of progress or the existence of such a thing as historical reason.

But our purpose here is to discover the real significance of the guerrilla wars of Latin America. In themselves, they embrace such a complex variety of cases and concepts that they require detailed study; it is impossible to make generalisations about them.

There is one state—Cuba—that claims to have been created by guerrilla warfare. There is also a theory, based on the Cuban experience, whereby this particular revolutionary method is seen as almost universally applicable throughout Latin America. Finally, there are a number of guerrilla groups in several regions of Latin America.

Our aim is to examine the nature and determine the size of these movements, then to place them in their international, continental and national contexts and finally to evaluate their rôle in the political and social transformation of the countries in question.

There is a copious literature on the guerrillas. A large part of it is propagandist, but there are also many dialectical writings. Books and pamphlets adopting anti-guerrilla positions are less plentiful, which is somewhat surprising in view of the fact that the Latin American press is, on the whole, openly and often violently opposed to guerrilla tactics.

There are, therefore, numerous and easily accessible sources whereby one can familiarise oneself with guerrilla 'ideas'. However, this plethora of written material holds a danger for the student: that of submerging him in a powerful environment, an almost watertight system that claims to provide a complete interpretation of events and of society.

On the other hand, information about the actual movements of guerrilla fighters is more scanty. Cables and official communiqués are short and unreliable. Reports often amount simply to panegyrics or vilifications. Reminiscences and memoirs have not yet been published, because of the relative youth of the guerrilla movement.

In order to arrive at as objective an understanding as possible of the future prospects of both the theory and practice of guerrilla warfare, we must try to establish a correct evaluation of the significance of the guerrilla factor in the political activity of each country and of the ability of each of the régimes that are being challenged to find the solution to its most acute problems. Clearly, the destruction of each and every guerrilla base by the police or army will not solve the essential problem, which is how to ensure that the peoples of Latin America join in the great movements of economic development and social integration that characterise the contemporary world.

In pro-guerrilla propagandist literature, the analysis of social problems is allotted only a little space. The tendency is rather to limit or even suppress altogether studies attempting to deal with class structure and relations. The call to arms is only likely to be heard if the opposing camps are clearly distinguishable from each other and apparently irreconcilable. Hence the extreme simplification in the presentation of political situations and definition of the forces to be overcome. All nuances, all elucidations of complex mechanisms are deliberately eschewed, as a detailed understanding, or simply an appreciation, of them would confuse the picture which must necessarily be kept simple.

The choice of guerrilla warfare implies the rejection of all other policies in which armed combat is only one among many means to be used, discontinued or employed in a limited way according to the circumstances. The refusal to analyse is in no way due to an inability to do so; it springs from a deliberate

3

decision that military considerations alone should henceforth underlie the public examination of the contradictions and tensions within the society which is to be overthrown. It is no longer a case of force being just one aspect of the struggle, as in other revolutionary traditions, but of all revolutionary effort being subsumed in the armed confrontation.

Propaganda, strike action, sabotage and assassination, all weapons whose use formerly depended on circumstances and opportunity, become means whose use is dictated for and by the guerrilla command.

Social change is seen through the perspective of a tiny power apparatus, dedicated to its own growth and to hardening itself in battle, until it is able to overcome and destroy the power of the government.

This conception is closer to a Counter-State than a Counter-Society, and it is here that its originality lies, as compared with the old classical definitions of the various types of socialist movements.

This process of introversion can be clearly discerned, whether in the writings of Che Guevara, Régis Debray, or in the proclamations, manifestos and theoretical material of the various guerrilla movements. While the guerrilla band concentrates within itself the most idealistic, clear-minded and determined elements of the nation and symbolises the qualities of the 'people', the power to be destroyed and superseded becomes an out-and-out enemy, utterly alien to the society it dominates. To strengthen this impression, propaganda will stress the government's dependence on a foreign power. In the final analysis, the actual character of the régime is unimportant: the Venezuelan parliamentary system is treated in the same way as the authoritarianism of the Bolivian army. There is no need to make use of politico-social analysis in drawing up this equation; on the contrary, it has more in common with the art of caricature, whereby a Leoni or Barrientos becomes quite simply a flunkey of North American imperialism.

There is no theoretical justification for this idea in any specific doctrine, even if its proponents lay claim to an intellectual tradition and argue that they have derived various formulas from it.

Apart from the use of a few stylistic devices, and a propensity to rely on the power of the state in shaping society, Marxist affinities do not mean much in Latin America, but to place oneself under the banner of Marxism-Leninism is rather more original. Even if it is conceivable that a Marxist should settle down to study the structure of society and production relations in Latin America—though, in actual fact, this has not happened —it is hard to see how Lenin's ideas can usefully be applied to Latin American problems. The fact is that the fierce pragmatists who call themselves partisans of the 'direct way' consider it essential to establish their spiritual or theoretical allegiance to Marx and Lenin. If quotations from the masters are of not much use to them, other 'Marxist-Leninists' often create difficulties in the realm of theory, and sometimes even in the field of action.

As regards over-all strategy, which is the chosen subject of the theoreticians of armed struggle, the international situation today is not as propitious as it might be. The partisans of guerrilla warfare hope for the establishment of numerous bases of rebellion throughout the Third World but particularly in Latin America. This would lead to the dispersal of the armed forces of the United States. The sapping of her military strength, the increase in unproductive expenses, the accumulation of economic burdens, the continually growing problem of raw material supplies, etc., would finally frustrate North American power in its struggle for world hegemony. Clearly, an attack on the part of hundreds of Lilliputians may theoretically bring down the giant. However, these Lilliputians must follow a common plan and co-ordinate their activities in order effectively to pierce the North American armour and weaken or neutralise its military potential. Or again, these centres of rebellion and resistance must co-ordinate their efforts with those of another great power, also with claims on world hegemony but unable to realise them without help from outside, which, under various forms, is waging war against Washington. In other words, the partisans of guerrilla warfare ought to be able to rely on the participation, if not the leadership, of the Soviet Union, or again on a strategy valid for the whole socialist camp.

Twenty or forty years after the heroic period of Soviet communism or of the Russian state, the theoreticians of guerrilla warfare have come up with the idea of world conflict, which is none other than the old dream abandoned by the Bolsheviks who have turned into bureaucrats. And as for new China, the very first attempts at co-operation reconfirm the truth of what has already been amply illustrated by the history of the Russian Revolution and the failure of the European revolutions, namely that state interests, even where the state in question is revolutionary and avowedly internationalist, take precedence in the present—which means permanently, as the present can be extended indefinitely—over the theoretically superior interests of world revolution.

The groups, fronts and parties ideologically in favour of armed combat split and quarrel among themselves when it comes to deciding on the right moment to initiate or take over the direction of the active struggle. The guerrillas themselves run into the reasons or state of the socialist camp and are held back rather than encouraged by the party machines, which represent the camp's local interests. Where the impetus is given by an already established régime, and where action favours the spreading of propaganda and means of rebellion, there is on the international level an immediate rupture with the logical beneficiary. Cuba is not supported by the Soviet Union in her generalised war and is unwilling to take orders from Mao Tse-tung's China.

Meanwhile, the guerrilla choice of an open confrontation with Washington and the challenge to the North American power in the field of strategy, which the latter considers of supreme importance, together with the rejection of the struggle for limited objectives, such as the elimination of the privileges or monopolies enjoyed by certain 'yankee' companies, produce a unified defensive reaction on the part of various interests in the United States, even though these interests are diverse, sometimes conflicting, and of differing degrees of importance to the State Department.

There is nothing left, therefore, but the faint hope, projected into a distant future and based upon doubtful geo-political considerations, of a potential revision in the international strategy of the Soviet Union or of communist China, a return to aggressive revolution, encouraged by the creation of numerous insurrectional bases within the United States' sphere of influence. Ernesto Guevara used to speak of 'two, three, four Vietnams . . . .'

Part I

Chemistry and Alchemy

I

Proclamations and Appeals

WHEN THE GUERRILLA feels the time has come for him to try
to reach the public through a proclamation or a message, he
has to use highly coloured language in order to convince it of
the intolerable nature of the prevailing social conditions
and the inevitability of a violent solution. Even if, up to then,
the signatories have been involved in movements or activities
with limited objectives, as soon as they have taken up arms,
they feel obliged to reject and condemn all forms of activity
that are not subordinate to the armed struggle.

What follows are three documents quoted *in extenso*. We hope
the reader will bear with us. They show the level of generalisation that guerrilla propagandists reach.

Here, first, is Camilo Torres, a former Catholic priest who,
in January 1966, sent a message 'from the mountains' to the
Colombian people, which was counter-signed by the representatives of the Army of National Liberation (ELN), Fabio
Vásquez Castaño and Víctor Medina Morón:[1]

For many years, the poor of our country have been waiting for the
word of command to throw themselves into the final struggle
against the oligarchy.

On each occasion, just as the people's despair was reaching its
limit, the ruling class found a way of duping, distracting, or pacify-
ing it with new formulas which always came down to the same thing:
suffering for the people and prosperity for the privileged caste.

When the people found a leader in Jorge Eliécer Gaitán,[2] the
oligarchy killed him. When the people wanted peace, the oligarchy applied force. When the people, unable any longer to endure

the régime, undertook guerrilla activity with the object of seizing power, the oligarchy contrived a military coup to trick the guerrillas into giving themselves up. When the people asked for democracy, the oligarchic dictatorship gave them a plebiscite and a national front.

The people will believe no more. The people no longer believe in elections. The people know that legal methods are exhausted. The people know that there can be recourse only to arms now. The people have been driven to their limits and are prepared to make the ultimate sacrifice, so that the next generation of Colombians shall not be a generation of slaves. So that the children of those who are now willing to sacrifice[2] their lives shall have education, shelter, food, clothing and, above all, DIGNITY. So that the Colombians of the future shall be masters in their own country, independent of the North American power.

Every genuine revolutionary must realise that armed conflict is the only way left. But the people are waiting for their leaders, who by their example and their presence will sound the call to arms.

I want to tell the Colombian people that the time has come, that I have not betrayed it, that I have travelled through town and village calling for unity, for the organisation of the common people in the struggle for power, for us to dedicate ourselves to the attainment of these ends even in the face of death.

Everything is ready. The oligarchy will be at its tricks again soon, with elections, with candidates vacating their seats and then going back on their decision; with bi-partisan committees; with a reform movement based on ideas and men who are not only old in years, but who have betrayed the people as well. Colombians, what else are we waiting for?

I have committed myself to armed struggle. I intend pursuing the struggle, gun in hand, in the mountains of Colombia, until the people's cause is triumphant. I have joined the National Liberation Army because I have found it imbued with the same ideas as the United Front. In it I have found an expression of the peasants' desire for and realisation of unity, without religious or traditional party differences, without the slightest tendency to oppose the revolutionary elements of any other sector, movement or party, without *caudillismo*.[3] It is seeking to free the people from the exploitation of oligarchies and of imperialism, it will not cease the struggle until power has passed entirely into the people's hands and its aims are consistent with the platform of the United Front. All Colombian patriots must put themselves on a war-footing. Gradually, experienced guerrilla leaders will emerge in all parts of the country. Meanwhile, we must remain on the alert. We must collect weapons and ammunition, train ourselves in guerrilla methods, contact those closest to us, make stocks of clothes, medical supplies and provisions, and prepare ourselves for a prolonged struggle.

Let us carry out these small tasks that are directed against the enemy and will ensure our victory; let us put those who call themselves revolutionaries to the test; let us rid ourselves of traitors; let us not cease our activities, but neither let us grow impatient. In a long drawn-out war, all will have to act when the time comes. What matters is that, at that precise moment, the revolution should find them ready and on guard. It is not necessary for everyone to do everything. We must divide the work. The militants of the United Front must be in the vanguard of the action. Let us wait patiently, full of confidence in our ultimate victory.

The people's struggle must be transformed into a national struggle. We have already begun, as there is a long day ahead of us.

Colombians: let us not fail to answer the people's and the revolution's call.

Militants of the United Front: let us turn our slogans into deeds.

We will fight to the death for the unity of the people!

We will fight to the death for the organisation of the people!

We will fight to the death for the conquest of power on behalf of the people! To the death, as we are determined to fight it out to a finish, until victory is ours, for a people that is willing to fight to the death must always triumph in the end!

To a triumphant conclusion, under the aegis of the National Liberation Army:

NOT A STEP BACKWARDS! LIBERATION OR DEATH!

Camilo Torres Restrepo.

One finds the same incisiveness, the same simplified description of a rejected society, the same vague definitions of those sections of the populace to which the guerrillas look for support in the National Liberation Army's proclamation, dated April 1967, at Nancahuazú, Bolivia:

13

Long is the history of poverty and suffering endured by our people. For hundreds of years, a steady stream of blood has gushed forth. Thousands upon thousands of mothers, wives, sons and daughters have shed tears in abundance. Heroic patriots whose lives were cut off are numbered in their thousands.

The men of this land have lived and still live as strangers in their own country; any yankee imperialist possesses more rights on the national territory that he calls his 'concessions': he can raze to the ground, destroy and burn Bolivian homes, crops and goods. Our lands do not belong to us; our natural wealth has served and still serves to enrich foreigners who leave only empty mines and deep cavities in the lungs of Bolivians. There are no schools, no hospitals for our sons; our living conditions are wretched, salaries and wages at a famine level. Thousands of men, women and children starve to death each year; the poverty in which the peasant in the field lives and works is appalling. In other words, we live like slaves, our rights and gains nullified and trampled under foot.

In May 1965, before the horrified eyes of the whole world, wages were reduced, workers sacked, imprisoned, exiled, massacred, and camps full of defenceless women and children shelled and sacked.

But if that is a fair description of our life, our people is a people that has fought, is fighting and that has never given in. How many heroes have there been among the miners, peasants, workers, teachers, professional men and students, our glorious youth, who have written glorious pages of our history in their blood?

Before our eyes and the eyes of the world rise the legendary figures of Padilla, Lanza, Méndez, Zudánez, Ravelo, Murillo, Tupac Amaru, Warnes, Arze; and also the incomparable heroines of La Coronilla, Juana Azurduy de Padilla, Bartolina Sisa, Vicenta Eguino, Simona Manzaneda—hundreds of men and women whose glorious example is cherished by our heroic people, ready to follow it.

If former generations fought hard for fifteen years to build a free and sovereign homeland, ridding our soil of the foreign master, in a few years new capitalist powers stuck their claws into the country created by Bolívar and Sucre. Peasants brutally murdered, from the foundation of the Republic up to the present, are numbered in their thousands, as are miners and workers whose demands were met with gunfire. And also in their thousands are numbered those 'valiant' generals and colonels who earned their promotion and their rank in this unequal contest, machine-gunning and shelling the defenceless people, whose only weapon, at times, was the invincible proud barrier of its own dauntless breast!

The memory of massacres, crimes and inflictions suffered by the Bolivian people remains fresh in our minds. Messrs Sbirrï[4] whether you are generals or not, yankee imperialists, your claws and fangs are dripping with the blood of the Bolivian people and now your end has come. Now the National Liberation Army is rising out of the pools of blood you have shed, the ashes of those thousands of patriots that you murdered, persecuted, imprisoned or sent into exile. Men of the fields and the towns, of the mines and the factories, of the colleges and universities, boldly take up arms. Tremble, murderers, for your end is at hand, and the voice of Justice, Welfare and Liberty for the Bolivian people is resounding invincibly in mountain and valley, on the peaks and in the forests!

Now that you have felt the first tremors, generals, call your mothers and your children to you; we also are sorry for them. But perhaps you imagined that those thousands of peasants, miners, workers, teachers and students did not have children, mothers and wives—those whom you murdered pitilessly in the streets of Catavi, Cerdas, Villa Victoria, El Alto, La Paz, Milluni, Siglo Veinte.

The ruling clique and its yankee imperialist boss are trembling in fear as the violence of battle begins; they struggle like wild beasts at bay, increasing the persecution, committing still more heinous crimes and violating the so-called democratic constitution that they have sworn to respect. Their anti-guerrilla hysteria leads them to ban left-wing political parties, as though it were possible to kill ideas through decrees. They prosecute, imprison and murder (they call it 'suicide') free citizens accused of being *guerrilleros*. They arrest and torture foreign journalists on the pretext of their being *guerrilleros*; they fabricate slanderous stories and their propaganda is interwoven with such ludicrous lies that the people holds them in contempt. This and every other attempt to stifle the guerrilla movement will fail, just as will every stratagem to hold on to power. Their end, as the ruling class, has come.

In our fight against thievery, corruption, injustice, against the crimes and prebends that profit a few, in our creation of a new classless society where justice will reign, with equal rights and duties for all, where the natural wealth will be exploited by the people and for the benefit of the people, many lives of officers and soldiers, useful to the country, will alas be lost, for it is quite clear that not all those sent into battle share the views of the pro-yankee clique in power. We ask all patriots, officers and soldiers to lay down their arms. We ask the glorious youth of the country to resist induction into the army. We ask the mothers to see that their sons are not sacrificed for the defence of a clique that has sold out to the foreign dollar, that surrenders our richest resources to voracious yankee imperialism.

The National Liberation Army calls on the Bolivian people to come together, forge a solid united front without distinction as to political shade or colour; it calls on those patriots who are in a position to do something and feel able to withstand the hard conditions of the battle to enter its ranks. It is also possible to help from the outside; there are thousands of ways of doing this and the creative genius of the people will uncover them in all their variety, from the smallest group of friends to the most audacious deeds. The main thing is to *organise ourselves* and to make the Bolivian soil tremble under the feet of the ruling clique and its yankee imperialist boss.

We are warning the people that yankee imperialism, in order to keep its hold on our country, will make use of new generals and new civilians, and even pseudo-revolutionaries, who will be replaced in their turn. We must guard against being taken by surprise and duped as has happened throughout our history. This time the battle has begun and will end only with self-rule by the people and the eradication of foreign domination.

The National Liberation Army hereby pledges itself to fulfilling the ideals of the people and, in due course, to punishing the present oppressor, torturer, informer and traitor, all those that are, with impunity, wronging the poor. The civil defence organisations are in the process of being formed. Secret people's courts will begin to function, to pass sentence and to punish.

Finally, the National Liberation Army expresses its faith, confidence and certainty in a conclusive and total victory over the ruling clique, its yankee imperialist masters, the invaders disguised as advisers, whether yankee or not. We shall neither cease our efforts, nor rest until the last portion of our land has been freed from imperialist domination, until we see a new age of contentment, progress and happiness dawning over the glorious Bolivian people.

Let us die rather than live as slaves!

Long live the guerrillas!
Death to yankee imperialism and its military clique!
Freedom for all patriots under restriction and in prison!

The revolutionary proclamation to the Peruvian people, signed, in July 1965, by Luis de la Puente Uceda, as general secretary of the MIR (Movement of the Revolutionary Left), Guillermo Lobatón, commander of the Central guerrilla zone, Ricardo Gadea, commander of the Southern zone, and Gonzalo Fernández Gasco, commander of the Northern zone, summarises the Peruvian situation. It is an attempt to influence political opinion on a national level, rather than the people specifically of those districts where the guerrillas are about to try to establish themselves. It is more like an attempt to vindicate the chosen tactics of the MIR than an appeal to the peasants:

From the unconquered mountains of Peru, the cradle and principal centre of our great pre-Hispanic civilisation, the armed MIR sends forth its revolutionary clarion call, its message of faith and summons to battle.

Our country is living through the most savage period of its history.

We are in the forefront among the nations of the world as regards hunger and malnutrition.

Our people succumb easily to endemic diseases.

Infant mortality is assuming alarming proportions.

Our average national standard of living is one of the lowest in the world.

The living conditions of the masses, in the towns and in the countryside, are really sub-human.

The Peruvian environment is fairly represented by the outer suburbs and the slum streets of the towns, by hovels built out of stones, dried mud and straw in the countryside.

We are a people that goes bare-footed and in rags.

Wages in town and, even more so, in the countryside are wretched.

The cost of living rises and the value of our money falls, so that real wages decline or remain static, despite the absurd rises manual and officer workers manage to obtain for themselves through hard economic struggles.

Unemployment and under-employment affect the majority of the population.

Begging is an institution in our country.

Poverty has in certain regions reached a stage where thousands of peasants have to sell their children or give them away to be spared the sight of them dying of hunger at home.

Our cultural level is abysmal.

Illiteracy is the lot of two-thirds of the population.

Nearly two million children do not go to school.

Secondary, technical and university education is a privilege.

Law and justice remain a dead letter, as the entire administration and judiciary is in the pay of the oligarchs.

The human dignity of the humble is continually abused.

Bourgeois freedom, without equality of means or opportunity simply means freedom for the exploiters.

Representative democracy represents only the privileged classes.

The parliamentary system is simply a caricature of popular sovereignty and serves only the ends of the exploiters.

Popular suffrage is a farce, because the oligarchs and their servants control the electoral machine and the majority of the people is prevented from voting.

The feudal-bourgeois state keeps our people in subjugation by all possible means in order to pursue the interests of imperialism, of the landlords and wealthy bourgeoisie.

Massacres of peasants, workers and students and repressions directed against militants and leaders of the left have become institutionalised. The people have shed much blood, there has been and will continue to be much suffering and weeping throughout the land.

The slaughterers, murderers, torturers of the Peruvian people are rewarded and promoted.

The moral crisis within the system becomes increasingly more severe.

Moral values are in a critical state.

Administrative corruption is assuming unbelievable proportions.

Maladministration is the surest and fastest way of becoming rich.

The bribe opens all doors.

The law, civil service, public offices, promotions, university and college entrances, etc., are manipulated by the highest bidders.

Money, whatever its origin, opens all doors and is the ladder to success in every career.

Flattery, servility and unscrupulousness are the key to success.

The crisis of confidence is assuming huge proportions in the minds of our people.

This is how the people see it: *Peru is lost and nothing and nobody can save it!*

Our youth is living through a very serious crisis because of the lack of prospects, of possibilities, because of the confusion reigning everywhere, the pollution of the political atmosphere.

Prostitution, sexual perversion, drug addiction and many other vices and signs of degeneracy are becoming more widespread and affecting society at all levels.

Delinquency is increasing day by day and the offences that are committed shock public opinion; the reason for them lies in the injustice permeating the economic and social structure, and the example of corruption and unpunished delinquency set by the privileged classes or the holders of power.

Every day imperialism strengthens its grip.

Our national riches have been handed over to yankee monopolies.

The misappropriation of mines, land, industries, transportation, trade, banks etc., continues at an increasing pace.

Through the system of loans, our country is finding itself mortgaged or sold to the imperialist master.

All national activities, such as education, agriculture, medical care, post and telegraphs, production, trade union organisation, the press, national defence, politics, etc., are permeated, controlled and run by imperialist bodies.

The semi-feudal régime impregnates the whole of the national life.

No limit is set to the accumulation of land.

Empiricism and large-scale cultivation of crops predominate on the big estates and generally in agriculture.

The political and judicial authorities, water boards, etc., favour the large landowners at the expense of the peasantry.

Hunger, exploitation and ignorance, perpetuated by the large landowners, ensure a regular supply of labourers to the mines, of agricultural workers to the coastal estates, and of workers to the urban factories.

The capitalist system and imperialist domination coalesce in the feudal structure of agriculture.

The upper-middle-class, whose wealth comes from landed property and the misappropriation of public funds, flourishes under the aegis of imperialism and on the basis of the feudal system.

The large industrial enterprises, the agricultural estates of the coast, the banks, the insurance companies, external and internal trade—particularly the wholesale side of it—transport, etc., are monopolised by small intermeshed groups that have control over the whole or a part of the apparatus of power, in collusion with the landowners and under the aegis of the empire.

The national bourgeoisie is powerless, shackled by the monopolistic upper-middle-class, the large landowners and imperialism.

The limitations of our internal market, the competition of foreign imports, the restrictions and scheming of all the credit institutions and the absence of state protection, etc., are at the basis of the stagnation of national industry, or its gradual plundering to the advantage of monopolistic capitalism or imperialism.

The petty bourgeoisie, composed of small and medium sized landowners, businessmen, industrialists, importers, artisans, teachers, students, etc., is becoming progressively impoverished, potential areas of development are blocked and it is oppressed by the large landowners, wealthy bourgeoisie and imperialists.

The intellectuals, professional people and technicians vegetate or are obliged to work for the oligarchy and imperialism, as the possibilities of making a patriotic contribution to the progress of the country are very limited.

The peasantry, numbering six or seven million, is the largest and most deprived class in Peru; it forms the basis of the social pyramid and is exploited, abused and subjected to all manner of sufferings.

The working class, originating in a peasantry stripped of its land and the impoverished section of the lower-middle class, is subject to bourgeois and imperialist exploitation; it receives famine wages employment is restricted and the unemployed or under-employed population swell the labour pool, thereby tending to bring wages down.

In addition, bureaucratic leaders and traitors to the working-class restrict its struggle and slow down the process whereby it becomes the class-conscious vanguard of the revolution.

This summary analysis suggests that what we are faced by is a national crisis of the utmost importance.

Who can deny that our country is on the brink of disaster, that bankruptcy is staring it in the face, that, despite all palliatives, all attempts to smooth things over and all the propaganda, the country, as a whole, is poised over the abyss?

History presents us with an inescapable dilemma: *either we accept our duty as Peruvians, our mission to save the country, whatever the sacrifice called for, or we become accomplices, whether active or passive, in that vile process that is imperceptibly destroying the fabric of our nation.*

Many are those that will chose the easier way, the way of indifference, that which consists in swimming with the tide, in leeting everything go to blazes, provided one is alright oneself. This is the way of individualism, egotism, shallowness of mind, cowardice, passive acceptance of privilege, betrayal of the sacred destiny of our homeland.

We, members of the Movement of the Revolutionary Left, in concordance with our resolutionary ideology and duty, accept our historical responsibility and summon all the exploited to battle, fully confident that our people will respond with heroism, at first collaborating and then engaging actively in the struggle, in order to conquer power and build a new Peru for all Peruvians.

As a genuine revolutionary movement, we have rejected the paths of compromise and negotiation with the exploiters, we have rejected bourgeois electoral methods, as we have no intention of playing the oligarchs' game; we have avoided throwing the unarmed masses into battle, in the countryside as well as in the towns, as still less do we want the hired assassins of the régime to be allowed to shed worker or peasant blood with impunity; and we have abandoned the traditional bureaucratic method of work with the masses, a method that has gradually turned into a mere pastime, serving to confuse the issue, resulting in a series of failures and providing a pretext for the usual political chicanery.

As a genuine revolutionary movement, we have chosen the path of armed struggle, knowing it to be the most difficult, the one that calls for the greatest sacrifices, the one that most infuriates the oligarchy and imperialism, but at the same time the one that constitutes the highest form of the popular struggle, the one that shatters the scepticism, fear and deception that have afflicted the masses, the one that brings out all the positive qualities of the nation at present submerged under corruption, exploitation and injustice, the one that restores the feeling of national pride and of

21

confidence in the greatness of the national past and its prosperous future and that leads inevitably to power.

As a genuine revolutionary movement, we are not driving the masses into battle, but we are urging them to strengthen their ideological and class consciousness in the heat of battle.

We are not leading our Movement, nor would we attempt to lead the masses, from the comfort of some office far removed from the scene of battle. The leaders of our Movement and its best cadres are in the field, learning and teaching, urging on the process and enriching their own experience, inspiring people with the spirit of idealism and sacrifice and forging real folk leaders. At the same time, our cadres and militants in the towns are helping at this particular stage, in the development of the process of armed struggle in the countryside, and are gathering their strength towards the fulfilment of new tasks in subsequent stages, working secretly, illegally, as well as openly.

Initially, we have chosen guerrilla warfare in the mountains, and we have already established three guerrilla zones in the North, the Centre and the South where we are ready to face any kind and any size of army that tries to repress us.

For the first time in the history of our country we shall show that it is possible to defeat the forces of repression of the oligarchy and of imperialism by making use of guerrilla strategy and tactics, and with the growing support of the peasantry, the working class and the progressive sections of the lower-middle-class and the national bourgeoisie.

The banners of freedom, justice and national salvation are raised high, and borne by the strong hands of those whose spirit is dauntless and whose conscience is clear, so that no mercenary will ever succeed in laying hands on them.

We are certain that many of our brothers will follow the path we are opening up and that, in the near future, the freedom songs of hundreds of guerrilla groups, their rifle shots, will be ringing through the country, giving birth to a Rebel Army, and that thousands of workers, peasants and students will join in the struggle, making use of all forms of popular warefare, until the oligarchy's armies have disintegrated and are in full flight, power has been seized and the nation liberated.

We are well aware that the police, the army, the navy and the air force are composed basically of workers and peasants and lower-middle-class elements, and, with the exception of small groups of high-ranking officers, that they form part and parcel of the people. We appreciate the deception to which they are victim, but we are convinced that armed struggle, popular pressure and ideological propaganda will make them realise that the homeland we are defending is their own, that it is the real homeland, that the enemies we are fighting are their enemies and the ones who are responsible for all the misfortunes of Peru, that the battle we are waging is being fought for them, their humble kith and kin, for their children's future, for the poor, for the real homeland.

As a genuine revolutionary movement, we are able to put our country, America and the world into perspective. We realise that the greatest scourge of the peoples of the earth is North American imperialism and that our country's wealthy bourgeoisie and land-owners debase themselves in the slavish pursuit of its interests and are there to exploit the people and keep it in a state of poverty and backwardness. The Revolution we are starting will, therefore, be the work of peasants, workers and the progressive and patriotic sections of the petty bourgeoisie and the national bourgeoisie, under the leadership of the Revolutionary Party which must be forged in the struggle and of which the MIR is a component part.

The National and Popular Revolution that we are starting is directed against the three great enemies of the people: imperialism, the landowners and the wealthy bourgeoisie.

Our revolutionary process is getting under way at a time when the world is passing through the most revolutionary phase in its history, when the colonialist chains are being snapped throughout Asia and Africa, when the socialist world is expanding and growing stronger, when the struggle for the liberation of the peoples is reaching its climax in all the continents, as is shown by Vietnam in Asia and Colombia and Guatemala in America, to name only the most sigificant cases, and when imperialism, hounded on all sides and a victim of its own growing contradictions, is adopting an attitude of barefaced aggression towards the peoples, as in Vietnam and the Dominican Republic.

Our revolutionary process is getting under way at a moment when all the contradictions of the present régime are reaching a critical stage, when the bourgeois government, concession by con-cession, finds itself utterly enslaved to the oligarchy and imperialism, when it slaughters peasants and workers to an extent that no previous government has ever done, allows the administration to become more and more corrupt, raises the cost of living to an intolerable level, persecutes all sections of the left and chiefly the militants and leaders of the MIR, shamelessly mortgages our country up to the hilt and tries to deceive our people with public works that, first and last, benefit the landowners, the wealthy bourgeoisie and imperialism.

Our revolutionary process is getting under way at a time when the bourgeois parties like APRA and *Acción Popular* are in a critical condition—in that it is becoming clear, within their own ranks and as far as public opinion in general is concerned, that their principles and electoral programs have been completely abandoned by the treacherous leadership of the parties—and when the supposedly left wing parties are suffering the fatal consequences of their own blind actions.

Finally, our revolutionary process is getting under way at a time when our peasantry grows conscious of its rights on a national scale; when it has acquired experience in the different types of struggle and is determined to win its complete freedom; when our manual and office workers are tearing off the blindfolds that stop them seeing the way and following the light; when the young in our secondary schools and universities are strengthening their revolutionary conscience and taking an increasingly active part in the peoples' struggles; and when the progressive sections of the petty bourgeoisie and the national bourgeoisie—who believed more strongly than any others in change through electoral and peaceful means and who have been cruelly disillusioned—are becoming aware that there is only one way left.

In these historical circumstances, the MIR is initiating the armed struggle on several fronts, in our mountains, raising aloft the banners of national liberation, of genuine social justice and of real democracy; it is turning itself into the armed vanguard of the people and summoning all the exploited to take part in this historical process, in whatever way they can.

The MIR, gun in hand, and in the certainty that it is speaking for our people, demands:

1. *The immediate dissolution of Parliament*, because, with a few rare exceptions, it is the refuge of landowners, wealthy bourgeois and lackeys of imperialism; because it has impeded all attempts to reform the structural injustices of the country; because it is a burden

on the national budget and consequently on the people; because it has demonstrated its uselessness and is also a totally negative element as regards the national interest and the interest of the people.

2. *A general amnesty* and freedom for all prisoners charged with political and social offences, and severe and immediate punishment of all those, whether civilian or military, responsible for the massacres of the people that have taken place in recent years.

3. *Genuine agrarian reform:*
—the final and total elimination of large-scale landownership, through the immediate and unconditional return of landed property to the peasants that work it;
—the immediate devolution of all the lands stolen from the indigenous communities and, at the same time, the payment of suitable indemnities against the damage done and the unlawful profits made;
—the immediate nullification of all pre-capitalist agrarian contracts, and the payment of suitable indemnities to the peasant victims of servile exploitation, based on the different restrictive clauses of payment in work.
—the appropriation of the latifundia, the large agricultural and stock-farming estates of the coast, the Sierra and the forest, including among the beneficiaries of the division or collective assignment the peasant groups dependent on the properties to be distributed, which are not to be above medium-sized.
—an exception to be made for the medium and small landowners who work their own land and contribute to its development, looking after their interests and helping them to increase the productivity of the land and of labour;
—priority attention to be given by state organs to all aspects of peasant work and life, so that the process of agricultural transformation should be co-ordinated.

4. *A living wage based on family needs* and tied to the cost of living, for workers, civil servants and business people, professional people and technicians.

5. *Urban reform,* to eliminate housing monopolies and their attendant abuses, to turn the present tenants into owners, making an exception for the small and medium house owners, who will receive special treatment.

6. *The immediate recovery of Peruvian oil,* with mandatory payment of indemnities against the illegal profits made by the 'International

Petroleum Co.', the revision and annulment of contracts affecting our national riches and made with imperialist enterprises such as the Marcona, Toquepala, Le Tourneau Companies, etc.

7. *The recovery of full National Sovereignty*, casting off the yoke of imperialism, expelling all the 'advisers' and other civil or military agents of the Empire, cancelling all the treaties and agreements that are compromising our national independence and our sovereignty, and establishing diplomatic, commercial and cultural relations with all the countries of the world.

The Movement of the Revolutionary Left is fully conscious of the historical process it is setting in motion; it understands the extent of its enemies' unscrupulousness and savagery; it is aware of the great difficulties and obstacles that it will meet with on the way, but, at the same time, it is more than ever convinced that the people is with it, that History and time are on its side, and it is absolutely confident that courage and heroism will manifest themselves to an extent unhoped for and hitherto unknown, that the battle will spread like a torch carried by the Chaco runners of ages past, by way of mountain, forest, plain, valley, desert, roads, suburb and town, until the time has come for the seizure of power.

The Movement of the Revolutionary Left declares war on behalf of all the people of Peru and assures you that our cause is invincible, that the future of our country is at stake, that doubt, fear or deceit must be cast aside, that all of us must take part, to the best of our abilities, and in a planned and disciplined manner, in this movement of national redemption.

The Movement of the Revolutionary Left calls upon the peasants, workers, students, intellectuals, small and medium landowners, businessmen and industrialists, artisans, office workers, rural and urban teachers, the honest soldiers, NCOs and officers of our armed forces, to form a large, single, anti-oligarchic and anti-imperialist Front in this struggle.

The Movement of the Revolutionary Left directs its insurrectionist appeal to the heroic, victimised Aprista masses, betrayed by traffickers, dealers and degenerates, who are serving as the henchmen of the oligarchy and imperialism and who, for over twenty years, during the course of a struggle full of hope, have paid no heed to the blood, anguish and tears of the Aprista people; and to the masses of Acción Popular, also betrayed by those who initially set themselves up as the standard-bearers of the 'anti-compromise' movement, that is as the opponents of the unholy alliance between APRA and the ultra-reactionary sections of the community, and who gradually followed their example, linked themselves with them wholeheartedly and worked for them by butchering the people more savagely than ever before, by mortgaging the country, at the same time disguising their true intent with demagogic gestures and placatory noises. We appeal to the workers, peasants, students, professional men of the middle ranks of APRA and *Acción Popular*, who have not been corrupted by the cliques that lead them, by intimidation, by the abandonment of principles and defeatism, to join in the struggle; the Revolution they were waiting for has begun and all the exploited and all true Peruvians will play their part in it.

The Movement of the Revolutionary Left adjures the parties of the left to express their ideological convictions in action, to forsake the paths of compromise, of procrastination, of political chicanery and subjectivism; it adjures them to put aside egotism and low scheming, so that they should not miss the boat of History in America once again. We are calling upon all for unity in action, for unity as a process in itself, for genuine revolutionary unity to create the great party of the Peruvian Revolution.

Finally, the Movement of the Revolutionary Left, weapon in hand, from the heart of the mountains, calls upon all revolutionaries, all patriots, all the exploited to join with it in flinging wide the gates of History.

Only battle will make us free!
Only liberation will restore to us our dignity!
Long live the Peruvian Revolution!
We shall conquer!

The most striking feature of the Peruvian and Colombian appeals is the high-flown, classless tone of argument; they evince a longing for immaculacy and purity, a rejection of repugnant political methods and the hypocrisy of the privileged and they reflect exasperation at the feuds and wranglings within the left itself. There is a symbolic air about these appeals 'from the mountains' and an adolescent feeling about the rejection of urban niceties and the platitudinous quality of society as it is.

Although most of the leading spirits of the guerrilla groups consider or call themselves Marxists, none of the appeals gives evidence of any real attempt to understand the structure of society and how this affects politics. There is nothing but a pot-pourri of generalised formulas. And if by chance a few paragraphs that seem to come to closer grips with reality are inserted, as in the Peruvian text, the confusion is, if anything, compounded, for how can one explain the growth of a wealthy bourgeoisie on a feudal basis? And where does one draw the line between the national and the monopoly bourgeoisies?

No doubt this imprecision makes it easier to appeal to the most diverse social strata and interests, by employing patriotic phrases, but it makes it more difficult—even for the guerrilla leaders themselves—to understand the main thrusts of complex and evolving societies like those of Peru, Bolivia or Colombia.

It is only in respect to foreign imperialism, a kind of common denominator, that the 'bundle' of mutually antagonistic groups and classes, all tied up in the national colours, takes on any semblance of unity. This makes for good propaganda, but bears only the remotest resemblance to an analytical treatment, whether Marxist or otherwise.

As regards the exploited classes—workers and peasants—the language used is more that of pity and indignation than what one would expect from organisations conscious of their social rôle and of their desire for real emancipation. Neither the vocabulary nor the slogans bear the stamp of the workers' or peasants' mentality. The text can only be the work of young intellectuals spelling out all the grievances, their own and those of the exploited classes, that can be laid at the doors of an unjust society.

Only the Bolivian appeal seems to follow some pre-defined plan. Although it is couched in cruder terms, it is more tightly 'constructed' than the others. It is more closely related to the idea of guerrilla warfare as a technique for the capture of power, at one and the same time agent and instrument, head and arm or, more precisely, a government in embryo.

2

Theoretical Difficulties

'ABOVE ALL', writes Ernesto Che Guevara,[1] 'it must be made quite clear that this type of struggle—guerrilla warfare—is a means; a means towards an end. This end, which is inescapable, inevitable for all revolutionaries, is the conquest of political power.'

In the same pamphlet, set out in note form, Guevara begins by rejecting the opposition between guerrilla warfare and mass warfare, since 'guerrilla war is the people's war. To try to carry on this type of warfare without the support of the population is to court inevitable disaster'.

After that, Guevara specifies three basic contributions made by the Cuban Revolution to the 'mechanics' of the revolutionary movements in Latin America:

1. the popular forces are capable of winning a war against the army; 2. it is not always necessary to wait for all the revolutionary conditions to be fulfilled: these can be created by the insurrectionist base itself; 3. in the under-developed parts of the Americas, the battle is fought principally in the countryside, the *campo*. Referring to the Second Havana Declaration, Che recalls that, in Latin America, the rural population has harder living conditions than the town workers; that this population forms a majority; that it constitutes a huge potential revolutionary force. The armies, for their part, are trained and equipped for conventional warfare and are impotent in trying to handle the particular kind of combat waged by the peasants, fighting in surroundings they know intimately. The small fighting units receive a constant supply

29

of fresh recruits, and the old order disintegrates. It is then that the working class and the urban masses enter the picture and determine the final outcome of the battle. It is the people's support that makes the initial groups invincible, right from the start, however disproportionate the numbers, strength and resources of the two sides. Nevertheless, the uncultivated and isolated peasant class needs the political guidance of the working class and of the revolutionary intellectuals. The national bourgeoisie, in Latin America, is disqualified from assuming the leadership of the anti-feudal and anti-imperialist struggle by its inefficiency and its fear of social revolution.

Guevara, therefore, considers revolution to be inevitable—and he quotes other passages from the Second Havana Declaration to back up this contention—because the living conditions of the Latin American are intolerable, because the revolutionary conscience of the masses is developing, because world imperialism is in a critical state and because the movement of the subjugated peoples of the world is now universal. The main problem is the organisation and leadership of the revolution.

Peaceful means are not to be rejected *a priori*. It is quite in order, when there is a choice between various tactics, for a theoretical discussion to take place which is instrumental in actual decision-making. But history makes no allowance for mistakes and the vanguard is recognisable by its position of leadership of the working class in the latter's quest for power, taking short cuts when necessary. Latin America is, moreover, precariously poised between oligarchic dictatorship and popular pressure. In the struggle for certain bourgeois freedoms, the essentials must not be forgotten, in so far as bourgeois legality merely masks the class character of the state, and the only valid struggle is that which envisages revolutionary power.

The rôle of force, therefore, is of prime importance; it is the midwife of the new societies. Force must be applied 'at precisely that moment when the people's leadership considers the circumstances most favourable'. In this respect the two relevant criteria are consciousness of the need for change and certainty of the possibility of affecting a change.

30

The idea that armed struggle must assume a purely defensive character is a mistake to be avoided. Guerrilla warfare is not passive self-defence; it is a kind of forward defence whose ultimate end is the conquest of political power.

What is of crucial importance is to force the class dictatorship to drop its disguise and show itself in its true colours, as an instrument of repression. 'The oligarchy-popular pressure equilibrium must be destroyed', says Guevara. And there must be no let-up, as a revolution that does not advance is a revolution that retreats. Battle fatigue and loss of faith facilitate pseudo-democratic exercises more easily acceptable than openly reactionary coups.

Another danger lies in trying to maintain conditions favourable to revolutionary action for as long as possible, by taking advantage of certain facilities offered by bourgeois legality. Too many leaders of progressive organisations have ended up by losing sight of the real objective: the conquest of power.

Why do present conditions seem to indicate that guerrilla warfare is the right course for Latin America? Che puts forward a number of reasons. First of all, if one can logically assume that the enemy will employ force to keep himself in power, it is obviously necessary to possess a people's army to oppose and destroy the forces of repression—and only long and hard practical experience can produce such a people's army. It springs to life and is nurtured in peasant localities. In the towns it would be continually exposed to superior forces, with no chance of defending itself or manoeuvring. In contrast, the guerrilla band, geographically and socially in a better position, 'ensures the survival and continuity of the revolutionary leadership'. Urban detachments can undoubtedly deal some telling blows, but their destruction would not entail the obliteration of the revolutionary 'spirit' and leadership of these are both preserved within the 'rural stronghold'.

Finally and above all, it is in the guerrilla zone that 'the future apparatus of the state charged with effectively administering the class dictatorship throughout the transition period' will be created.

Guevara is very clear on this point: 'The longer the struggle, the greater and more complex will be the problems of administration; it is in trying to resolve these that cadres will be trained for the difficult task of consolidating power and economic development at a later stage.'

Another line of argument is the increasingly explosive character of the Latin American peasant struggles against feudal institutions, in the context of a social situation where foreign and local exploiters are in alliance with each other.

And finally, the fight must be continental in scale. It is inconceivable that the emancipation of Latin America should come about as a result of conflict between two local forces in a limited arena. The North Americans are bound to intervene because their own interests are threatened and because the issue is vital to them. In fact, they are already intervening, but in future they will use all their strength and all the means available to them. Victory therefore cannot be won and consolidated within the framework of a single country. The war must be conceived and carried out on a continental scale, and if it is impossible to foretell the course it will run or its duration, there can be no doubt as to its outcome, since it is the product of a particular set of historical, economic and political circumstances. Wherever the fighting begins, it is bound to lead to further developments influencing the whole revolutionary war.

It is plain that each argument put forward by Guevara, each stage in his reasoning and even his logic itself are debatable. What must be remembered for the moment is the conviction that history is moving in the direction that Che wants it to, and that everything is a matter of organisation and political tactics. This, in turn, is utterly dependent upon the existence of a 'nucleus' of revolutionaries. Neither the working class nor the peasantry can produce this nucleus. But Guevara does not specify its class nature or social origins. 'Guides of the people', 'revolutionary leadership', 'cadres being forged in the struggle' are so many expressions descriptive of neither a worker nor a peasant vanguard but an intellectual one. A new power apparatus, whose growth means the decline of the official legal power and whose victory would enable it to control the whole of society, must be created outside society, from an external position; this must not be a new society, because that could not take the place of real society.

The continual reiteration of the main aim—the capture of power—is not a mere technicality; it is also a question of exorcism, a manifestation of the fear that the partisans of reform or revolution might discover ways and means of affecting change on the basis of the existing society and within its bounds, whereas the guerrillas' only chance lies in making all change and all improvement depend on the victory of a new power.

In this connection, the argument emphasising the dangers of piecemeal reform and the preference for a violent solution— even if the latter reinforces and stiffens the reactionary power— is significant. In the same way, speculation on a long drawn out conflict allowing the guerrilla cadres to serve their apprenticeship as statesmen, is especially revealing.

In spite of references to the sacred Marxist and Leninist texts, it is clear that Che's theory no longer has much in common with Marx's views concerning the proletarian succession to capitalism, inevitably written into the development of capitalism itself, nor with Lenin's views—at least those of Lenin the theoretician—with their emphasis on the representative and organisational rôle of the Party in the affairs of the working class.

A Marxist analysis of the guerrilla movements and the 'theories' of its instigators ought not to start with quotations from Marx or Lenin, but with an attempt to identify their social components and the social purpose that informs the revolutionary 'cadres'.

Such an analysis is even more urgently needed in view of the fact that Guevara's ideas are not the product of theoretical speculation but were worked out after the event, not just after Batista's fall from power—a period when the programme of the July 26 Movement was still closely related to the propagandistic slogans of parliamentary democracy and not just after the establishment of the new power as it exerted its authority over the forces and organisations representative of the different sections of Cuban society on its emancipation from the old régime—but long after the new power had discovered its own dynamic principles and evolved its own structure.

The need to simplify involves a denial, or at least a by-passing of the complex strains and contradictions inherent in present-day society. Vagueness and generalisation create the impression of a situation fully justifying the use of force. This simplistic viewpoint does not admit the validity of programmes of reform and change. Finally, it allows no exact knowledge to be gained of the nature and rôle of the representative worker and peasant organisations, as regards the present situation or the future.

The re-structuring of society will take place once the new government has been established, just as the ideology and the choice of tactics will be laid down *pari passu* with the survival and consolidation of the new power. Society is a laboratory.

In Che's 'Diaries', there are very few references to political or social conditions in Bolivia, whereas there is plenty of information and discussion about the guerrilla war as such, as though it was something quite apart from the national situation, though capable of transforming the latter.

There are three lines (June 8, 1967) on the massacre of miners that took place on the Feast of St John, an event that indicated the extent to which the Barrientos government was willing and able to apply force, and, moreover, in the traditionally most explosive region of Bolivia: 'There is news about the state of siege and the threat from the miners, but it is all hogwash.' One last point. Che never returns to this matter except to note, on June 30, that 'they accuse me of being the instigator of the rebellion in the mines, as well as being responsible for the incident on the Nancahuazú River'. In actual fact, there was no liaison with the miners. The only contact took place at a Havana level with Juan Lechín who had escaped to Chile; he appeared 'enthusiastic' and asked for money. An ELN (Ejército de Liberación Nacional) communiqué aimed at the miners, emphasised that mass struggle was tactically wrong, warned against jeopardising the forces in actions where success was not assured, and ended with an appeal for recruitment (Communiqué No. 5, *Punto Final*, July 30, 1968).

As regards the peasants, it is instructive to follow the monthly analyses in the *Diaries*. The April one actually states '. . . the peasant base has not yet been developed although it appears that through planned terror we can neutralise some of them; support will come later'. The May report: 'Complete lack of peasant recruitment, although they are losing their fear of us and we are beginning to win their admiration.' In June: 'The lack of peasant recruits continues. It is a vicious circle: to get this enlistment we need to settle in a populated area and for this we need men.' But for the same month, he writes: 'Militarily the Army's action has been nil, but they are working on the peasants in a way that we must be very careful about as they can change a whole community into informers, either through fear of our aims or through trickery.' In July: 'The peasantry still is not joining us, although there were some encouraging signs from some peasants we know.' In August: 'We still have not incorporated the peasants, which is logical when one considers the little contact we have had with them in recent weeks.' And finally in September: '. . . the Army appears to be more effective in its actions, and the peasants do not give us any help and are turning into informers.'

This acknowledgement of facts that entirely contradict the theoretical argument and imply a failure, does not seem to lead to any adjustment being made in the theory. Superficial echoes of the struggle, caused by propaganda that was no doubt provoked, but whose apparent beneficiaries ended by being fatally taken in themselves, seemed sufficient to strengthen faith in a method that experience itself belied. The *Diaries* are full of purely propagandistic victories that scarcely affected the situation. 'The clamour over the Debray case has given more belligerency to our movement than ten victorious battles. . . .' 'The legend of the guerrillas is acquiring continental dimensions: Onganía closes the border [of Argentina]; Peru is taking precautions.'

Between the world of reality and that of propaganda, Ernesto Guevara continued building up his forces, at least on paper. In his plan for work in the towns (D111, documents published in the *Punto Final* supplement, Santiago de Chile, July 30, 1968), he specified: 'Urban action will be increasingly linked with the [revolutionary] army as the latter approaches the particular urban zone, until it turns into suburban guerrilla warfare, subject to the army's authority.' The very concept of revolutionary action in the towns subordinates it entirely to the armed power: 'Personnel must strictly adhere to the line of conduct established by the army leadership, through the command centres, but with complete freedom to follow this line in its practical application.'

Régis Debray, whose only practical experience consists of a few short expeditions into the Latin American *'maquis'*,[2] is more exact and categorical than Che Guevara in his definitions and condemnations. Unlike men of action, he does not seem to experience any doubts as to his judgement. In everything he exhibits the self-assurance and occasional naïvety of a graduate of the École Normale Supérieure.[3]

In *Revolution in the Revolution*,[4] the theory of guerrilla warfare acquires the clarity of a thesis: 'In Latin America today a political line which, in terms of its consequences, is not susceptible to expression as a precise and consistent military line, cannot be considered revolutionary. Any line that claims to be revolutionary must give a concrete answer to the question: How to overthrow the power of the capitalist state? In other words, how to break its backbone, the army continuously reinforced by North American military missions? The Cuban Revolution offers an answer to fraternal Latin American countries which has still to be studied in its historical details: by means of the more or less slow construction, through guerrilla warfare carried out in suitably chosen rural zones, of a *mobile strategic force*, the nucleus of a people's army and of a future socialist state.'

This is the only acceptable theory. All others should be rejected: armed self-defence ('the failure of armed self-defence of the masses corresponds on the military level to the failure of reformism on the political level'), a certain interpretation of armed propaganda ('To consider the propaganda of force as a stage distinct from and prior to military operations is, it seems, to provoke the enemy unnecessarily, to expose the comrades working as propagandists to assassination or the need to escape, and to expose a future or possible zone of guerrilla action'), and finally guerrilla adherence to the Party, as a kind of arm of its peace-time organisation ('The subordination of the guerrilla force to urban political leadership not only creates practical problems for the *guerrilleros* but also a sense of dependence and an inferiority complex').

The traditional idea of the party is transformed: '*In certain conditions, the political and military are not separate but form one organic whole, consisting of the people's army whose nucleus is the guerrilla army. The vanguard party can exist in the form of the guerrilla base* (foco insurreccionál) *itself. The guerrilla force is the party in embryo*. This is the staggering novelty introduced by the Cuban Revolution.'

Is this *a posteriori* theory, based on one extensive experience involving several programmatic changes not the product of a particular set of circumstances? Debray asks this question himself and answers it with an emphatic: 'Quite the contrary'. Indeed, in his view, the Cuban example, thanks to the new leaders of the various guerrilla formations, all of whom are Marxists, all 'having as their aim an unequivocally socialist and proletarian revolution', makes it possible to end the old dichotomy 'between Marxist theory and revolutionary practice'.

The social origins of the guerrilla fighters do not seem to cause the young French theoretician any concern: 'The worker-peasant alliance often finds its link in a group of revolutionaries of bourgeois extraction, from which derives a large part of the guerrilla leadership.' It is true that Debray considers class selfishness incapable of enduring the conditions required by life in the field.

In *The Long March*,[5] Debray subjects each Latin American guerrilla movement to a critical examination in order to deduct certain principles. This study does not conclude with different

sets of tactics for each situation. The work is an attempt to
find a way of applying the same tactical principle in different
sets of circumstances. Besides describing Venezuelan, Colombian, Argentine or Bolivian conditions, he tries persistently to
reject everything that contradicts the simplistic formulas. In the
final count, the argument is based on the following reasoning:
the Castroist method has triumphed in Cuba and is, therefore,
right. In the other Latin American countries, the revolutionary
attempts were clearly based on incorrect principles, as they
ended in failure. There is some doubt about those still in
progress, but it is easy to see that the author has a whole battery
of explanations ready to account for defeat as well as for victory.

The book is not without contradictions. For example, having
already spoken of the Peruvian leader Hugo Blanco, 'a man on
his own and with no permanent domicile in the region',[6] he
says that he was able to escape persecution. 'The peasants,
therefore, felt they had been betrayed. No one was protecting
them against the army. As between life and trade-unionism,
they preferred life: rent would again be paid to the landowners.' All of which is a somewhat off-hand way of dealing
with Hugo Blanco's activity, whatever one might think of the
latter. A few paragraphs further on, he admits that 'the
recapture of a small outlying area of fertile land belonging to a
landowner is better propaganda for agrarian reform than
a hundred illustrated booklets on Ukrainian sovkhozes'. In
fact, as it happens, peasant pressures in the Cuzco area have,
without guerrilla assistance, led to the recapture of numerous
outlying tracts of land.

The complexity of the social situation frequently baffles
Debray. Facts embarrass him and he explains them away as
best he can, occasionally even taking liberties where the
circumstances are well known. To take only the case of Uruguay,
there is the passage where Debray talks of the 'three hundred
students who, in September 1964, withstood a police siege after
demonstrating against the rupture of relations with Cuba'.
Anyone living in Montevideo would know that it is disin-
genuous to quote this episode as indicative of the students' place

in the vanguard of the revolution. In reality the students were supplied with food, under the very eye of the police and, indeed, with its full permission, and the only result of the 'siege', which took place without any violence, was a traffic hold-up in the capital's busiest thoroughfare. (It would seem that the meaning behind this kind of demonstration lies in the fact that the students are demanding special class privileges such as freedom from police interference, privileges which are in any case granted them but which are never, for example, in any circumstances, granted to the workers.)

Still on the subject of Montevideo, Debray claims that a large anarchist trade union centre is in existence there. He must have got his facts muddled, as all that is left of the FORU (Regional Federation of Uruguayan Workers) in Uruguay is about a dozen militant libertarian ancients, keeping alive the memory and preserving the rubber stamp of what was thirty years ago a large workers' organisation.

More interesting than what he tells us about Latin America is what Debray says about the rôle of the party, or the party in embryo, or of that organisation which is not easily definable but which has all the necessary qualities. In *The Long March* again, he states that 'in this connection, the Cuban Revolution has shown that if it is essential to have an organisation and firm political leadership (July 26 Movement) at the insurrectional stage of the revolution, it is possible to dispense with a Marxist-Leninist vanguard of the working class'. Where will the men who make up this organisation, with its strong political leadership but which is not a party, come from? The answer is to be found in a quotation from Lenin providing another formula: 'A minority organisation of professional revolutionaries, theoretically indoctrinated and fully trained in the practice of their art.'

On every page Debray betrays the social origins of the professional revolutionaries: they are students and teachers, members of the lower-middle and professional classes. These urban elements will never fully commit themselves or become revolutionaries totally dedicated to the seizure of power until

39

they have passed through the school of rural guerrilla warfare.

The idea of revolutionary voluntarism, of the political-military apparatus does not, therefore, spring from an analysis of the situation in each Latin American country, but is a generalisation based on the experience in Cuba and the international situation interpreted in a very simplified form.

The fact that no serious attempt has been made to study Cuban society and its component parts, that no interest has been shown either in its social structure, the nature of the army, or in the very real dependence of the island's economy on the United States, in no way inhibits the proponents of guerrilla tactics from suggesting that they are the only valid tactics for the whole continent, while acknowledging in extreme cases that certain conditions are more favourable than others.

Nevertheless, one would think that, as it is the official military machine that has to be faced, it would be necessary to acquire some insight into the nature, rôle and operational methods of the armed forces. Batista's army was characterised by certain features which were not necessarily shared by the armies of Brazil or Mexico and apart from the fact that in some countries, notably Chile, it was not the army but special police detachments that constituted the forces of order in the first instance (the 22,000 Chilean carabinieri, found even in the smallest villages), they cannot be compared to the few thousand practically raw recruits of the Bolivian army as of April 1967.

Most of Fidel Castro's admirers or supporters made no secret of the disintegration of the Cuban army following his victory. Jacques Grignon-Dumoulin, for instance, in the notes prefixed to each important speech made by the leader or his principal lieutenants, describes the situation in the last quarter of 1958 as follows: 'From late October 1958, Fulgencio Batista feels that the situation is getting out of hand: his sole concern now is to make good his escape and enjoy the huge fortune he has amassed through his plundering of the Treasury. . . . He is therefore trying to save face by getting a successor, nominated by himself, elected in the fixed elections of November. But the prospect of a questionable interregnum is demoralising to an army that is less and less disposed to fight, while it encourages the rebel forces and the majority of a population oppressed by a terrorist régime.'[7]

Fausto Masó, one of the few Cubans who was unaffected by the blandishments of either Havana or Miami and stuck to his job as an intellectual, a job which consisted of an objective study of reality, recalls that 'the Cuban guerrillas did not destroy Batista's army in one battle, but that the latter surrendered only when demoralised by the results of a terrorism which formed the official response to violence in the towns'.[8]

One must also bear in mind that the politico-military definitions of guerrilla warfare are of recent date. They emerged only after the victory over the dictator Batista. As the new power gradually took shape, it fell back on Marxist-Leninist phraseology and abandoned its earlier formulas. This development took time, and only unquestioning Fidelistas accepted it.

Let us remember that in New York's Central Park, on April 24, 1959, Fidel Castro declared: 'We are genuine democrats, because democracy that talks only of theoretical rights and forgets man's needs is neither genuine nor real. No bread without freedom, or freedom without bread. No dictatorship of man, or dictatorship of class. No dictatorship of groups, dictatorship of castes, or oligarchy. Freedom with bread and without terror. That is humanism.' At the meeting of the Economic Council of the Twenty-one, in Buenos Aires, on May 2, 1959, the same Fidel Castro did not inveigh against North American imperialism; he felt that the United States had a positive rôle to play in the emancipation of Latin America: 'The Cuban delegation, the technicians of the Cuban delegation have calculated that the full economic development of Latin America requires an investment of 30 million dollars over a period of ten years. There is no reason to be alarmed at this amount; the figures are there, we know our needs ... we know what normal growth requires, the number of millions needed to provide a set number of workers with work. ... To whom can we turn for capital? To the United States, and to the United States alone. In what form must it come? In the form of public loans, as experience has shown that other methods meet with practically insurmountable obstacles and as the United States has approved of this method in respect to the countries of Europe and the Near East. Moreover, we believe that this will be to the advantage not only of Latin America, but, in the end, of the United States herself.'

In recalling these words, these statements, hopes or illusions, we have no intention whatsoever of making a value judgement about the Cuban leader's ideas at this period, nor of disregarding subsequent events or underestimating the part played by pressure groups and the United States Government in the changes that took place afterwards in the behaviour and policy —and the arguments used to back them up—of Havana. What seems important to stress at this point is that the arguments put forward by Ernesto Guevara and Régis Debray, including all the literature distributed in Latin America and in Europe, do not spring from the July 26 Movement nor do they relate to any set of tactics as defined by Fidel Castro. They result from an *a posteriori* interpretation as much of Cuban events as of the international situation.

In the same way, they cannot be considered as the fruit of mature judgement enriched by experience. Until there is any evidence to the contrary, they must simply be regarded as an extrapolation on the most recent arguments employed by the Cuban government, the previous ones, as regards internal policy being in support of a return to parliamentary democracy, a programme of social reforms and, as regards external affairs, of collaboration with the United States or, if needs be, of the neutrality proper to a small nation—witness Raúl Roa's speech at the sixteenth session of the General Assembly of the United Nations.

The elemination of mass organisations and bodies (trade unions, peasant associations and student leagues) not subordinate to the guerrilla nucleus, and of opposition groups and currents within the guerrilla movement itself (Huber Matos, William Morgan) and the removal of potential leaders (Che Guevara, Anibal Escalante) are not the result of legal or *de*

facto organisational decisions. They relate to the eternal law of
states concerned with their own self-defence and preservation,
and all ideologies are borrowed from and every emotional
device used in attempting to justify them.

The most striking example of an opportunistic argument is
supplied by Fidel Castro in the public speech that set the stage
for the 'liquidation' of Anibal Escalante, but that was, in
principle, aimed at any political organisation that might rival
the power of the leader himself. It is also a good sample of
Castro's style: '. . . we shall all dedicate ourselves to the task
of organising this party. Each one of us here has fulfilled an
infinite number of tasks in one or another sphere, each one
doing his best, preparing to confront the imperialist enemy,
fighting the imperialist enemy, joining battle in the field of
culture, in all fields. At last, great battles have been joined,
that have consumed our enthusiasm . . . no, not consumed it,
we must use another word, that have absorbed it—as enthusiasm has not been consumed and never will be—the
enthusiasm of the leaders and militant comrades of the Revolution.

'Others laboured at the task of building the Party. And the
Party took shape, and the ORIS[10] took shape. But were we
constructing a real Marxist party? Were we creating a real
working class vanguard? Were we really integrating the
revolutionary forces? We were not integrating the revolutionary
forces. We were not organising a party, we were organising a
system of bondage. We were not organising a party, comrades,
we were organising, creating or fabricating a strait-jacket, a
yoke. We were not setting up a free association of revolutionaries, but an army of domesticated and tame revolutionaries.'

3

Variations in the Cuban Government's Position

THE TRICONTINENTAL CONFERENCE that took place in Havana in January 1966 revealed a number of contradictions within the Latin American camp. If, on a tactical level, the groups classified as Castroite had generally made use of the Chinese line of argument (primacy of the armed struggle, need for a regional body to co-ordinate the movements in Latin America), Castro's diatribe against Chinese 'procedures' and Chinese 'imperialist' mentality clearly indicated the Cuban Government's determination to resist the pull of a new international centre.

The Soviets had manœuvred skilfully: they had accepted their duty to support guerrilla struggles where they were of real significance (Venezuela, Peru, Colombia and Guatemala) but, in exchange, had succeeded in getting Fidel Castro to condemn those who could not be controlled: Trotskyites or non-combatants ranking with combatants.

On the one hand, Fidel Castro kept his distance as regards Peking and counted it as a gain that the Soviet Union should be giving practical assistance to the 'National Liberation' movements and not just talking about it; on the other hand he insisted on the validity of his thesis: 'We believe that, on this continent, and for all or nearly all the nations, the struggle will assume a violent form.'

Beneath all this verbal thunder, there was a subtle process going on. Manœuvring between the two socialist colossi, Castro

44

was trying to mark out his own zone of influence, to preserve and strengthen his own apparatus and, as far as possible, to escape the consequences of the dangerous games being played by others in distant lands.

When the OLAS (Latin American Solidarity) conference met in the summer of 1967, the Castroite position had improved, at least as regards the very special world represented at Havana. A number of communist parties refused to take part in the meeting—notably those of Venezuela and Brazil—while the other official parties were on the defensive and avoided taking any very definite decisions: the Uruguayan, Arismendi, particularly, worked to this end. In order to set the tone of the conference, the stress was laid on Che Guevara's return to active combat, even if apart from representatives of the CP, there was no delegation from Bolivia where the guerrillas were challenging army patrols.

It was possible to stress the 'withdrawal' of certain Latin American parties, such as the Venezuelan one. A vigorous attack was mounted, not against Soviet policy as a whole, but against some of its regional aspects.

The magazine, *Teoría y Práctica*, published by the Cuban CP's Schools of Revolutionary Instruction, criticised not only the attitude taken by the CP in respect to certain minor matters or under certain circumstances, but its whole political activity in Latin America. Félix de la Uz made a direct attack on the tactics of alliance with the national bourgeoisies: 'The [Brazilian] Party has placed too much trust in the national bourgeoisie and, in actual fact, has surrendered to it, not knowing how to maintain an independent line in the face of its waverings and faithlessness. . . .[1] Only a little while ago, in an article published in *L'Humanité*, Luís Carlos Prestes undertook to show that the Party line was still strongly influenced by bourgeois tactics.'

Fidel Castro's speech at the closing session of the first OLAS conference, August 10, 1967, is no model of clarity or logical construction but, nevertheless, contains a number of unequivocal statements. These refer, in no uncertain manner, to the absolute necessity for and superiority of the armed struggle[2] and also to the special position occupied by the Cuban CP within the family of CPs and, generally, among the revolutionary movements:

The phrase without content is as bad as the bogus content of certain phrases. That's how it is with forty-year-old theses like the well-known one concerning the rôle of the national bourgeoisies. What a job it has been thoroughly to convince ourselves of the absurdity of this notion in the context of our continent. How much paper, how many words, how much chatter has been wasted as we wait for a liberal, progressive, anti-imperialist bourgeoisie! ... Of course, according to certain 'illustrious' revolutionary thinkers, we are nothing but petty bourgeois adventurers who have not matured as revolutionaries. It is a good thing that the revolution came before maturity! Because, in actual fact, the mature ones, the super-mature ones have matured to such an extent that they have rotted away. But we regard ourselves as a Marxist-Leninist party, we regard ourselves as a communist party. ... It is with joy and not with nostalgia, with happiness and not with sadness that we see the ranks of the revolutionary movement swelling, revolutionary organisations multiplying and the Marxist-Leninist spirit, that is Marxist-Leninist ideas, making headway. ... All this means that there exists, on this continent, a much broader movement than the one consisting simply of the Latin American communist parties, that our obligations are towards this huge movement and that we will appraise these organisations not according to their claims but according to the actions by which they prove themselves. We are full of joy at our party's wholehearted identification with a broader movement as represented by this first conference of ours.

... The guerrilla band is destined to become the primary nucleus of the revolutionary movement. This does not mean that the guerrilla movement can be launched without any preparatory work; this does not mean that the guerrilla movement can do without political leadership. ... We do not deny the rôle of the guiding organisation; we do not deny the rôle of the political organisation. The guerrilla band is organised by a political movement. ... What we consider to be incompatible with a true conception of guerrilla warfare is the claim that the guerrillas can be led from town. And in the conditions of our continent, it would be very hard to eliminate the guerrilla's rôle. . . .

Some are wondering whether it is not possible to achieve power in a Latin American country without an armed struggle. Of course, theoretically and hypothetically, once a large part of the continent has been liberated, there would be nothing strange in the revolution very occasionally attaining an easy victory in a particular country. But this does not mean that the revolution will triumph without a struggle taking place in any country. The blood of revolutionaries may not run in a particular country, but the victory will have been made possible by the sacrifice and blood of the revolutionaries of a whole continent. . . .

As for those who really believe in the possibility of a peaceful path in certain countries of this continent, we cannot understand what they are referring to, unless it be a path in harmony with imperialism. . . . Those who believe that they will beat the imperialists in elections are simply being naïve, and those who believe that they will be allowed to assume power on the day they win the elections are being more than naïve. . . . The revolutionary, in accordance with his revolutionary concept and aim, makes use of the different types of struggle. The main thing is to know whether we are going to persuade the masses that the revolutionary movement and socialism will come to power without a struggle, that they will come to power by peaceful means. This is a lie. And those in Latin America who assert that they will come to power by peaceful means are deceiving the masses.

If one tries to interpret these arguments and assertions in terms of power politics, it becomes clear that Fidel Castro is striving, on the one hand, to maintain his position within the socialist camp, in view of his defence requirements against the United States threat, and, on the other hand, to avoid following the political line of the leaders of that camp, wherever and whenever it threatens to confine him to his rôle as head of government of a small Caribbean country, whereas in fact he likes to think of himself as the potential leader of a continental revolutionary movement.

He claims to be faithful to Marxism-Leninism, but reserves the right to interpret the doctrine in his own manner. He speaks in the name of the Cuban Communist Party, but the latter merely acknowledges his authority and he has taken good care not to allow it to organise itself on the model proposed by Escalante. He is anti-imperialist, in so far as this anwers to the needs and opportunities of the present-day Cuban economy. He chooses guerrilla tactics, because this alone can win him allies that the traditional communist apparatus cannot control, but that he can maintain and that will turn him into a Latin American leader. The reason for Fidel Castro's choice is not to be found in the social conditions of the Latin American countries—that is why he was unwilling to take the slightest risk in Santo Domingo—but in the realities of his own power in Havana.

At the OLAS conference, there were no more diatribes against the dissident revolutionaries, against the Yon Sosas or the Adolfo Gillys. The only jabs were made at the communist parties, which, no doubt, disputed Fidel Castro's interpretation of the holy texts, but also, and above all, questioned his control over the machinery of power and access to it. The virulence of Castro's speech against the Venezuelan CP is indicative of its self-defensive nature. It is not simply a question of Fidel Castro discussing tactics with the militants of another country; it is Fidel Castro struggling against the threat from the Soviet Union to the whole basis of his power. The support and maintenance of a certain type of general dissidence become the only guarantee of his political survival in Cuba.

4

Reservations of the Extreme Left

ON THE ONE HAND, there are the revolutionary proclamations, as a rule intemperate; on the other, the assertion of a new theory by those who consider themselves the true representatives of Castroite thought or methods. 'Guevarist' manifestos are not necessarily received enthusiastically or even favourably in the fermenting and intellectually agitated world of the Latin American left and extreme left. Controversy is very active and takes many forms, leading to organisational shake-ups—splits, expulsions, denunciations.

This not only concerns those parties that claim leftist descent and inclinations and that belong, in a manner of speaking, to the tradition of political struggles against the oligarchy and for the establishment of parliamentary democracy, such as APRA in Peru, Acción Democrática in Venezuela, Liberación Nacional in Costa Rica, the 'Colorados' and their numerous related sub-groups in Uruguay. There is also the host of organisations that has sprung from these parties as a result of splits and differences over doctrine or tactics, and there is the proliferation of tiny groups, of associations with a more or less limited life span, but which are reborn and replace each other *ad infinitum*, leading one to attribute greater significance to them than their ephemeral existence would otherwise seem to call for. The different schools of thought, ranging from extreme nationalism to Maoism, proliferate, with masters and

49

pupils who remain curiously alike, even in their way of ex-communicating each other.

The question of guerrilla warfare has, evidently, been widely debated on an academic but highly emotional level. Even though all this has taken place in a revolutionary environment, conservatism has also played its part and reservations with regard to the 'theory' of guerrilla warfare have appeared, in the first instance among those who already possess *their own* doctrine.

For example, in *Las Guerrillas*, booklet published in La Paz in 1963 by Guillermo Lara, the title on the cover is followed by an explanatory subtitle that is quite unambiguous: 'The Marxist conception as opposed to adventurist *golpism*.' This thesis belongs to the Trotskyite POR (Revolutionary Workers' Party) of Bolivia. It goes into a certain amount of historical detail in order to show that there is nothing new about guerrilla warfare '. . . when Indibil and Mandonio raised the Iberian peninsula against the misdeeds of the Roman praetors and proconsuls . . .' but quickly moves on to the main issue of the day: 'The guerrilla war cannot be considered apart from the political stage reached by a particular country, and still less apart from the laws of social progress, seeing that armed struggle arises out of the revolutionary process which is itself determined by these basic factors.' Therefore, the choice of the right moment for insurrection is not determined by military con-siderations, but by a strict political analysis of the situation. This ignores the fact that guerrilla bands may spring up, not as a new weapon in a period of class struggle when the masses are on the offensive, but also as a desperate defence measure at a time when a government is sending its troops in to crush what is left of the beaten and disorganised popular forces.

The main argument against Che Guevara is 'that a type of struggle which may be positive in certain political circum-stances becomes inappropriate in others'. Here it is expressed with crystalline clarity: 'At this particular moment (June 1963), guerrilla bands in Bolivia would be inadequate, and to nurture them artificially would be seriously to damage our cause as well as Cuba's.'

The controversy over the value of Ernesto Che Guevara's theory of guerrilla warfare is sometimes complicated by the fact that attempts to put this theory into practice are censured by the supreme authority in Havana.

This is what happened after Fidel Castro's speech at the Tricontinental Conference in 1966. Castro condemned Chinese policy towards Cuba in very harsh terms and acknowledged *grosso modo* the Soviet Union's leading rôle on the international stage. He violently attacked the Trotskyite factions and rounded on the Guatemalan guerrilla movement, MR-13 (Movimiento Revolucionario 13 de noviembre), whose guiding spirit was Yon Sosa.

So the followers of Che Guevara's tactics found themselves being denounced by the Cuban leader. The strangest confusion reigned in the world of Latin American coteries and revolutionary reports; the 'official' Trotskyites of the Fourth 'authentic' International published open letters to Fidel Castro stating explicitly that those Trotskyites he had attacked by name were not affiliated members (Felipe Alvahuante, Posadas) and sometimes were not even Trotskyites at all (Adolfo Gilly). The Argentine, Adolfo Gilly, replied in an article published by *Marcha* of Montevideo and reprinted by several socialist organs, notably *Arauco* of Santiago de Chile in which he asserted that the commonplaces and untruths enshrined in Fidel Castro's speech in fact reflected the latter's submissiveness to Soviet policy; that his attacks on the MR-13 echoed the exasperation of the Soviet leaders and their inability to stem the rise of revolutionary movements in Latin America. For Gilly, Castro was betraying the revolutionary cause in treating the Guatemalan fighters as enemies, 'because the leaders of the Guatemalan revolution are taking their decisions in the midst of fighting in the streets and in the mountains of Guatemala and not in the Hotel Habana Libre'. And the question 'What have you done with Che Guevara?' put in political terms kept on coming up meaning: what has become of your revolutionary policy? Why did you not support the Dominican revolution? Why are you breaking with the Chinese? Why do you condemn those who are faithful to the revolutionary struggle?

The polemics were to concern themselves more and more with factual situations and real experiences, and mere literary exercises made way for the study of real battles with their toll in flesh-and-blood victims. In Peru, as in Venezuela or in Colombia, it was no longer matters of doctrine that were under discussion. In Peru alone, guerrilla activity broke out at Jauja in May 1962, between 1962 and 1963 in the region of La Convención and Lares, in the early months of 1963 in Puerto Maldonado, and in July 1965 with the attempt to open a number of fronts. The bases were destroyed by the forces of repression, which really meant the army. They found no firm support in the towns and peasant solidarity did not help them. They did not, in fact, shake the influence of the traditional parties or undermine the authority of the democratic régime.

Debate within the revolutionary left concentrated on the analysis of various attempts at action. Américo Pumaruna[1] saw in this 'foquismo' a manifestation of ill-advised, vague revolutionary voluntarism, only marginally relevant to the realities of Peruvian socio-political life, in short, devoid of the basic background understanding. In plain language, for the author, the MIR had mistaken its wishes for reality: '... the MIR was making a purely subjective and extremely fallacious evaluation of the objective conditions of the peasant masses.' And worse still, the MIR was inclined to entertain illusions about the attitude of the 'progressive national bourgeoisie' towards the guerrilla movement, to believe that the latter might favour the growth of the struggle of rebellion. A number of different organisational aspects of guerrilla warfare were criticised equally severely: the isolation of the politically articulate sections of the population, confidence in the supposed zones of 'impregnable' security, absence of mobility, etc.

The following critical observations, published in a magazine issued in Paris, are made by one of the active participants in the guerrilla war. The document is reproduced *in extenso* as it is eloquent of the state of mind of the fighting man, crushed by the forces of repression and in addition being taken to task by his left-wing 'comrades' who regard themselves as being as radical as he, only more enlightened:

Open letter to M. Américo Pumaruna, Paris.

Respected master: I venture to write to you, in all humility, after reading your judicious essay *Peru, Revolution, Insurrection, Guerrilla Wars* in the November issue of that bible of revolutionary thought, *Vanguardia Revolucionaria*.[2] And my humility is no pretence, as I myself have taken part in a crazy guerrilla adventure which today I am able to deplore and reject, thanks to the light shed by your article. This forces me, in addition, to write to you under a pseudonym, as it is my misfortune to be hunted by the PIP and the GC[3] and I have not had the opportunity of escaping to Europe there to carry out a serious investigation into the revolutionary situation in our country.

And, in all humility, in the face of the expertise that is yours, I shall proceed with my analysis of the events that have taken place in Peru and that have, to such little purpose, claimed the lives of sub-lieutenant Vallejo, the amiable Mayta, the poet Javier Heraud, Luis de la Puente, Guillermo Lobatón, Maximo Velando, Raùl Escobar—the latter's death doubly purposeless, as I believe he had left Paris to take part in the guerrilla struggles—Rubén Tupayachi, well . . . one could go on for ever. Now you have made me realise that all of them were lacking in theoretical training or ideological understanding, having failed to learn the lessons of Fidel Castro, Che Guevara, Mao Tse-tung, etc., and that they threw themselves into a suicidal struggle against the oligarchy and imperialism without consulting you. This is a mistake that I, at any rate, will never in any circumstances repeat. Furthermore, to help spread the word, I am taking the liberty of quoting a number of significant passages from your work, so that those in Peru who have taken the wrong path and followed a bad example may see themselves in this mirror: 'The theoretical and organisational weakness of the groups of the left, together with their violence and impatience to see justice done have been tried and tested. Guerrilla "foquismo" is the legacy of Castroism misunderstood, and the classical Peruvian examples also form part of the Latin American revolutionary's equipment.

53

... The main idea in Che Guevara's book is wrongly understood.'

But I defer with even greater admiration to your eloquent analysis when you turn your attention to the Cubans, having exhausted the subject of the Peruvian revolutionaries. As you say: 'Many Cuban comrades are responsible'—swallow that Fidel—'for having informally, unwittingly and through their lack of a true understanding, spread dubious stories such as that of the twelve men of the Sierra, Fidel's superhuman qualities, the comparability of the Sierra Maestra and Cordillera of the Andes . . . among innumerable Peruvians—fortunately, thank God, you were not among them— won over by the topicality of the words in the absence of analytical equipment and theoretical grounding,' etc. And as for Jauja, I have never found a more judicious appraisal than yours, Master: 'What manner of empirical reasoning led them to engage in such a totally erroneous action? No doubt this relates to those factors we set forth at the beginning of this work; almost total misunderstanding of the Marxist method, of revolutionary theory and also of the real processes of the socialist revolution: a distortion erected on the basis of a false interpretation of the Cuban process in particular and almost complete isolation from the masses.' Poor Fidel Castro! Does he understand? If Américo Pumaruna, after his Moncada failure, had, as a Cuban, examined this blunder in the light of theory, we may be sure that Fidel would never again have risked making another.

But it is not only the men of Jauja who get their just deserts; there are also those young National Liberation Army puppies at Puerto Maldonado who will benefit from your advice . . . 'they had no more taken the trouble to examine the relation between the situation and circumstances of the Convención-Lares region and the rest of the country than to study in detail the particular conditions prevailing in the region itself.' I am entirely in agreement with you. These ignoramuses were bound to get what was coming to them for failing to consider the consequences of such an absurd action, and to make a thorough-going theoretical preliminary study, with the help of maps, compasses and all the necessary equipment.

I am very pleased as well that you are giving that riff-raff of the FIR and Hugo Blanco, for example, what they deserve: 'The entire political apparatus (of the FIR) was inextricably and unfortunately bound up with the relatively powerful military apparatus and only

54

tenuously linked to the other revolutionary axis composed of the peasants: the Cuzco leaders and the mass of people in La Convención province.' How could it be put more plainly, dear Master? That's the stuff to give these improvisers, who had the temerity to carry on a peasant war without consulting you, you and your well-known gifts. You could at least have told them which elementary handbooks to look up before launching themselves into such lunatic actions.

But that is not all. With the authority that your extraordinary revolutionary work, the sacrifices you made in the years 1963–65, have given you, you put the entire national left in its place when you say that, at the outset of the MIR guerrilla struggle, 'all the disorientated sectors were waiting for some kind of explanation of what it was all about and were hiding in anticipation of new events.' Luckily, a single bright star, exactly like that of Bethlehem, was shining in this black night; it was, it could be none other than *Vanguardia Revolucionaria*. As you yourself so aptly put it: 'At this stage, the only position that reflected an extensive and profound study of the rebel organisation and the conditions in which it would have to develop was the one adopted by *Vanguardia Revolucionaria* in *VR* No. 4.'

And here I have one regret. Unfortunately, I was in the mountains with these ignorant revolutionaries and was unable to read it . . . and I did not return home! There is another thing: no doubt it was because of the great efforts that went into this historical publication, that you and your friends forgot to inform Héctor Béjar and the young people of the ALN that instead of taking to the mountains in order to help the MIR rebellion, they would have done better to have started analysing, reflecting, diagnosing, prophesying, observing, commenting, etc., following the illuminating example and the brilliant thought of Professor Américo Pumaruna and his comrades of *Vanguardia Revolucionaria*.

I should like to continue by drawing attention to the gems in which your magisterial study abounds, but I do not wish to over-extend this piece. You may rest assured, dear Master, that I have learnt the lesson well: no more guerrilla warfare without a full-scale preliminary grounding in Marxist-Leninist theory, which will take years to acquire, even at the risk of seeing the revolution postponed indefinitely—no matter; never again to ignore the lessons of China, Cuba, Algeria, Vietnam, etc.; no further action without consulting you, you and *Vanguardia Revolucionaria,* beacons that illuminate the way for us, that teach us the alpha and omega of revolution.

I have forgotten one other thing. Stay in Paris, or in Rome, analysing the mistakes of those who venture to carry on a guerrilla struggle. Imagine our misfortune if, in addition to suffering defeats, to dying in battle like those madmen of the MIR and ALN and of so many other bodies that have not yet learnt their lesson, we would have to bear the loss of someone like you, with your ability to write critical epitaphs on the guerrillas. So, in all sincerity, I beg you do not come! We do not want to risk finding ourselves fatherless.

Your very humble follower Silvestro Américo (February 1967).

Once battle had been joined, the different positions of the discordant revolutionary groups could be expressed only with extreme caution. Thus it was under the heading, 'In defence of the Bolivian guerrillas', that *Política Obrera* (April 26, 1967) raised objections that were, in fact, fundamental. What, asks the author, is the position of the Bolivian masses? 'The mining proletariat, the only one in Latin America with a real revolutionary tradition is going through a period of exceptionally severe repression in consequence of the rout of May 1965, the date of Barrientos' murderous attack on the workers' movement. For its part, the peasant mass, the great combustible mass of April 1952, is mostly paralysed, and a section that, in the Bolivian context is semi-privileged has given in to the government.' In these circumstances, the Bolivian guerrilla struggle can be defended only because it opens an important front, diverting the forces of repression and reducing the pressure of the army on the mining vanguard. Guerrilla warfare is looked upon as a contributing factor, a secondary means dependent on circumstances, the decisive factor remaining always the reorganised working class.

5

The USSR and China in Latin America

ARE THE REAL reasons for the conflict between Moscow and Peking over tactics to be used in Latin America to be found in the vast and wordy documents issued by the Soviet and Chinese communist authorities or the endless statements made by the national communist parties? No doubt they are, if one succeeds in disengaging from the repetitive and incantatory hotchpotch the scraps of phrases or odd words that draw one's attention to a certain policy line or show up the importance accorded a particular manœuvre when compared with earlier versions.

This activity is the preserve of specialists and is based on the existence of a language for supposed initiates, as, for the ordinary reader, it is hard to differentiate between pro-Chinese or pro-Soviet formulas: anti-imperialism, the struggle for national liberation, denunciation of oligarchies, appeal to the progressive forces and, more particularly, to the poor workers and peasants.

A potentially distorting factor in the exegetical work that interpretation of the official texts requires is the belief in the real value of the arguments used by either one of the world centres, whereas these arguments are just so much self-vindication.

It is, nevertheless, quite clear that the Soviet or Chinese Latin American departments are not run by militants, armed with good solid texts and information about social conditions, trying to determine the best ways and means of securing the rapid victory of socialism on the continent, but that they function as state departments and their activities, like their long or short-term objectives, are related purely and simply to the interests of the state they serve.

The relationship between the representatives of the 'socialist' states in Latin America and those who act upon their theses, applying them to local problems, must therefore be looked at carefully. One must also bear in mind the extent to which any particular Latin American national situation or the effect of the Latin American continent as a whole on the international situation might influence the foreign policy of those powers which, like the Soviet Union or People's China, have aspirations to world hegemony.

When Peking buys several hundred thousand tons of wheat from the Argentine and pays cash down, as in 1966, she is giving provisional assistance to a régime elsewhere condemned as pro-imperialist and oligarchical. In 'moral' terms, this operation is no different from a trade agreement, for example, between the Soviet Union and Brazil, which is another country classified as belonging to the oligarchical and pro-imperialist camp. And, it must be added, there is no 'revolutionary' justification for the commercial relations established beween Madrid and Havana.

It is important to find out what means, in effect, are at the disposal of the Soviet Union and People's China, in Latin America, for the execution of a foreign policy basically determined by state interests.

As regards the USSR, one must remember the trade contacts that she is naturally trying to extend; her marginal position in a field dominated by the United States, followed by Europe; her desire to overcome the numerous obstacles to a normalisation of relations with the countries of Latin America. She has constantly to apply a double standard: on the one hand maintaining good relations with countries open to the exchange of raw materials and merchandise, and, on the other, exploiting the competitive and negative feelings that exist between the United States and the nations of Latin America, which implies support for a policy of national independence.

58

On a general level, there is nothing revolutionary in the Soviet position and the twin objective is not in itself contradictory. But when one returns to the particular context of each nation, numerous difficulties crop up. The very idea of trading with the Soviet Union produces an immediate reaction, not in business circles but in organs of public opinion and also, of course, among those economic groups that co-operate with the United States, Great Britain or the European countries. In these circumstances, anti-communism becomes a theme that, for financial reasons, it is easy to harp on. And one can well believe that there must also be tensions and antagonisms manifesting themselves in the various Russian departments, with the foreign trade experts showing little respect for the political agitators, even if the latter are pro-Soviet. Anti-yankee propaganda may have its uses, but for the treaty and trade agreement negotiators, it must be instrumental in securing immediate and concrete results, and not lead to total opposition which, in present-day conditions, would simply show up the weak position of Soviet foreign trade.

What the Soviet Union does control is a chain of political organisations, legal or clandestine communist parties that have some importance as groups capable of exerting pressure or of intervening in political affairs. For the most part, they are run by elderly bureaucrats who owe their survival to their faithfulness to the Soviet machine. They have grown old in harness and no longer display any initiative or spirit of adventure. These parties have never been able to take anything more than a subsidiary part in the combinations of the Popular Front or the nationalist-inspired alliances. They have scarcely any illusions left about a victorious future. In short, despite the fact that they were originally a foreign import, they have become a 'creole' element in political life.

The superiority of communist parties to the other revolutionary bodies that claim kinship with Marxism or Leninism lies in the continuity of the apparatus, in their permanence when compared with the continuous turnover and in the 'tropical' character of the various groups and revolutionary trends. The

59

leading cadres are conscious of this—hence their fidelity to the Soviet Union.

The old leaders have seen too much of the birth and death of organisations not to appreciate the importance of a head-office guaranteeing continuity. On the other hand, their survival is restrictive. No CP can prevent the unending proliferation of groups and organisations, arising naturally out of the intellectual ferment of the middle classes, which look to Marxism and the revolution and which 'established' communism can neither win over nor restrain.

Much of the energy of the CPs goes into preventing the development of rival factions, keeping them in under a leash, eliminating them. If, by chance, some rival organisation manages to get the backing of a popular movement, the basic problem becomes how to get control of this movement, regardless of the means. Knowledge of organisational techniques at least has remained from the long Stalinist tradition: alliance with the rival in order to get the better of him in the end, infiltration of his apparatus, alternating denunciations with the establishment of communist cells.

It is hard to know to what extent the political leadership in the Soviet Union regards the Latin American communist machines as useful and usable. It is conceivable that they are only maintained because they have existed for so long, because it is always tricky to liquidate local branches without calling the parent body into question, and also because their disappearance would leave a vacuum which the left and extreme-left groups would find no difficulty in filling; this would further complicate the already tortuous pattern of political forces which no outside participant in the game can afford to ignore. It seems likely that the method will remain unchanged for the time being, that is to counter everything that is distinct from the CP and to try to take over everything that cannot be eliminated.

In the great market place of international relations, in the shameless struggle for spheres of influence, it is, even if Latin America does not, at present, offer very fertile ground for

Soviet foreign policy, always good to have at one's disposal a few shock groups or key positions. This is something that is always negotiable.

Carl Schmitt, in his *Theorie des Partisanen*,[1] sums up the basic reasoning of the great powers, intent on manipulating others: 'In the shadow of the present atomic equilibrium of world powers, under the protective covering, so to speak, of their vast means of destruction, a theatre of limited and self-contained wars could be established with conventional weapons and even the control of the use of means of destruction through a public or informal agreement between the world powers.'

A good example of the kind of balancing act of which a communist leader is capable, when his powerlessness makes it impolitic either to follow or reject any course, can be found in the booklet by the Brazilian, Carlos Marighella, *A crise brasileira*.[2] The whole art lies in speaking about the guerrilla wars, going into the historical background, giving a detailed account of their significance, placing them in the general context of social struggles, syphoning off the sympathy that they are capable of arousing, and all the while showing how serious the dangers of a false interpretation could be, concluding in a way that is both redolent of approbation and condemnatory.

Brazil is a country occupied by the present military *entreguista*[3] dictatorship and United States ruling circles, in whose service are the traitors that have seized power.

In these siege conditions, the Brazilian guerrilla band, with its clearly political significance can do no more than register a protest, act as an instigatory force behind the popular struggle. It would be unpardonable if it were to be deprived of its continuity, of its necessary life span, through exposure to risks of a superior concentration of enemy forces, through being allowed to venture into battle or take part in crucial engagements with the forces of reaction.

No one expects guerrilla warfare to be the signal for a popular uprising or the immediate proliferation of insurrectional bases. Nothing of the kind. Guerrilla warfare will stimulate the resistance struggle everywhere.

Another sample of the illuminating language of these theore-
tician-tacticians was supplied by Armando Hart at the OLAS
conference in August 1967 when he was giving the Latin
American revolutionary movements the benefit of his advice
with regard to the possibilities and opportunities of the path
of armed struggle:

... we must point out that in Latin America the conditions for the
development of the revolution are present. This holds good for most
of the countries of the continent, for almost all of them, as far as
continental and overall strategy is concerned. When it comes to
individual countries, it is not possible to be so categorical. Moreover,
we must be specific when we talk about revolutionary conditions.

On occasions, our claim as to the existence of these conditions
has been confused with the Leninist concept of the revolutionary
situation. When we were talking about conditions, we were not
referring to what, in a strictly Leninist sense, might be termed a
revolutionary situation. If we insist on what Lenin called a revolutionary situation, we might conclude that no such situation exists
anywhere on the continent. Nevertheless, there are economic, social
and political conditions in Latin America that, with the development of the people's war, might lead to revolutionary situations. To
sum up, continentally and for most of the individual countries, conditions are ripe:

   1. For the initiation and extension of revolutionary war against
the power of the oligarchies and of imperialism;

   2. For the people's army that has sprung from this revolutionary
war to defeat the armies of the oligarchies, over a greater or shorter
space of time.[4]

From all points of view, People's China has fewer ties with
Latin America, and those that exist are not very long-standing.
Even though there has been an increase in trade, the total
volume is relatively insignificant in the Latin American as
well as Chinese contexts.

This want of commerce between China and the outside
world, only partially modified by large but irregular purchases
of cereals in Canada, Mexico or the Argentine, or by treaties

of a political nature, with a number of countries of Black Africa or with Cuba, is partly explicable in terms of Peking's desire for national self-sufficiency, at least if one is to believe an accredited representative, Nan Han-chen. The latter declared, at the Algerian Afro-Asian Training Centre, in 1965, that the Chinese example, to exploit human resources, to live frugally, to adopt a collective economy, to reduce imports from imperialist and neo-colonialist countries, was a good one to follow in the struggle for independence.

China's attempt to exert influence in the political sphere is naturally of recent origin and is still confined to radio broadcasts (in 1957, one hour of programmes every two days for Latin America; in 1960, one per day in Spanish and one in Portuguese; in 1967, a total of 38 hours per week, 14 hours for Central America and Cuba, 14 hours for South America, $10\frac{1}{2}$ hours for Brazil, in Portuguese); to distribution of informative matter put out by Hsinhua (news agency) and of various magazines, of which the most important is the bi-monthly *Pekin Informa*; to the showing of a number of documentary films; to the arrangement of trips for political leaders and prominent professional people; to the establishment of China Friendship Societies.

Is there an organisation operating systematically within each country and dedicated to establishing a pro-Chinese group, trying to gain acceptance for the Chinese theses, setting up communist parties that take their lead from Peking? It is not easy to answer this question, but it is noticeable that most of the movements that have followed the 'Chinese' line have not originated from within the communist parties; they have arisen from the merging of a number of small organisations that were already on the fringe of the communist party or opposed to it and that sprung from other political currents. It was only in Peru and Brazil that pro-Chinese parties owed their birth to a split in the original organisation.

What after a relatively short period of time looked like a flowering of Chinese-inspired associations and publications was largely in fact an amalgamation, under Peking's banner, of cells and groups that already existed. This tendency originated in the desire of isolated groups to belong to a new international, heir to the revolutionary tradition, and was not the result of recent activity. Subsequently the internal difficulties of the Chinese régime had the effect of further reducing the size of the Latin American 'machine'.

Neither in fact nor theory, therefore, can the guerrilla wars be reasonably attributed to Chinese influence, and still less can they be claimed as products of a Chinese 'international'. Just because some funds have been put at the disposal of the militants and there has been some attempt to establish organic links, there are not sufficient grounds for concluding that a pro-Chinese apparatus on a continental scale exists.

It is on the other hand quite clear that the Chinese arguments have been exploited in the discussions between various revolutionary groups and movements. They may indeed have added fuel to the fire of controversy, but it is unlikely that they provoked it in the first place.

Guerrilla warfare is a phenomenom, the explanation of which lies in the political and social conditions of Latin America. It owes far more, no doubt, to the behaviour and state of mind of academic intellectual circles than to the reactions and aspirations of the labouring classes. Where Washington, Moscow and Peking make the same mistake is in seeing guerrilla warfare as the fruit or subject of a propaganda campaign, whereas it is only a manifestation of a more general phenomenom, a reaction to the problems and dilemmas of Latin American societies.

So what are the ultimate facts about the Sino–Soviet quarrel in Latin America?[5]

The differences basically relate to the evaluation of the possibilities of offensive warfare against the United States. The Soviet Union does not believe in the feasibility of a frontal attack requiring the permanent mobilisation of all the opposition forces in a climate of war and violence. In Soviet eyes it appears more sensible to encourage the anti-imperialist elements to keep up a steady pressure and thus progressively modifying the power ratio. Coexistence assures the growth and consolidation of the socialist camp while allowing the contradictions in the American one to mature.

China, on the contrary, regards the pacification policy as allowing the United States a breathing-space, enabling it to concentrate its forces wherever and whenever danger threatens, to take on and defeat the peoples struggling for independence one at a time.

The USSR remains attached to a working class phraseology, to the formula of the party as vanguard of the industrial proletariat, and also to a conception of inevitable stages in the progress towards a socialist society, beginning with the working class spurring on the economic rôle of the middle class, then acting as the motive force and finally coming out on top. The social struggle is centred on the towns and industrial regions. The Chinese argument emphasises the revolutionary character of the great peasant masses that are capable of maintaining the party of the vanguard and supplying it with recruits. If the Third World enters into Russian calculations, containing, of course, elements that can be made use of, it is for China a natural ally that could prove decisive in the struggle with the United States.

The Soviet Union warns its supporters of the danger of throwing away the advantages to be gained from simply allowing the international situation to develop, that is by avoiding the kind of action involving nuclear weapons which might precipitate a total war or probable collective suicide. China is not haunted by this fear. On the one hand she condemns nuclear blackmail that is to the advantage of the United States alone, and on the other she insists on the superiority of the masses in every type of war and their ultimate ability to win through to socialism whatever the ups and downs of the struggle.

In practice, the organisations that follow or claim to follow the Moscow line feel that it is essential to join in the bourgeois democratic game wherever possible, given a certain minimum of guarantees, that their basic task is to accelerate what is a natural process: the establishment and extension of a large-scale movement that will include all the national forces and confront the obsolete, inefficient ruling cliques and the groups subject to United States imperialism. Rejecting this line of reasoning and these prognostications, the pro-Chinese groups consider the Latin American middle-classes to be incapable of carrying out their historical mission and too dependent on the interests of United States imperialism. As a result, they feel that the only course lies in setting up a front of the deprived and dissatisfied social classes: proletariat, peasantry and lower-middle-class.

Even so, it must be pointed out that the pro-Chinese groups or parties do not automatically support the local guerrilla movements. For example, in Peru, *Bandera Roja*, the organ of the pro-Chinese Peruvian PC, did not breathe a word about the call to arms of Luis de la Puente and Lobatón and the setting up of 'fronts' in several parts of the country.

As regards Bolivia, Inti Peredo, who took part in the pre-parations and in Che's fateful insurrectionary action and who, having survived the massacre, intends taking up the struggle again, gives a very clear indication of the rôle of the pro-Soviet and pro-Chinese CPS. In his July 1968 manifesto, 'The Bolivian guerrilla movement is not dead',[6] he recalls:

'The parties that claim to be the vanguard of our people in its anti-imperialist struggle are duty bound to behave honestly and to render an account of their actions to the people. They are also duty bound to acknowledge their mistakes if they consider that they have been mistaken, or to give an explana-tion of their behaviour if they think it right.

How may one explain the fact that these parties can pay tributes to fallen guerrilla fighters whereas in reality they attacked them when they were preparing for the struggle? How can one explain the fact that Monje warned the militants of his party against a 'fissiparous group' that was deviating from the 'line' and that, for the same reason, Zamora expelled comrade Moisés Guevara from the pro-Chinese PCB, when the latter, together with others, was rallying to the guerrilla cause?

6

Origins of the Guerrilla Fighters

WHERE DO THE MEN who make up the original cells of self-conscious revolutionaries, who establish and run the guerrilla bases, come from? Are they the products of a clearly identifiable class or section of the population? The theoreticians of guerrilla warfare use traditional revolutionary terminology: the proletariat and poor peasantry are the exploited classes and it is they who are the progressive elements in society; their emancipation both justifies and demands a battle. But on the other hand and even though it is never admitted in so many words, most of the writings of the proponents of guerrilla warfare and their very way of reasoning suggest that one cannot count on the enlightened vanguard or revolutionary leadership emerging from the ranks of the working class or the landless peasantry. There are even factors inherent in urban and rural working class conditions that inhibit or prevent a full comprehension of the deepest class interests and therefore, of the means whereby they may be protected and promoted.

The propaganda pamphlets or theoretical works are frequently written by professional revolutionaries, which does not mean militants who have been selected to devote themselves entirely to agitation or fighting, following the pattern of various organisations and parties at the end of the nineteenth and beginning of the twentieth centuries, but simply self-appointed spokesmen with a talent and vocation. The cell or embryo of the party is like a team of technicians specialising in the conquest of power. In *La longue marche* Debray, without apparently attaching too much importance to it, so self-evident

67

does it seem to him, speaks of '. . . Ten to thirty professional revolutionaries entirely dedicated to the cause and with the seizure of power as their objective . . .'

These are not members of the privileged classes going to the people in the spirit, say, of the *narodniki*, to serve it, merge with it and sacrifice themselves. On the contrary these are men who are conscious of their rôle as leaders, determined that the exploited lower orders should be controlled, politically indoctrinated, organised and used.

When one analyses, the 'cells', it becomes immediately apparent that they are, for the most part, composed of intellectuals, professional people and students. There are neither working class nor peasant elements, rather sons of middle class people, civil servants, and members of the liberal professions.

In a remarkable work,[1] the sociologist Orlando Albornoz set himself the task of determining what relations exist between the student body and the national political life of Venezuela for example, as regards the struggle against the dictatorship of Pérez Jiménez, the creation of a political ruling class, the birth of a guerrilla movement, in other words, the important changes that have occurred in the country over the last twelve years.

His conclusions could not be more clear-cut:

Basically, the Venezuelan guerrilla movement is a university or at least university-inspired movement. There is not the slightest doubt about the relationship existing between the guerrilla movement and the Central University. Human and every other kind of material for guerrilla warfare came, for the most part, from the universities, the national universities, of course. Over the years 1962–65, the universities in contact with the movement of subversion were the strategic centres for the maintenance of the guerrilla bands. Funds were collected at the entrance to the Caracas students' hostels centre and in the corridors of those university departments sympathetic to the armed movement; what is more, the autonomous status of the Central University made it the ideal place for meetings and the starting point for recruitment and indoctrination drives.

Does the University and the student world represent only one

68

side of the guerrilla movement, the 'flank', as it were, of something rooted in the people? This does not seem to be the case. It is mainly from this sector and not from among the workers and peasants that the idea and organisation of guerrilla warfare have come.

Must one put this revolutionary spirit down to a kind of second generation revolt, students from humble backgrounds giving vent to the aspirations of their class? An analysis of the social origins of the students disposes of this hypothesis:

... it seems clear that class and the educational system are so geared to each other as to make it generally impossible for the lower classes of the population, workers and peasants, to reach the upper levels of the primary school, whereas the middle and upper class parents can give their children a higher education with opportunities that improve the higher their social status. This phenomenom, which is more or less common to the whole of Latin America, means that the Central University, for the most part, contains students of middle or upper class families.

These observations, which seem to us of crucial significance, do not contradict what the inspirers of the revolutionary movements themselves believe, in spite of their adherence to a language borrowed from European socialism. There have been attempts to supply this *de facto* situation with a doctrinal basis. Orlando Albornoz quotes Humberto Cuenca, a professor at the university and militant member of the MIR, who, in his books, *Revolutionary University and Army*[2] and *University and Revolution*,[3] points out that in Venezuela the revolutionary vanguard is represented by the students and that this phenomenon is tending to become general to the whole of Latin America. Nevertheless, it must be realised that Cuenca considered that the students would have only an 'instrumental' part to play in the revolution.

Two remarks of Orlando Albornoz also seem noteworthy. In the first place he points out that if the Venezuelan parties support student groups, the latter frequently take up positions that are distinct from and opposed to those of the parties themselves, to such an extent that, in extreme cases, the central leaderships of the parties are forced to dissociate themselves from 'their' university branches. In the second place, he shows that if the extreme positions of the groups of activist students are viewed with sympathy by the university population as a whole, which becomes evident when there are internal elections, the practical attitude of the majority of the students is different: most of them, as individuals, are trying to integrate with society as it stands.

If one acknowledges that the various intellectual revolutionary groups, including that advocating the method of guerrilla action are in fact giving expression to a class concept, then there does not seem to be any contradiction between the various attitudes of the students, bent on taking the place due to them in whatever type of society.

Is the Venezuelan case an exception? It would seem rather to be a model. It is in the university centres of Lima, Buenos Aires and Santiago, in the young intellectual circles of Rio, Bogotá and Mexico City that groups upholding the theory of guerrilla warfare are to be found. And one has only to peruse the lists of militant guerrilla fighters to see immediately that, with a few exceptions, they are composed of students and university graduates.

Analysing the guerrilla movement of 1965, Héctor Béjar, an officer of the ELN (National Liberation Army of Peru), points out that the year 1964 was apparently calm, but that Fernando Belaúnde's experiment, which tried to create a 'national bourgeoisie' and had raised lower middle class hopes before disappointing them, was failing. 'All this . . . is connected with the new insurgent groups of the lower middle class which shattered the *status quo* of bourgeois legality by means of the armed attacks of 1965. These political groups were the MIR and ELN, both of them strongly influenced by the mystique and ideology of the Cuban Revolution. They originated in APRA, the communist party and the new university syndicalism that harked back to Marxism-Leninism.'

There is one section of certain guerrilla movements, i.e.

army, navy officers taking part in guerrilla 'fronts', that deserves special study. In his analysis of the Venezuelan revolution, Douglas Bravo, the guerrilla leader of the State of Falcón and former member of the Political Bureau of the Venezuelan PC, emphasises the important part played by the group of 'patriot officers', which he saw as one of the four 'pillars' of the Armed Forces of National Liberation (FALN):

> In 1962, at a time when these guerrilla fronts were coming into existence, a group of officer patriots in Carupano, on May 4, took up arms against the government of Romulo Betancourt, instigated a rebellion in the town of Carupano and organised a heroic resistance ... A month later, ... on June 2, 1962, in the town of Puerto Cabello, the sailors rose. ... Remember the heroic battle of the Alcantarilla, where the patriots of the navy, together with workers and student patriots, held out in an extraordinary manner. ...[4]

Another example of participation by members of the armed forces is provided by the sailors, and especially the petty officers, of the Brazilian Navy. Even though, initially, it had to do with demands for promotion, the protest movement, partly tolerated and partly exploited by President Goulart, was to be wiped out by the military *coup d'état*. Some of the leaders were to come together again subsequently in the attempts to set up small *maquis* groups, notably in the Matto Grosso in 1966.

It is important to determine to what extent manifestations of rebellion in the armed forces correspond to that civilian phenomenon whereby members of the petty bourgeoisie who find themselves frustrated in their search for social advancement and who are losing faith in the normal machinery of promotion resort to violent means.

Official propaganda frequently stresses the 'criminal' character of certain terrorist groups or guerrilla bands. It would be as futile to deny the instances of 'gangster' participation in revolutionary operations or of peasant bandits joining guerrilla groups, as to try to generalise from these cases, treating them as indicative of the social composition of the movements of rebellion.

Bank raids or attacks on cashiers to secure funds for the politico-military organisation are common to most revolutionary movements. These illegal operations can only be successfully executed with the help of specialists, who are not necessarily political sympathisers. The destines of individuals are never simple.[5]

It goes without saying that the schoolboys and students flocking into the guerrilla groups are motivated to a large extent by sentiment. Reaction against the older generation, disgust for the contemptibly materialistic behaviour of adults, rejection of official hypocrisy, all help in determining the attitude of youth. These emotions cannot of themselves create and sustain an actual organisation. Nevertheless, they contribute, in no small measure, to producing the right climate. They play a considerable part too in innumerable cases where, for example, the representatives of the politically repressive régime are connected by family or friendship with young people who are involved in or, to some extent, responsible for subversive action.

7

Military Methods

THERE IS NO DOUBT that guerrilla warfare as such has a long pedigree and that it assumes different forms according to the locality, the origin of the men involved, their motives, the kinds of weapons available, etc. What is new is the deliberate creation of guerrilla groups as an instrument for the conquest of power.

Is there anything novel about the military techniques developed by the Cuban guerrillas? Are they considered applicable to the politico-military struggle in other countries? Have they, in actual fact, been copied and, if so, what have been the results? These are the questions that spring immediately to mind.

The much-lauded Cuban 'model' was not the creation of the leaders of the July 26 Movement. So-called Castroite propaganda theorises on the basis of an experiment, a model, that was never actually put into practice.

In fact, one does not find even an approximation to what is now presented as the Castroite 'theory' or 'method' in the recollections of those who took part in the first insurrectional attempts of the July 26 Movement.

According to Alberto Bayo, ex-general of the Spanish Republican Army and himself a native of the island, it was after discussion about the importance of the topics and tactics to be taught the Cuban volunteers training in Mexico for a Cuban landing that the idea of guerrilla warfare commended itself. 'Fidel himself said to me one day, "General Bayo, . . . I'd like you to tell them how to advance under enemy fire, how to attack in formation, how to retire, how to protect one's rear".'

'Of course I will teach them all this for the sake of their general military education, but I will also advise them never to use normal military tactics, because if we fight like that we will not last a month after the landing in Cuba, and I want to go on living.'[1]

The training being carried out in Mexico showed that none of the volunteers had any previous military experience, which sheds much light on the nature of the struggle that was to take place in Cuba. There is no large body of men, as in Europe, that has active experience of war or at least of military training, so that even a passing acquaintance with methods of combat gives its possessor an advantage over most other people. On the other hand, after 1933, Cuban military cadres were thoroughly revamped. The expulsion of the dictator, Machado, the installation of the provisional President, Carlos Manuel de Céspedes, followed by the seizure of power by Fulgencio Batista (then a sergeant) led to profound changes in the military command. The old generals were eliminated and a wave of promotions began that favoured the young officers. This new military hierarchy no longer depended directly on the old oligarchy, on the large landowners. It was tied to Batista's star and he was to make use of his 'captains and lieutenants' in the March 1952 *coup d'état*. However, this new generation of officers lost the popular support it had enjoyed at the time of Machado's fall. It was the prop but also the client of the Batista dictatorship, a partner in its corruption and decadence.

In the Cuban situation, therefore, the factors we have isolated as regards the military set-up are a population with no military background and an army linked to no clearly identifiable social class or even to the oligarchy.

In the preparatory 'Mexican' period, as during the early and most difficult months when the first group was getting a foothold on Cuban territory, and even afterwards when the July 26 forces were expanding, sponsoring new columns, and in control of certain areas, it was quite natural for most of the

74

energy to go into learning how to survive and fight. One is often reminded of the 'Soldier's Manual' when looking through the memoirs of the leaders. 'I immediately started on my course in theory. I spoke of the absolute need for discipline, the foundation and pillar of the army, of respect for the hierarchy, of obedience towards a superior whoever he may be, ... of the impermissibility of grumbling about the leaders.'[2]

Even in Bayo's *150 questions to a guerrilla fighter*[3] published in 1960 after the victory and a widely distributed soldier's manual, definitions like the following are to be found: 'Closed order consists of exercises that instil habits of discipline into the body of troops. The closed order conditions the guerrilla fighter in such a way as utterly to eliminate his will, to make him obey his commander, whoever he may be, implicitly, in the field ... At attention he must be like a statue, not moving an iota once the order, "eyes front!", has been given, and the salute must end in absolute immobility, arms raised to the same height and fingers in the same position.'

This attitude is common to military establishments throughout the world, from Camberley to Tataouine, from naval colleges to Red Army academies.

The first contacts with native soil, after the disastrous 'Granma' landing of December 2, 1956, were heroi-comic. The cargo was lost; there were only a few rifles left, and some sodden ammunition; the first guide was an informer; the survivors chewed sugar cane for food, scattering bits all along their trail like Tom Thumb. The first attack found them cut off from each other and in a state of exhaustion; it was to take the little parties of survivors several days to regroup. There is a certain humour in Che Guevara's account which, one should note in passing, contrasts with the verbose writings of the 'committed' writers, that is to say 'committed' after the event and over-fond of hyperbole: 'Night fell and we set out again. Drawing on my recollections of astronomy, I spotted the North Star, and for two days we guided ourselves by it, moving eastward towards the Sierra Maestra. Months later I was to learn that the star we used to find our way was not the North Star!

It was simply good luck that we took the right direction and arrived at dawn below some cliffs near the coast.'[4]

The emphasis which the 'doctrinaries' subsequently placed on the need for suspicion is understandable when one remembers the number of times the anti-Batista fighters were deceived, starting with Fidel Castro himself, who was convinced there was no traitor in the Mexican training group when in fact there was one of Batista's intelligence men on the course. Shortly after the landing, when the group had only just re-formed and won its first victory, it was Fidel again who permitted one of his men to go and visit 'his sick mother'. Provided with the money Fidel had given him, the good son made contact with the soldiers of the regular army, and the very next day the position was subjected to an aerial bombardment.

'Our small group, basically non-military, lived in the Sierra Maestra but was not adjusted to it: we went from hut to hut, we ate only when we could pay for it, we were tolerated but nothing more . . . We spent several months like this, wandering among the highest mountains of the Sierra Maestra, descending from time to time on brief raids and returning at once to the *maquis*. Life was very hard there.' This is how Che described the first period of the guerrilla war,[5] still a long way from the abstract picture of the perfect guerrilla that was to be projected after the victory.

Even in the manual subsequently published under the title of *Guerrilla Warfare*, dealing with theory and practice, there is rather a strange mixture of traditional precepts, an elementary exposé of the principles of military training for NCOs and recruits, nostalgic descriptions of life in the open air among men, and the kind of enthusiasm engendered by ex-service men looking back. In particular, there is a sort of exaltation of sweat, steaming feet, and suchlike, which would bring back memories for any 1914–18 veteran or infantryman with experience of something besides asceptic war:

Thus the guerrilla fighter will live for days without encountering any inhabited place, avoiding all contact that has not been previously arranged, staying in the wildest zones, knowing hunger, at times thirst, cold, heat; sweating during the continuous marches, letting the sweat dry on his body and adding to it new sweat without any possibility of regular cleanliness. . . . During the recent war, upon entering the village of El Uvero following a march of sixteen kilometres and a fight of two hours and forty-five minutes in a hot sun (all added to several days passed in very adverse conditions along the sea with intense heat from a boiling sun) our bodies gave off a peculiar and offensive odour that repelled anyone who came near. Our noses were completely accustomed to this type of life; the hammocks of guerrilla fighters are known for their characteristic, individual odour.[6] Within the framework of the combatant life, the most interesting event, the one that carries all to a convulsion of joy and puts new vigour in everybody's steps, is the battle. The battle, climax of the guerrilla life, is sought at an opportune moment either when an enemy encampment sufficiently weak to be annihilated has been located and investigated; or when an enemy column is advancing directly toward the territory occupied by the liberating force.

The conditions under which a column such as Camilo Cienfuegos' moves reflect the very special circumstances of Cuba and it is clear that one must be very cautious in trying to apply the same principles to other regions and other politico-social conditions.

To begin with, let me say that since we left the region of Cauto behind, travelling westward, we have been marching for forty days without resting a single night, most of the time without a guide, following the compass and with the south coast as our landmark. The journey was particularly hard in this region: for fifteen days we walked in water or mud up to the knees; and at night we had to take care to avoid ambushes and troops stationed at various points and cross-roads that lay on our route. During the thirty-one days it took to cross the province of Camagüey, we ate only eleven times, although it is Cuba's richest region for livestock farming. After four days without anything to eat at all, we had to slaughter a mare, the best of our few mounts, for food. Nearly all our provisions had been lost in the swamps and quicksands of the south coast.[7]

In the same report, Cienfuegos observed, 'Several days afterwards we learnt that there had been a group of soldiers stationed at the place we had passed, that they heard the shot and the sound of our marching but did nothing to stop us. This is concrete proof of the reluctance of Batista's army to fight, of its steadily declining morale.'[8]

If Ernesto Guevara's manual contains endless details and advice on life in the *maquis*, on the rôle of women, liaison, communications, discipline, etc., the problems of the rebel army, that is to say of larger more distinct units, relating to logistics, general tactics and strategy, are dealt with perfunctorily in a few generalised paragraphs. The reason is that the experience is lacking. The military collapse of Batista's régime occasioned no confrontation between large forces. It is always the beginning, the settling in that is stressed:

Relatively small nuclei of people chose places suitable for guerrilla warfare, either with the intention of launching a counter-attack, or to test the way the wind is blowing, and that is where the action begins. We must be quite clear about what follows. In the first period, the relative weakness of the guerrilla band is such that it must concentrate on getting a footing, finding out about the district, establishing contacts with the population and fortifying places that, in case of need, might be transformed into inlying pickets.

There are three conditions of survival for a guerrilla band that starts off in these circumstances, constant mobility, constant vigilance, constant suspicion.[9]

In contrast, the political character of the guerrilla nucleus is emphasised from the beginning. If it is hard to find anything at all original from the point of view of military technique, of the mass organisation of the struggle, when other periods and other regions have been very productive in this respect (witness the Ukrainian *Makhnovshchina*, or Vietnam), there is something new in the conception of the rôle of the guerrilla band: it is the school of power and its conquest. 'The guerrilla band now has an organisation, a new structure. It is the head of a large movement with all the characteristics of a small government.

A court is established for the administration of justice, laws may be promulgated and the work of indoctrination of the peasant masses continues, extended also to workers if there are any near, to draw them to the cause ... '[10]

There is one set of tactics Guevara does make much of but that would seem practical only in the case of an army reluctant to fight. Here is how it works:

In the first stage of guerrilla warfare, enemy columns will penetrate deep into insurgent territory; depending on the strength of these columns two different types of guerrilla attacks will be made. One of these, first in chronological order, is for a fixed number of months to cause systematic losses in the enemy's offensive capacity. This tactic is carried out on the vanguards. Unfavourable ground impedes flank defences by the advancing columns; there must therefore always be one point of the vanguard that, as it penetrates and exposes the lives of its components, serves to give security to the rest of the column. When men and reserves are insufficient and the enemy is strong, the guerrilla should always aim for the destruction of this vanguard point. The system is simple; only a certain coordination is necessary. At the moment when the vanguard appears at the selected place—the steepest possible—a deadly fire is let loose on them, after a convenient number of men have been allowed to penetrate. A small group must hold the rest of the column for some moments while arms, munitions and equipment are being collected.

Further on, Guevara points out that one of the results of these tactics is that soon there is no one willing any longer to be in an advance party, 'and it is clear that a column without a vanguard cannot advance ... '

Possibly these tactics were, in fact, applied and proved effective in Cuba, but there is some doubt as to their value in other places and in different circumstances; they put one in mind of the expedient of removing the end-carriage in a train as a preventive measure against the accidents to which such carriages are more prone than others.

The Cuban plan outlined by the theoreticians of guerrilla warfare was followed by none of the guerrilla movements of

Latin America, even in a modified form as to place and circumstances. This is not at all surprising, as the basic features of the Cuban situation in the 50s were duplicated in no other region.

The Venezuelan guerrilla movement resulted from the impossibility for revolutionary groups of pursuing their activities in the towns, mainly Caracas; but its survival always depended on maintaining a recruitment, information, liaison and financing base in the capital—or more precisely, the university centres.

The Colombian guerrilla bases were the product of the disintegration of the old activist peasant movements—and the attempt by political groups of the extreme left to take over what survived of them. The Guatemalan guerrillas originated in military factions. As for the many Peruvian experiments, these looked more like syndicalism reaching a point of confrontation with the régime, as in the case of Hugo Blanco's movement, or adventuristic attempts at *coups d'état*, like that of Luis de la Puente. Everywhere else, whether in Argentina or Brazil, it was only a case of the after-effects of urban movements or the short-lived adventures of a few handfuls of students.

There remains Bolivia, always supposing that it was not a case of an international training camp rather than a national politico-military base, up to the moment when the regular forces fell on the guerrillas. There, at least, there was a weak army, a discredited government, working-class districts in the towns and mining areas that were in favour of a change of régime. However, agrarian reform has been an established fact ever since 1952 and this does not fit into the scheme. It is inconceivable that the peasantry should be mobilised against a landed oligarchy that has vanished from Oriente region, where there is no land problem.

8

Theories and Techniques of Counter-Guerrilla Warfare

As SOON AS one looks at the problem of guerrilla warfare from the general viewpoint of revolutionary violence and in a world perspective, the issue threatens to become confused. This is the impression one often gets from articles in the North American and European press.

There are some happy exceptions. One of these is provided by Captain Samuel Griffith of the United States Marines who, in 1940, translated Mao Tse-tung's pamphlet, *Yu Chi Chan* (Guerrilla Warfare) published in China in 1937. This military man, no innocent in such matters, links the tactics of speed, surprise and guile in combat, advocated by the communist leader, with the tradition and influence of the Chinese military philosopher Sun-Tzu, who wrote the *Book of War*, some 2,400 years ago. He finds no difficulty in appreciating the fact that 'guerrilla warfare was not invented by the communists; guerrillas have existed for centuries'. He is quite clear also about the difference between a regular army recruit and a guerrilla fighter: 'In the United States, we take great care to keep soldiers out of politics, and even more so to keep politicians at some distance from soldiers. The guerrillas do the exact reverse. They take the utmost pains to ensure that their soldiers are politically educated and fully aware of the issues at stake.' In 1961, and now a brigadier-general, Griffith's clear-sightedness was still in evidence, witness the new preface to his translation, in which he says: 'A revolutionary war is never confined to military action.' In the same way, he differentiates between 'partisans' and 'guerrillas': 'The basic difference between the patriotic resistance of partisan wars and the revolutionary movements of guerrilla wars lies in the fact that the former usually lacks the ideological content that always informs the latter. Resistance is distinguished by its spontaneous nature: it begins and then gets itself organised. A revolutionary movement organises itself first and begins afterwards.'[1]

First pouring scorn on those who believe that there are certain types of modern weapons that can eliminate guerrillas, and pointing out the feasibility of victory for guerrilla movements given a number of political and social as well as military factors, Griffith then turns his attention to counter-guerrilla operations. In his view, they can be summed up in three words: location, isolation and eradication.

In fact, counter-guerrilla activity has no chance of success unless it turns guerrilla tactics against the guerrillas themselves, subjecting them to endless assaults, harrying them, causing desertions and taking prisoners. As against Mao and despite the events on which the latter bases his opinion, the collapse of the White armies in Russia for example, Griffiths believes that it is possible to create 'counter-guerrilla forces' under certain conditions, but he admits that this largely depends on extra-military factors.

This acuteness and realism is not to be found in the work of James Eliot Gross[2] where, despite or maybe because of the wealth of historical references, so many examples are given that the picture becomes blurred: a huge file is opened under the heading, 'Non-conventional wars'. A whole series of factors are isolated from the Arabs in Lawrence's time, Spain under the Napoleonic occupation, the mutineers of the *Bounty*, the defence of the Warsaw ghetto and the East Berlin rising of 1953, making the reader's head spin in the end. The conclusions reached illustrate this, witness the following unilluminating observations: 'It is important to realize that the support given a guerrilla movement does not necessarily indicate the enthusiastic and spontaneous support of a large majority of the population.' Or: ' . . . [this] people grows very aware of the importance of choosing the safe side.'

The definitions given of the various movements are, in any case, questionable. The Organisation of the Secret Army (OAS), for instance, is described as 'an essentially urban resistance movement'. If the collection of facts or experiences taken from all over the world and from different periods of history does not reveal what is common to all 'non-conventional wars' and serves only to show how hard it is to theorise, at least the chapter devoted to military technology might shed some light on what is probably taught in the schools of counter-guerrilla warfare.

Stress is laid on one factor that favours the government side, namely an extensive railway network enabling the authorities to move their forces about quickly and easily. But there is a danger of 'logistic intoxication', which may lead to a weakening of the government's forces, as a result of their inability to do without means of transport. The same goes for the advantages and disadvantages of the road network: road convoys allow for easy penetration, but they are more exposed to ambush. In practice, sabotage of trains, bridges, railway tunnels is more effective and causes more extensive damage than harrying or attacking convoys or mining roads.

Similar attention is devoted to the communications system in the authorities' hands, especially the telephone and radio network. Except where they can rely on a station situated on foreign territory, the guerrilla forces are in an inferior position here.

For the location and destruction of guerrilla groups, James Eliot Gross regards the aeroplane as being too fast, and thinks that the helicopter, although more vulnerable, possesses certain advantages. It is the helicopter that can serve as a means of transport for small units and also keep them supplied.

As for weapons, it is stated that most heavy arms are unserviceable for this type of fighting. Apart from nuclear weapons which cannot be used for various reasons, the main one being that the political damage caused would outweigh the military gain, there are undoubtedly certain techniques for raising 'hot barriers' against infiltration; but there again, their use would meet with political objections. In the final count, it is the type of weapon used by the individual, the supply of ammunition, the soldiers' marksmanship that are important.

'In short,' the author concludes, 'the introduction of modern infantry weapons into guerrilla battles has produced some changes in the tactics of both sides but has not basically modified the ratio of strength between regular and irregular combatants.'

These are commonplaces and it is hard to see of what use they could be to officers and technicians studying at the Fort Gulick Center for guerrilla and counter-guerrilla tactics in the Panama Canal zone; of no more use, one would think, than are Lenin's commentaries on Clausewitz's *Vom Kriege* to the guerrillas of the Peruvian valleys or the Amazonian *selva*.

In practice, and in spite of the vast literature on psychological warfare, or on the particular tactics suitable for guerrilla warfare, that has been and still is circulating, methods of repression have scarcely altered at all. To take only the case of Peru, in 1965, when fronts were opened in the North, South and Centre, it is clear that the army's methods were as simple as could be. When a guerrilla base had been located, either through direct observation or information supplied, the place was pinpointed on a military map and a zone was marked out with compasses and subjected to saturation bombing. After that, there were no guerrilla fighters left and sometimes no inhabitants either.

The crudeness of the means employed should not make us jump to the conclusion that the Peruvian military men have no political sensibility or are unaware of the nature of the social problems. It cannot be too strongly emphasised that the army is one of the few official institutions where contact with the peasant, the Indian, is an established fact; many officers are intimately familiar with the mentality of the valley-dwellers. Furthermore, it is usually in the army barracks that the peasant first becomes conscious of so-called civilised living: bed, shoes, hygiene, etc., and also of the concept of a nation, with all due reservations as to what that term signifies. It is, in fact, in the army that the peasant realises that his local power game fits into a larger, state-sized context, that the army is the state as much as, if not more than, the 'politicians'.

A volume issued by the Peruvian Ministry of War in 1966[3] certainly contains sufficient contemptuous references to 'agitators', 'bearded ones', etc., but there is also precise data on the interdependence of local interest groups, peasant questions, the mentality of the Indians of the *selva*. This familiarity with the people, the land and its problems was to allow the forces of repression to operate with greater agility, added to their already superior armaments.

The terms used to describe the population of the 'troubled' areas might have been taken out of an anti-oligarchy propaganda pamphlet: 'Whether Indian, half-breed or forest-dweller, with all his concomitant virtues and faults, with all his hopes and agonies, his difficulties and anxieties, pliable and hard-working, whether magnificent soldier, worker or farmer, he has a deeply rooted ancestral love for the land, is religious to the point of superstition and is today getting on his feet and beginning to sense his strength and ability.' And ' ... The indigenous population of the Sierra, exploited for centuries, with no means of becoming educated, with a low standard of living, enduring the poverty of the soil or of the locality where he works, devoting his life to hard labour and continual sacrifices for the sake of his daily bread.'

This was the kind of individual that the army was to put its stake on. And in the end, it was the 'Campa' Indians of the forest who provided the forces of repression with information and guides, something the guerrillas had never been able to obtain from them, except initially when they were establishing themselves. The army distributed supplies, provided medical care, in short took full advantage of its superiority in means and resources.

As soon as the government acknowledged that the crisis had reached the point where the army would have to take over, the

Supreme Decree of July 2, 1965, the military command set to displaying its efficiency in putting down guerrillas, but also demonstrated that it was more than just a governmental instrument, proving that all the political machinations of the parties were incapable of safeguarding what was vital to the nation and the state, whereas it could be safely entrusted to a vigilant army.

The army was ready and all it was waiting for was the decree. Apart from strictly organisational measures, steps had been taken to isolate the guerrillas from the population:

' ... The armed forces are carrying out an intensive information and propaganda campaign, broadcasting messages in the native language over loudspeakers carried in aeroplanes and helicopters, dropping thousands of leaflets, telling the peasantry, whether literate or not, to refrain from collaborating with the guerrillas out of ignorance or fear ... ' Finally, to avoid there being any innocent victims in the region, women and children were advised to keep away from any suspect.

The army was on the offensive in the valleys from the start, stationing small platoons of soldiers in all the hamlets and at crossroads, locating, pursuing and destroying guerrilla groups. In this hunt, the local peasantry no longer gave the insurgents any help; the latter were harbingers of disaster and, with their backs to the wall, they were virtually reduced to making demands, issuing threats and dealing out punishment.

Since 1960 specialised centres have existed in the training and education programmes of the Latin American armies established by the armed forces of the United States, where about 1,500 men a year have been trained for the anti-guerrilla struggle, according to the figures quoted by the *New York Times*.

Another police-type training centre is the International Police Academy in Washington, which contains a high proportion of Latin American students. This institution is not directly linked with the programme of military aid, but it is involved in certain tactical anti-subversive exercises.[4]

According to information supplied by the United States Defense Department in May 1967 the number of Latin

American soldiers trained in the various colleges of the North amounted to 1,323 for the year 1966, and those trained 'abroad', that is to say outside US territory but following North American programmes, to 4,692.

It is probable that training camps for guerrillas have operated and are still operating in Cuba, but it will be some time before we learn much about their nature, size significance and the difficulties affecting them. At present, the information issued is too often propagandistic in character.

What is clear now, even in the absence of the relevant information, is that both these training schemes are much more closely related to a kind of activism and instinct to spend state funds than to clearly demonstrable needs. It would be interesting, and doubtless highly revealing, to know exactly how many 'specialists' trained in the North American colleges have been called on to fight in Latin America and, where this may have happened, what use their training has been to them in their engagements with guerrillas. It would be just as interesting to discover the number of guerrilla hopefuls who have trained in Cuba, and to find out from those who really tried to engage in guerrilla activity in their country, to what extent their Cuban 'period' was useful to them.

We can be certain that there is as great a distance between the courses at Fort Gulick or on the Island of Pinos and the continual improvisation of battle, as there is between the books of Mao Tse-tung and the experiences of those French officers in North Africa who combed his writings for the key to victory.

The 'experts' of the national armed forces in Latin America tend to identify every opposition movement that threatens the established order, which they are pledged to protect (and sometimes make trouble for if the prestige of the officer corps is threatened), with international communism.

The official intelligence statements and documents generally treat pro-Chinese communists, pro-Soviet communists, extremist nationalists and rebels of every kind of ideological persuasion as coming under the same heading. There are certain advantages in this, as it eliminates all hesitations and

87

drastically simplifies the work of repression. The military is thereby saved from having any doubts on the matter. This is an instinctive reaction. Nevertheless, there are certain drawbacks too, even if only because all these different elements are driven, at least emotionally, into extremist positions, and the changes that all societies must undergo are forcibly delayed and therefore tend to be more violent when they do occur. Finally, the adjustments taking place willy nilly in the military establishment itself are ignored, so that the tensions of society as a whole manifest themselves in the very structure of the army.

Even if the logical reaction of military régimes like those of Argentina, Brazil and Paraguay to the threat of rebellions in neighbouring territories is to exchange information with each other, strengthen liaison between general staffs, station frontier troops to prevent infiltration and supply those faced by guerrillas with war materials, it is nonetheless inconceivable that this defensive solidarity against a common enemy should lead to the establishment of supra-national organisations. There is still the greatest suspicion of any scheme that would limit the freedom of each military establishment, or rather of each militaristic society, and that would subject it to overall control.

Neither the Organisation of American States, nor the Inter-American Defence Junta, nor the schemes for inter-American Forces have been able to function, except in so far as they provide a framework that facilitates meetings and limited agreements between cautious and still reserved voluntary members. The grandiloquent declarations, the publicity that surrounds the continental conferences cannot hide the fact that each military establishment is intent on remaining master in its own house. Anti-yankee feelings are not the monopoly of the guerrillas.

9

Guerrillas Within the Political System

THE GUERRILLA theoreticians' conception of a ruthless war presupposes the existence of two powers quarrelling over the control of the population. The official state uses all the means at its disposal to maintain the social structure intact, which means preserving the dominance of the oligarchic classes that have the advantage of the support of United States imperialism in the defence of common interests and privileges. The Counter-State, that is the politico-military guerrilla establishment, wages a war to the death with the official authority, grouping the exploited elements of society and making use of the tensions inevitably set up by social injustice and presumptuous foreign intervention.

This Sorelian concept is rarely borne out by the facts (any more than the French trade union movement corresponded to George Sorel's ideas, for the very good reason that it in no way owed its inception and development to the theoretician). Social change is an infinitely complex phenomenon that cannot be explained simply in terms of a duel between two powers, nor are its multifarious aspects necessarily reflected in the vicissitudes of an armed confrontation.

The simplistic formula of the state as instrument of the oligarchy, which is itself the accomplice and partner of US imperialism might satisfy the intellectual élites with their eye on the conquest of power. And propagandistically, as a stratagem whereby all the various strands of discontent may be brought together, it has its value. Nevertheless, it is inapplicable to everyday political and social life where and when the determining factors in the behaviour of the various classes of the population operate normally, marginally and often in opposition to the ideologies.

The guerrilla bands are conditioned by this real situation even where they are the direct result of the conscious effort of a group of men seeking power. Their leaders live in constant fear of seeing their clichéd black-and-white explanations being given the lie by political developments. Their permanent hope lies in the blindness of officialdom. It would be disastrous if a settlement were to preclude confrontation, so that there is profound relief when the enemy controlling the state machinery hangs on to power and refuses to make way for a liberal régime. In his account of the revolutionary war, Ernesto Guevara recalls: 'A qualitative change had occurred; there was a whole zone that the enemy army avoided so as not to meet up with us; it is true that neither were we too eager to clash with them. At that time the political situation was full of possibilities for opportunists. Thus there was on Batista's side a similar will to continue the struggle, the only thing we agreed on, as we too were determined to continue it at all costs.'

In the March 1966 'Iracara Manifesto' Douglas Bravo felt obliged to go into details about Venezuelan political arrangements, the parties and groups that had for some time been gambling on a violent outcome to strengthen their opposition to the Acción Democrática government ended by joining it on the formula of a 'broader base'. This is what happened in the case of an important section of the political front which consisted of the party of the MIR leadership, the National Democratic Front and the Republican Democratic Union. The Christian-Democratic movement (COPEI) on the other hand held back, not in a revolutionary sense but as a prospective alternative government, and always keeping to the rules of the parliamentary game. In plain terms, this showed that the financial resources, the means at the disposal of the state were sufficient to satisfy not only the clients of Acción Democrática but also of the parties close to it, and that there was still something over to put into a programme of agrarian reform, a workers' housing plan or the development of new industries.

It is in connection with these developments that we should interpret Douglas Bravo's remarks: the lower-middle-class, the favourite environment for guerrilla propaganda, is not frustrated and social mobility and advancement can be guaranteed by the régime.

Politically, imperialism has maintained itself in power by means of the different *service* governments. That is why the enemy, at this stage, is the coalition government, against which we must erect a huge resistance front composed of all opponents of the régime, including certain sections of the governmental side that have some reservations about 'gorilla-style' politics,[1] with Betancourt dominating a coalition government.

Nevertheless, we must remain on our guard and not lose sight of the fact that the COPEI is now one of the principal weapons in the class enemy's struggle with the liberation movement and that it is probably destined to become the main stand-by of imperialism and the Venezuelan oligarchy.

As regards the other reformist parties, one must distinguish between the popular basis that they still influence and control, and the conservative, reformist, opportunistic leadership, that has utterly betrayed the people's interests; and one must be even more careful to make this distinction with regard to the COPEI. As a matter of fact, as well as furnishing the clearest example of the internal class enemy, it has a homogeneous organisation and a programme that unites its supporters and therefore constitutes a special danger for the workers' movement.

In reality, many advocates of the AD, URD and FND, parties that have abandoned their principles, might once more be deceived by the false theoretical prospects of COPEI, utterly alien as they are to the objectives of liberation.

We cannot deny the skilful use the COPEI makes of its presumed and entirely verbal opposition to the government, in order to diguise its concurrence in the coalition's policy of repression, torture, encirclement and rounding up of guerrilla bases, because the COPEI, AD, FND and, in general, all the traditional reformist parties,

91

are identical as regards their support for the neo-colonialist system
that prevails in our country.

Given the fact not only that there is a coalition government
which still runs the country, but also that its difficulties and
problems do not improve revolutionary prospects and do not
lead to a heightening of the guerrilla struggle, but only to the
regular parliamentary succession of another democratic party,
the dualistic technique of the counter-government proves
ineffectual. It becomes necessary for the guerrilla politico-
military leadership to stress the external enemy, the United
States, as it cannot make the legal government look like a
universally detested monster with no prospects: 'A basic
method of combatting guerrilla fronts and of carrying out
repressions against the peasantry is by encirclement. This is
the technique chosen by the Pentagon in its tactical and
strategic struggle against the guerrillas, the people and liberation movements throughout the world.'

When Luis de la Puente who, in 1961, had been working on
an agrarian reform bill, of which the main objective was to
'eliminate all aspects of feudalism in order to encourage capitalist agriculture and cattle-breeding', becomes convinced, in
1965, that armed struggle alone can bring about the social
transformations Peru needs, he is, as an individual, taking a
crucial step. The main point is to find out if significant sections
of the population, in real conditions of exploitation and sub-
sistence living, are following this path as rapidly.

In 1961 too the leaders of the Venezuelan MIR, Humberto
Cuenca and Domingo Alberto Rangel, condemned the
Acción Democrática–COPEI alliance, called for a union of the
MIR, URD and PC to fight Betancourt's 'despotism', and expressed
the opinion that there was only one alternative to the crisis:
dictatorship or revolution.[2] For a year after this, terrorism
raged in the towns. Guerrilla bands were on the increase. In
1966, with the experience of it behind him, Rangel suggested
from prison that a lesson should be learnt from the failure of
the movement of violence and a return made to other, less

systematically insurrectional methods. There again, must one assume that the choice of and variations on tactics reflect the state of mind and aspirations of the people, or that they are attributable only to those with ambitions to take over the state?

However firmly the proponents of the direct path forecast the long or short-term outcome of future events as allowing increasing scope to the counter-state and creating more and more difficulties and dilemmas for the state, the facts do not lend themselves to this interpretation and frequently run counter to the predictions. This is especially so when the latter begin looking like scenarios based mainly on imagination. Here, for the last time, is Régis Debray:

This growth, from an isolated minority into a minority with a popular base, being transformed into the driving force behind the final violent flood-tide, gathers rapid momentum after the initial impulse. The first contact with the peasantry of the mountains, in which the guerrilla band settles for reasons of security and natural defence, is the most difficult one to establish and consolidate. These isolated peasants, small-scale owners of deforested, barren land (the *conuqueros* of Falcón in Venezuela or the Indian crop-sharers of the northern Agentine) are also the most devoid of political consciousness, the most difficult to guide and organise because of their very dispersion, their illiteracy and initial suspicion of strangers whose presence, they believe, heralds nothing but bombardments, pillage and senseless repression. But later, once this class has been won over, the guerrilla *base*, already firmly established as regards supplies, information and men, will go out to meet the agricultural wage-earners of the *low lands*: the sugar-cane workers of the Argentine north, often 'imported' from neighbouring Bolivia; the unemployed of the large towns of Falcón; the wage-earning workers of the northeastern coast of Brazil; that is to say, a much more receptive and materially formed class, by reason of its concentration. chronic unemployment, total dependence on the fluctuations of the capitalist market, etc. Finally, in the nearby towns, contact will be made with the small, already politically conscious concentrations of workers in the local manufacturing industries, without need for the slow preliminary work essential initially in the mountains.[3]

93

This 'Nevsky view' of guerrilla warfare was put into effect neither in Cuba, nor elsewhere. Must one, therefore, conclude that guerrilla wars are simply transient phenomena, in no way affecting the societies where they originate? It would be just as wrong to underestimate them as to give them a central place in the scheme of things, firstly because they are often the product of perfectly comprehensible politico-social circumstances, also because they afford one greater insight into the 'class character' of a number of aspirants to power, because they focus the moral if hypocritical reactions of student youth, and finally because they play a not inconsiderable, even if incalculable, part in the changes taking place in Latin American society.

To borrow the graphic expression of a Peruvian leftist intellectual and quoted by François Bourricaud,[4] in certain circumstances 'guerrilla warfare constitutes a new form of political wire-pulling'. In terms of Peruvian political life this means that, if guerrilla warfare fails to turn the country upside down and transform it, it simply becomes another factor in the power struggle. In 1965 when the fronts opened it was the conservative daily *La Prensa* that devoted its front page to the negligence, impotence and inefficiency of Belaúnde's reformist government and it was APRA that shrieked in protest and attacked the presidency! Although the incumbent government is naturally the first target, if the guerrillas have any real strength at all, the ministers do their utmost to minimise the danger, even going so far as to deny the existence of a *maquis*. They speak of *bandoleros*, bandits. The army, for its part, looks on with detached amusement. It waits for the parliamentary comedy to play itself out in the struggle with the guerrillas, knowing that, in the end, the parties will turn to it to put a stop to the activities of the local 'Castroites'. And, indeed, once Belaúnde appealed to the armed forces, the fate of the guerrillas was sealed. The proclamations, Marxist-Leninist arguments, observations on oligarchy and US imperialism, pamphlets full of good advice made no earthly difference.

Belaúnde was only the more convinced of the need to

accelerate the reforms, extend agrarian reform, increase the drive for social advancement, speed up the disintegration of the old oligarchic strongholds. The generals and colonels emerged surer than ever of their irreplaceability as guardians of the nation's highest interests. Several thousand young people, in school and college, sought a different means to reach the positions that would give their qualities of leadership full scope. A few hundred would mourn fallen comrades and help the imprisoned militants. And, seeking cohesion and decisiveness, Peru would continue to adjust herself haphazardly to a changing world.

Similarly in Venezuela a larger number of parties and groups were given a share in power at the same time as slow, cautious but significant steps were taken in the universities to ensure that the natural heirs to power came to respect the rules of the game.

As for Bolivia, where the multiplicity of parties reflected the extreme instability of alliances, it seems that the irruption of guerrilla bands into the politically confused situation did not basically alter the dismal picture.

Force has been readily employed on the *altiplano*[5] and in the valleys since the revolution of 1952, and the bulk of the population is now showing signs of weariness rather than ardour. The disintegration of the MNR, with its majority of half-castes, which was the great party of renewal and, for better or for worse, did provide the country with an administration, has also tended to encourage scepticism. It is a question now of waiting for a period of organisation, of normalisation that would give the political groups and cliques a breathing space and allow them to make a bit more sense of a chaotic situation.

To illustrate this distintegration of political life, one has only to list the parties that sprang into activity at the time of the July 1966 elections. There were those, of course, that gave President-General René Barrientos his majority. The Barrientist People's Party, Real (Authentic) Revolutionary Party, People's Christian Movement, Social-Democratic Party, Party of the Revolutionary Left and Socialist Revolutionary

Party joined together in the Front of the Bolivian Revolution for electoral purposes. Under the title of the Democratic-Christian Community, the opposition united the Bolivian Socialist Phalanx, Democratic Revolutionary Alliance and National Association of Democratic Professional People. Also in opposition were the Party of Socialist Republican Union, Liberal Party, Democratic Institutionalist Alliance, Revolutionary Nationalist Movement and Paz-Estenssorist Movement. Further to the left—though this term has a special meaning in the Bolivian political spectrum—stood the National Liberation Front, with one important participant, namely the pro-Soviet Communist Party of Bolivia. There was in addition a People's Democratic Committee, which brought together the abstentionist groups, the Communist Party of Bolivia, this one pro-Chinese, the Trotskyite Revolutionary Workers' Party, the Revolutionary Party of the Nationalist Left, the Revolutionary Nationalist Movement and finally the Espártaco group.

In most of these alliances, one can find a combination of nationalistic, Marxist and Christian elements, and the revolutionary is omnipresent.

There is one major consideration here that overrides everything else: the support of the Confederation of Peasant Workers of Bolivia for the Front of the Bolivian Revolution, i.e. General Barrientos. This means that the only state machine, the army, can depend on an organisation representing the largest section of the population: the peasants. There are endless political arrangements possible in filling ministerial vacancies, but the two principal sectors, the army and peasantry, cannot henceforth be ignored and it is only by taking great care not to provoke them that the old foxes or young wolves of the innumerable parties can win over those in power or at least those who run the administrative machine.

In these conditions, a guerrilla movement can only be a precarious contributory factor in any scheme to gain apparent or limited power, a means of blackmail in the hands of men who undertake to liquidate it once they have gained their objectives.

Guerrillas Within the Political System

The paradox about the guerrilla war in Bolivia is that, in spite of a theory that stresses the rôle of the peasantry, it has to find its fighters, apart from the intellectual leaders, among the miners, or more precisely the former organisers of the miners.

There is no question about the willingness of the opposition, beginning with former President Víctor Paz Estenssoro, to take advantage of the guerrilla factor in carrying on and developing its struggle against General Barrientos. But this is not to help the guerrilla movement as such; it is to make use of it in specific circumstances. The declarations of the former MNR leader, from his place of refuge in Lima, are eloquent to an extreme. While giving due weight to the significance of the guerrilla base as a manifestation of disapproval against the military régime, a reaction on the part of understandably discontented citizens, etc., the argument touches on the inability of the army to deal with the problem of the armed base, when a really popular government could do so equally well.

In a statement to the Italian journalist, Carlo Coccioli, who came to visit him in his Lima exile to find out what he thought about the Bolivian guerrillas, Paz Estenssoro said: 'It is a mistake to believe that the future of Bolivia lies either in the victory of the military government or in that of the guerrilla movement. There are other possibilities ... The guerrilla war must have the sympathy of all democrats today, to the extent that it contributes to the weakening of the régime of the military men. But that is all.' In his view, the military men in power were 'anti-popular and unpopular, which explains the growth of the armed rebellion, especially in the mining area. But should the rebellion take a really Castroite turn, the rural population which is helping it at present, though without any great enthusiasm, would inevitably come to reject it in theory and practice: Bolivia is not fertile soil for Cuban propaganda.'[6]

In an article devoted to the Bolivian situation, Ted Cordova Claure quotes Paz Estenssoro's reply to the question: what is the MNR's attitude to the guerrillas?

I cannot deny that the party militants are favourably disposed

towards the guerrillas. Several miners' leaders have travelled here
to ask what should be done. I asked them if they felt active help
should be given the guerrillas and they think it should; and this
reply is understandable, since the activities of the guerrillas give
grounds for hope whereas there was none following the military
coup. Officially, I cannot give any support to the guerrillas. But as
long as the MNR has no presence in Bolivia, no one can prevent some
militants from sympathising and even going so far as to collaborate
with the guerrillas.[7]

On a more searching academic level, the Colombian, Orlando
Fals Borda, a sociologist specialising in the study of the
phenomenon of force, has tried to identify what corresponds
to the rejection of an obsolete, unjust and inefficient society, as
well as the will to construct a better one, in the insurrectional
activities of what he calls the 'anti-élite'.

He believes that the guerrilla bands, together with the trade
unions and university movements, are the direct heirs of the
socialist utopianism of the first quarter of the present century,
in terms of values like supranationalism, technicism and
humanism, and in terms of 'norms' (mobility, technical control,
etc.). This neo-socialism is autochthonous moreover and acknowledges the place of rebellion in a political strategy that envisages
a total transformation, thus differing from the politics of reform
or evolution.

The artificially and painfully maintained political balance
between traditional parties can only delay the necessary changes,
as all it does is to increase the tensions till they reach breaking
point, that is the point of violence. The social forces of inertia
(the oligarchy and landowners) prevent the normal integration
of the new élites (i.e. the younger generations), thereby transforming them into revolutionary 'anti-élites'.

Indeed, it is the strait-jacket of official force that prevents
the necessary structural reform and finally leads to revolutionary violence. The first assault on inertia may well result
from a mobilisation of the masses around demagogues or
caudillos, but it will be followed by the people-antipeople
confrontation.

Guerrillas Within the Political System

There is, without doubt, a side of the question that fits Orlando Fals Borda's flexible and non-sectarian thesis, namely the absolute need for change, the impossibility for a society structurally retarded in every field of technical development to preserve its mechanisms, its élites and the pattern of interdependence between interest groups at different levels of the social scale.

In this respect, it is clear that the pressure for change, including guerrilla warfare, is a response to the natural, spontaneous demands of revolution.

One begins to have certain reservations when the author[8] associates this type of revolutionary change with socialist and communitarian progress. It is true that he sees the future not in terms of a centralised and dictatorial power but, after the initial thrust, as being determined by the interplay of social, economic and historical forces, liberated at last; in other words, in terms of a society representing a new and higher synthesis. It is also true that he does not despair of seeing the present élite making the kind of effort towards a new understanding that could preclude tragedy.

Over and beyond the eddies and sporadic crises, however, he believes in historical progress. One can only hope that events prove him right, even if history itself furnishes us with more reasons for scepticism than optimism.

Part II

The National Situations

IO

Venezuela. The Long Way Back to Legality

FOR SEVEN YEARS, Venezuelan political life has provided the international press agencies with an endless supply of sensational items: incidents of terrorism, armed attacks, battles between revolutionary groups and police detachments, assassinations, kidnappings, hijacking of planes and boats, street executions, capture of arsenals, imprisonment of members of parliament, escapes and more or less voluntary suicides, mountain ambushes, military rebellions, formation of guerrilla detachments, birth of opposition fronts, splits in the revolutionary parties. There is enough material for a hundred reports and a dozen films, for a voluminous and rumbustious chronicle if there were only someone to write it.

A mere enumeration of the events would run into many chapters, in a welter of names of militants and victims, lovers of justice and killers, parties and groups, an earthy mixture of heroism and denunciation, an endless list finally growing monotonous, like the cries of dying men. So, even the mechanical assignation of responsibility and the appeals to moral principles become incongruous, inhuman because too logical or decorous, whereas the individuals concerned, nearly all of them young, were dependent neither on these rapturous emotions nor on the condemnations of propaganda. This is why one must try to understand both their aspirations and the net result of their struggles, excesses, tactical genius and valour.

When the dictator Pérez Jiménez fell, in 1958, the Venezuelan Communist Party (PCV) followed a straightforward political line, namely support, if critical, for the Rómulo Betancourt government. While the party had been illegal, some fairly lively in-fighting had gone on, but the upper échelons remained faithful to the Soviet lead. In 1960, they supported Khrushchev.

In a Venezuela where democracy is becoming established, where parliamentarianism is flourishing, the leader of Acción Democrática, Betancourt, is playing a difficult game, but he holds some strong cards. The task is to shape a new and modern nation, and to see that the last vestiges of the old régime are swept aside, while avoiding unnecessary clashes, by harnessing the enthusiasm and ambitions of the new middle-class generations to the establishment of a state administration and by giving the leading spirits behind the social, political, trade union, intellectual and academic struggles, who were responsible for toppling and destroying dictatorial power, jobs and real functions in this administration. The parties and democratic organisations are in effect being asked to take part in the construction of a new country. Income accruing from a lucrative oil industry undoubtedly facilitates agrarian reform, industrialisation and the organisation of an efficient state system. And this amounts to real social reforms.

If the communists are keeping quiet, numerous left and extreme left-wing currents are pressing home their demands. Many activists both inside and outside Acción Democrática show a preference for the simpler and more direct policy of sweeping away the vestiges of the old régime and building a machinery of government that would turn the state into the dynamic force behind economic development. The Cuban course, which placed power in the hands of the bold, seems more straightforward than political manœuvring, electoral-based compromises, schemes worked out by groups of leaders. In this period of new projects, of rural migration to the towns and of job allotment, grievances come quickly to light and splinter groups are easily formed. The apparatuses of the democratic parties are neither yet complete nor stable, and this in a country where opinion is in a state of flux and the masses are on the move.

In October and November 1960, the dissidents of Acción Democrática who created the MIR (Movimento Izquierda Revolucionaria), the groups that supported Admiral Wolfgang Larrazabal who was a determined opponent of the dictator Pérez Jiménez, and revolutionary groups of every shade and colour took action. They condemned the 'entreguista' policy of the coalition government (Acción Democrática and COPEI, Rafael Caldera's Christian-Democratic-inspired party), its caution with regard to the interests of the propertied classes, its tendency to promote the creation of a new middle class, its pro-American views, its savage repression of student demonstrations, its inability to get the national economy moving.

An explosion of violence that no one could call a 'popular insurrection' put paid to left-wing opposition hopes of bringing about a change in government and policy.

The break between Betancourt and Castro and their exchange of homeric speeches served to create an overheated climate unfavourable to the dispassionate evaluation of problems. However we are speaking about Venezuela and if the opposition groups which were caught in a web of bidding and counter-bidding, of adolescent violence and repression, which must resort to semi-secrecy, terror and counter-terror, if they showed a certain youthful dash and boldness, President Betancourt coped with a mixture of skill and force.

The warm nights would echo to the sound of gunfire directed at police patrols, in the districts where the most recently urbanised would congregate, in the residential blocks where political pressure groups, local caudillos of the large parties and hard-liners had established social organisms with their own special code of laws. In the very middle of towns, cars manned by activists would pepper with machine-gun fire a militia whose meagre pay is no incentive to them to put up much of a fight. The social origins of most of the left-wing leaders and their recent entry upon the political scene led to an extreme mobility, blurring the boundary line between government and opposition, and allowing the young revolutionaries to find out exactly what was happening or was being planned in official circles.

The PCV was caught up in this whirlwind and felt itself being overtaken on the left and found a new generation launching itself into the attack without bothering about the 'party line'. In spite of serious opposition from the old-guard, the PCV decided to take part in movements of violence so as not simply to disappear as an organisation.

The AD-COPEI coaltion government and President Betancourt, in the first instance, would surely come to blows. In actual fact, the new régime had two solid bases of support, the Confederation of Venezuelan Workers (CTV) and the peasant federations. These were two active organisations, firmly rooted in industry and in the rural areas, and staffed by militants whose future was always linked with the struggles, and today the victories, of the democratic organisations.

The police forces and the forces of repression were new and neither robust nor experienced. The army, at the mercy of conflicting sentiments and exposed to numerous political influences, tended to intervene only if the government showed itself hesitant or ineffectual. In fact it was the trade unionists and militant peasants who were, through their participation in mass meetings and processions of machete-carriers, to provide crucial support for the still shaky régime.

Looked at from a purely class point of view it could be said that, throughout the years 1960–63, the working class and peasantry were defending a moderate but active government against assault from political groups composed, for the most part, of intellectuals, students, career-politicians and people who had come down in the world.

Alert, bold, proud of its spectacular successes, the revolutionary movement would have to establish itself in secret and, starting from a largely unforeseen objective situation, to improvise new forms of organisation, work out the tactics to be used, and justify its existence theoretically. At the same time, the temptation to seize immediate power was ever-present.

The governmental parties were always prepared to forget individual cases and leave the door ajar. The corridors of power, with all their machinations, might be repugnant to the young revolutionaries but nevertheless exerted a certain attraction.

Up till now, force has been simply a form of political activity and, in the last analysis, has aimed at exerting an influence within the context of the general political system. The polarisation of a legal government and an illegal counter-government disrupts the rules of the game.

For a short period, the extreme left had an ally. On May 4, 1962, a military rebellion broke out at Carupano. On June 2 of the same year, another rebellion was attempted at Puerto Cabello. Both were crushed. The armed forces did not let themselves be seduced either by a possible ultra-nationalist policy proposed by the revolutionaries, or by the opportunity to pose as arbiter or saviour of the state. The fever that affected some officer circles resulted only in a few professionals placing their technical knowledge at the disposal of the revolutionary groups.

Nothing of any significance was happening yet in the peasant regions. In the province of Falcón a clandestine radio station started broadcasting in October 1961. At the beginning of 1962, *cimarrones* (uncontrolled elements) made their appearance in the Sierra de Coro, but, as always, it was in the towns that the terrorist networks were most active in the construction of their organisation, serving a hard apprenticeship.

A turnabout, or rather demonstration of public opinion, marked the end of 1963. In December the electors were to pronounce on the régime, select new members of parliament and choose Betancourt's successor. The revolutionary fronts denounced what they called an electoral farce and set about making consultation impossible.

Two incidents were to provide the government with material for a massive propaganda campaign, right in the middle of the election period. The first was the terrorist attack on a train full of trippers, at a place called El Encanto, between Caracas and Los Teques. Five national guardsmen were killed. It was hard to find any revolutionary justification for this particular instance of violence, but it suited the administration and democratic parties down to the ground. The second was the discovery and seizure of three tons of weapons and war materials of Cuban origin, on the shores of the Paraguana peninsula, in Falcón state. The press, radio and propaganda networks made capital out of this proof of Castroite interference.

On December 1, 1963, a huge majority of the electors turned up at the polling stations and registered their votes in spite of the threats and outrages. That day, it is likely that many of the political leaders who had gambled on the terrorist groups in the hope of being carried along on a wave of popular support decided to return to less dangerous methods and to try to find their way back into the 'system'.

The opportunity for this was to be provided by the new President Leoni, who put his theory of 'broad-based' government into practice. A large section of the opposition was to take the opportunity of sharing in the responsibilities and also, of course, the advantages of power. And if there was the usual rigmarole of exits and entrances, of grievances and settlements, it all took place at least without the use of machine-guns and bazookas.

From now on, two tendencies bearing on terrorism were discernible: firstly, that of the 're-enterist' groups, who claimed to be able to pacify, then to bring about the reintegration of certain extremist sections; and secondly a contrary tendency to turn revolutionary violence into the only method of seizing power and to win the urban and guerrilla groups over to the idea of the counter-state.

One suspects that some rather extensive changes have taken place in the internal life of the parties and the revolutionary movements and groups, even if the language of propaganda itself has not changed and even if the European and North American press continues to describe the situation in the same terms, as though it were immutable.

The MIR, a succession of whose leaders had been arrested,

possessed no reliable network of international contacts, and having had to create its machinery out of nothing and to protect itself from the encroachments of the PCV was in a permanent state of crisis. A number of its leaders, such as Domingo Alberto Rangel, were of the opinion that the lessons of defeat should be taken to heart and insurrectionist tactics revised. Numerous groups which had supported the MIR when it seemed further to the left than Acción Democrática severed their connection and strove to establish fronts, embryos of new political organisations.

The papers of the MIR for internal use are frequently more critical than attacks from the outside. They are translucently clear as regards factual information, technically sound as regards the analysis of problems, and quite positive as regards organisation or work. But this intellectual excellence contrasts with the poor results actually obtaining. In August 1964 a document for circulation among the cadres admitted that, 'It would seem that our party and, to a lesser extent, youth have failed in the task of uniting with the masses. Party organisations have no idea how best to carry this out.' Another document, this time intended for party militants, which dealt with the armed struggle and concentrated especially on the armed forces, analysing their composition, tendencies and rivalries, pointed out both the possibilities of influencing NCOs and men and the absence of any serious attempt to do so. A note of complaint sounds through all the private or confidential reports —resources are slender, inadequate even for essential tasks; the necessary help could come from the 'friendly countries'. It is within this context that general political moves such as the creation of a public opposition front together with the PC and various minority organisations must be seen. This was, in effect, an engine of war, a façade making it possible to use legal means for the attainment of revolutionary ends. In practice, it was also a way of taking part again in normal political life.

The guerrilla fronts, though theoretically essential elements in revolutionary strategy, the nuclei of a people's army, could not at this time (towards the middle of 1964), claim to be making progress or even to be of any great significance:

The executive committee's policy of guerrilla warfare has not been a success. It is the most backward area of the armed struggle. The reasons for this are: 1. excessive dispersal of efforts; 2. deficiencies in the selection of combat personnel; 3. bad use of technically qualified personnel; 4. absence of good political leadership in the bases, and of leaders at a regional or national level; 5. inadequate finances and absence of permanent funds to cover the requirements of the bases, resulting in lack of continuity in logistical aid to the latter; 6. inadequate party propaganda for the bases and their political leaders; 7. weakness of bases in attack; 8. lack of initiative on the part of guerrilla detachments in carrying out their own plans for controlling and reconnoitring the physical areas in which they operate, and lack of overall executive control; 9. lack of a consistent policy of solidarity with the guerrilla groups, as much within the party as outside it; isolated attempts to help have had negative results; 10. lack of a consistent effort by the party and its executive to awaken enthusiasm in favour of the guerrilla struggle both within and outside the organisation; 11. very scanty collaboration between party groups and guerrilla bases, little co-operation in the recruitment and selection of fighting personnel, little use of regional organisational facilities of the party on behalf of the bases; 12. lack of proper liaison between the guerrilla and peasant fronts and, as a result, incoherence in the basic work of the strategic areas.

In conclusion, the MIR report continues: 'the existing bases have limited themselves to keeping going . . . It cannot be said that our bases have got beyond the embryonic stage and even as far as the stage of establishing a guerrilla zone.'

What about the PCV? Its leaders were in gaol and trying from there to hold the party together and make its policy prevail. But there was lively internal conflict, and differences over a basic issue, namely the continuance or termination of the armed struggle, were openly discussed.

In June 1964, instructions issued to the cadres were still unequivocal: 'The Communist Party affirms that there is no

alternative to the armed struggle pursued with the greatest
determination, ... to opposing Leoni's government resolutely
and creating a strong national movement towards the establishment of a patriotic and democratic government.' The self-
criticism was to the point: 'Underestimation of the guerrilla
detachments, ... lack of planning and of a spirit of war, ...
lack of harmony and co-ordination between guerrilla activity
and general policy, ... priority given to propaganda at the
expense of direct action against the enemy, ...'

The striking thing is that a year later there seemed to have
been no improvement in the situation. In the words of a PCV
militant, the group leader in the eastern zone:

Three years ago, I had occasion to raise the question of sending
personnel from the mountains abroad, to follow courses there. This
was because I realised that we who were fighting the war did not
even know how to use rifles, and knew even less about the techniques
and tactics that would enable us to fight more effectively. This was
not appreciated, and the choice of those who were to travel abroad
was made unsystematically. . . . What I felt was that courses abroad
should be kept basically for people from the rural districts, naturally
selecting the best of them. This does not mean that urban cadres,
who join subsequently, should not be sent as well. The former,
however, are a better bet, as they are men already used to the
rigours of guerrilla life and there is no fear of their 'beating it' as
has happened with people sent to us after following courses abroad.
. . . The decisions of the Seventh Plenum state that we have taken
advantage of the truce to get ready. I do not agree. In my view, we
have failed throughout the war to take advantage of favourable
circumstances to set up fronts while the enemy with his tactic of
encirclement always finds us untrained and weak, precisely because
we have not made use of the long periods of respite. In my view, we
have not yet fully mastered the art of war.[1]

There was worse to come. Before being arrested for the second
time and hanging himself in his cell, the communist leader
Fabricio Ojeda, known by his aliases, Pedro, Lucrecio, Roberto,
or Tulio, had got himself appointed President of the FLN-FALN,
i.e. the heterogeneous political organisation and its military

arm, uniting the MIR, PCV and a number of other groups. So
Ojeda was appointed president, and Douglas Bravo chief
commander of the FALN. But the two appointments had not
been agreed to by the party of which these two militants were
members. The Political Bureau of the PCV therefore condemned the decision and declared it illegal.

The fact is that the commanders of the FALN, Douglas Bravo,
Pedro Vegas Castejón, Elias Manuit Camero, Gregorio Lunar
Márquez and Fabricio Ojeda, had decided to take over effective
control of the guerrilla groups in view of the fact that several
members of the high command were dead, abroad, or in prison.
This meant giving the FLN-FALN the leading rôle. The group
took up its position in December 1965. An explanatory letter
was sent to the Political Bureau at the end of April 1966. The
other 'commandants' were also informed, in their places of
detention: 'The death of Commandant Ponte Rodríguez, your
imprisonment and the temporary absence of those who are
abroad have left a huge vacuum in the central command, and
are having considerable repercussions on the general state of the
movement. In order to resolve the problems that beset the
revolutionary movement the *utmost importance* must be attached
to the lack of effective political and military control guiding
and leading our forces ... '

The communist leaders let it be known from San Carlos
prison that they were not fooled: 'It seems to us', wrote one
of the Political Bureau members under the pseudonym of
Guillermo, 'that the resolutions in question simply reflect the
desire to set up a centre of power outside the Communist
Party ... ' They rejected the nominations by way of the
supreme commander of the FALN, Juan de Dios Moncada
Vidal, but the latter was in prison.

The MIR, or at least that section of it that favoured armed
struggle, was more flexible in its attitude. No doubt its leaders
were not sorry to see the rival party shedding its monolithic
façade. Under the pseudonyms of José and Castillo, two
Mirista officials replied to Fabricio Ojeda's letter in these
terms: 'We understand that you are proposing the setting up of

provisional organisations with those who are at liberty and in the country. It would be appropriate, therefore, to add the word "acting" to the titles of nominees to prominent positions.'

From the handwritten and duplicated material circulating in vast quantities through the entire underground network, among militants and leaders at every level of the PC, it emerges that the split had been latent for over a year, that Douglas Bravo had the backing of a majority in the primary organisations, while the majority of the top apparatus favoured a 'disengagement', that is a new tactical course aimed at reintegration in the democratic political system and allowing guerrilla activities to become dormant.

Finally in 1966, after five years of costly effort, a politico-military leadership more or less corresponding to Guevara's theory was developing on the basis of the weak guerrilla detachments that were still extant and on what was left of the MIR hard-liners and the dissidents of the PC. Its only chance of survival depended on the support of the Cuban comrades.

When, in May 1967, a group of volunteers landed and was caught in Machurucuto, an unknown place that was to receive extensive publicity, no one involved in Venezuelan political life underestimated the significance of the fact that among these volunteers there were three Cubans. One of them was killed, the two others were taken prisoner. They had accompanied eight Venezuelan volunteers trying to join up with the guerrillas. The Cuban Communist Party, in a very long declaration, 'makes common cause with the altruistic, revolutionary, internationalist and heroic gesture' of the young Cuban killed on the beach at Machurucuto.

There has been a gradual retreat from the direct path to power on the part of the revolutionary organisations. The resources and possibilities of the system have regained favour. In the great enterprise, the only sound element had been the urban fighting organisation, which was being slowly but surely reduced by a police force that had also learnt how to fight.

The PCV refused to send a delegation to the OLAS conference, whereas Douglas Bravo sent the following message: 'To

Commander-in-Chief Fidel Castro: From the mountains of Venezuela our fighters hail your intervention at the OLAS conference as the best and loftiest moral stimulus to our revolutionary struggle. We shall fight on to victory!

Douglas Bravo, Commander-in-Chief of the FALN, Mountains of Venezuela.'

II

Argentina. A Trial Run

AT A PLACE called La Toma, or El Molle, situated in a heavily
wooded region near the settlement of Santa Rosa, twelve kilometres
west of the Saucelito railway station, personnel of the Orán
detachment of the national gendarmery arrested, on the day before
yesterday, at 13.30 hours, six members of a Castroite cell who were
engaged in guerrilla training.

It was in this police-report style that news of the existence of
armed groups in the northwest of Argentina, on the borders of
Bolivia, was broken by the Buenos Aires press on March 6, 1964.

Other arrests were to follow in the Salta and Córdoba areas.
Two munitions and war-material dumps were found near the
camp. There were anti-tank grenades, hand and rifle grenades,
gelignite, Belgian rifles, camp bedding, medical supplies and
instruments for minor surgical operations, a transmitting-
receiving set and, of course, a large number of books and
pamphlets on guerrilla warfare.

Without giving away much information, the national gendarmery carried out reconnaissance and round-up operations in
the provinces of Salta and Jujuy. They located small armed
groups, engaged them in combat, took prisoners, chanced on a
camp where there was a large stock of material. They also
found three guerrilla graves and learnt from prisoners that
two of the bodies were those of *guerrilleros* who had been
sentenced by the group and executed. The 'Diary' of Captain
Hermés, killed in battle, has a few words to say about this type
of trial.

The main guerrilla unit was composed of twenty to twenty-five men, under the command of 'Commandant' Segundo. The gendarmery was sent off in pursuit of them. Several clashes took place and one gendarme was killed. It was only at the end of May that the final official statements were issued. They let it be known that the guerrillas had dispersed and stated that the leaders had come from Bolivia and that several of them had trained in Cuba.

From information published at the outset, it emerged that most of the prisoners were students, some of whom had come from the federal capital and others from Córdoba. There were also two office-workers, a waiter and a printer. There was no information on the 'officers', except that they were not local men and that one of them, 'Captain' Hermés, was probably of Philippine origin.

One other detail: the guerrillas were wearing olive-green trousers and shirts and had grown beards. This ritualistic behaviour leads one to ask what it is basically that impels these young people to choose the path of revolutionary action. Is it the romantic attraction of a Robin Hood type of existence or the conviction that Argentina's social problems can be resolved only through the intervention of a new force with no roots in the past?

It was only the national gendarmery, in charge of the frontier regions, that took part in the repression. It did so effectively, being a force made up of professionals and not recruits.

According to Gregorio Selser, a specialist in the study of these movements, a group did not contain more than thirty people, 'including students, office workers, workers, the majority being middle class, non-communists or ex-communists, plus a few Peronists, all of whom claimed to belong to the national left'.[1] This observer doubts whether the men had time to operate effectively as guerrillas. Of the forty or so named, seven died in battle, seven or eight while escaping and two or three 'vanished'. The gendarmery set six prisoners free, the Tucumán tribunals released seven and the Salta court ten or a dozen.

Selser's argument is that the intelligence services were aware of the activities of the group and had infiltrated two agents into it. Even though they knew about the initial activities as early as June 1963, the gendarmery intervened only after February 1964. The reason for this, according to Selser, was that the 'guerrilla danger' was used as an argument, in the discussions taking place with the United States, to secure additional armaments for the Argentine Army.

This short-lived adventure was the only one bearing any relation to the theory of guerrilla warfare except, of course, that no peasants were involved. It was a very small affair in comparison with the proliferation of pro-Castro, pro-Chinese and national-revolutionary groups and publications in Buenos Aires, and derisory when considered in relation to the tradition of violence that had existed in the federal capital for nearly a century.

It seems likely that if a terrorist base were to be established, it would be a product of the town and not of the rural areas. The Argentine delegations taking part in international meetings on the organisation and support of guerrilla movements contain only urban leaders. The strangest and most persistent of these spokesmen is the former chief of the National Liberation Alliance, an extremist branch of the Peronist movement, John William Cooke. This individual provides an example of the variety of political philosophies claiming a connection with Castroism or supporting movements like the OLAS. Here is Cooke on his 'doctrine':

... Peronism, by virtue of its social composition and its struggles, is basically revolutionary. And if there exists within it a revolutionary Peronism, it is because the régime, through its manipulations of the state and cultural machine, is preventing the masses from becoming aware of the causes of the tragic situation in which they are involved and the policy that could put an end to it. The so-called Peronist bureaucracy is, in short, a ruling class that shares the enemy's values and, for that reason, is incapable of leading the masses in the seizure of power without which there can be no solution either for the labouring classes or for the country, as we have already entered upon a stage where bourgeois nationalism no longer exists, only social revolution and national liberation, non-divisible objectives, twin aspects of a single indivisible process.[2]

12

Colombia. Putting Violence to Some Use

BETWEEN 1949 and 1957, Colombia's lot was one of continuous violence, not just the violence of an oppressive government or of a rebellious victim, but violence for its own sake, in all the peasant districts, the violence of nightmare and *grand guignol*. The tale of massacres, sadism, rape, disembowellings and dismemberments resounds like a litany through the history of those terrible years. The dead were counted in their thousands, some said two hundred, others four hundred thousand.

While the country was beginning to advance, with new industries developing after 1925, with the birth of a middle-class, the organisation of a trade union movement and with the methods and ideas of political and social change beginning to make an impact on public opinion under various ideological guises and preparing the ground for the necessary reforms, the conflict between Conservatives and Liberals took an insane turn.

On April 9, 1948, the leader of the modernist Liberal current, Jorge Eliecer Gaitán, who symbolised the desire for change and was aiming at the presidency, was assassinated. The explosion of rage and destructiveness that followed and was to turn Bogotá for a few days into a battle field, was, however, abortive because there were neither primary organisations nor any stable progressive parties.

The Liberals did not dare infringe the constitutional rules—though these were no longer respected even formally—but subsequently refused to recognise the legitimacy of Dr Laureano Gómez's election to the presidency. From that moment, gun and 'machete' law reigned in the country. There was an official authority in Bogotá, with its police force and its troops, but throughout the length and breadth of the country there was nothing but bloody struggles between local forces, rival bands, guerrillas of every kind.

The fighting, disembowelling of women and butchering of children and old people had nothing to do with a political programme or orders from above; it was to avenge the dead of yesterday, to avoid being killed oneself; it was the product of fear and habit.

This fever of destructiveness did not prevent deals taking place. Thousands of properties changed hands, always guaranteed by documents before a notary, but with the signatures frequently extorted at knife point, casual witnesses brought in for the occasion, or help of an accomplice in an official position. Landowners hired gunmen to protect their lands, and, when required, to extend them. But there were also armed groups that levied tithes on the rich *hacendados*.

One had only to be a Liberal to attract the murderous hatred of the Conservatives and the only good Conservative, as far as the Liberals were concerned, was a dead one. Hatreds hardened as the number of killings rose. Verse, songs, proverbs, even jokes, all contributed to this atmosphere of bloodshed and murder.

The development, advancement, adjustment of structures and techniques to fit the exigencies of a changing world were halted. The vast amount of energy that went into this senseless war was simply dissipated. The government survived only by relying on the pull of reaction, on the most conservative instincts of the Colombian establishment, namely latifundists, Church and army. The 1953 coup of General Gustavo Rojas Pinilla brought a four-year period of stern military rule, one of whose objectives was the ruthless eradication of all guerrilla activity and banditry. But it did not in itself heal the breach between Liberals and Conservatives. A meeting and agreement to put an end to their mad rivalry had to take place between representatives of the Liberal and Conservative Parties, far from the blood-stained country, in the Catalonian resorts of Benidorm and Sitges, before a new era could begin. The pact between Lleras Camargo and Gómez envisaged a period of 'democratic convalescence'. In effect, a civilian government was to exercise power in the name of the two parties, the presidency alternating between a Conservative and a Liberal nominated by common agreement.

This agreement made it possible to check and reduce violence; it is a force for peace. Clearly, it was not seen as a basis for drafting and putting social reforms into effect.

What was the position as regards armed groups in Colombia during and towards the close of those terrible years? According to an inventory drawn up by Mgr Germán Guzmán Campos[1] there were fourteen detachments in the region of Antioquia alone: three Conservative, six Liberal, the others owing allegiance to 'independent' leaders; these detachments contained five to twenty men each. In the Boyaca region, there were four detachments—two Conservative, one Liberal, one Independent. In the region of Caldas, there were fifteen armed groups, divided equally between the three categories. In the Cauca region, there were eleven groups with between four to three hundred men; there, the largest contingents were connected with the Colombian Communist Party (PCC). In the region of Cundinamarca, there were seven groups divided between Liberals and Communists. In the region of Huila, there were nine groups, some being Communists, others Conservatives. In the region of Meta, there were seven groups, mostly Liberal but with a strong Communist contingent and a Conservative group. In the province of Santander, there were fourteen groups, divided between the Liberals and the Conservatives, the largest belonging to the Liberals. In the region of Tolima, there were about forty groups, ten containing ten to three hundred men, with a large contingent of Liberals, about a dozen Conservative detachments and three numerically important Communist groups, including Manuel Marulanda's

(*Tiro Fijo*) in the region of Marquetalia, and Yon Isauro's (*alias* Lister) in the same region. Finally, in the region of Valle, there were about forty groups, mostly Liberal, with a strong Conservative detachment.

It goes without saying that this inventory drawn up in 1963 must not be regarded in the same light as a report on the strength of a regular army. The groups and detachments altered rapidly, increased or diminished considerably in size according to circumstances; their political affiliations were often in doubt or unstable; the extent of their activities varied: some were in control of their particular area, others were manipulated and some were hunted and on the point of disintegrating. A large dose of personal adventurism on the part of the leader, the thousand and one local obstructions and the direct or indirect intervention of the central forces further complicated the classification.

On the other hand, there were some genuine attempts to find a way out of the chaos, to organise some kind of ordered life in those areas where Bogotá's authority did not run. Thus the Law of the Plain (*Ley del Llano*), drawn up in September 1952, attempted to lay down a number of principles and rules governing the defence of the region, inter-personal relations and the definition of the rights and duties of the various *de facto* authorities. It amounted to a kind of constitution, drafted by the so-called *Comando Guerrillero de los Llanos Orientales*. Based on Liberal precepts or at least noting that the regions with Liberal majorities were abandoned to their fate by the dictatorship in the capital, the 'Law' laid down the salaries of officials —administrators of justice, civilian and military authorities— and defined the forms of government: a general assembly and a civilian and military Junta. Problems of law and order, of property and its protection, of armed struggle, of taxes and fines, of agricultural work and of animal husbandry were examined, and rules and regulations drawn up. Special attention was given to the exploitation of all available land and the establishment of collective farms which were to supply the guerrillas with provisions.

A second law, promulgated on June 13, 1953, was more extensive. It contained 224 articles and was entitled Law Organising the Revolution in the Eastern Plains of Colombia. There were seven sections: on the civilian population, popular government, higher civilian and military authorities, offences and penalties, administration of justice, armed forces and troops, and miscellaneous provisions. In this medley are to be found the right to freedom of conscience and religion, the recognition of civil and religious marriage, the sanctity of the home, but also the priority of 'war needs' and the division of the population into two sectors, armed forces and civilians.

Some of these articles give one an insight into the identity of the people who organised themselves in this manner, how they were distributed, what their preoccupations were, their taste for direct democracy: 'Once a month, there will be an open assembly where free discussion will take place and the problems common to the whole *vereda* will be debated, so that each one may express his opinions and criticisms.'[2]

This example shows how the regional and local situations cannot be fitted into any general definition and can only be understood in their own particular contexts. As regards our central theme, it can be stated categorically that guerrilla activity, whether in a flourishing or decaying state, was in no way comparable to the Cuban experience, or to the politico-military theory subsequently erected on it.

The National Front agreement between Liberals and Conservatives, and its administrative application according to the rule of parity, had obvious repercussions in the field of law and order. Gradually, though with extreme savagery, the armed bands were reduced, dispersed, crushed. The government made an attempt to eliminate or at least soften the violently disputed differences existing between old and new landlords, the despoiled or profiteers of both sides. The public purse was shared out between the supporters of the formerly hostile parties. The movement was characterised by a certain standardisation of political life and the more recent idea of creating a single party uniting Liberals and Conservatives.

This trend was related to the discovery of a community of interests between the privileged classes. It reflected a certain conservatism, whereas the problems of modernisation, economic development, a more equable distribution of national income required initiative, planned programmes and structural reforms.

It is not surprising, therefore, that the restoration of relative calm in public life was not accompanied by any improvement in the social sphere. On the contrary those elements favouring social change that had been thrust into the background by the wave of pure violence again came to the fore, insisting that the restoration of peace should not simply mean a return to the past but that it should provide the right conditions for the final dismantling of that past. As a result of this, new political movements came to life, for the most part left-wing, and within the liberal party itself there were stirrings of a profound disquiet, particularly on the part of the younger generation. There was also a rapid development in one of the most traditional sectors of Colombian society, the Catholic Church, a development that took place by fits and starts and at the cost of bitter internal conflicts, encouraged by the new spirit of the Vatican, and which, on occasions, produced something sensational, like the Camilo Torres affair.

What is particularly significant in this priest is not his rôle as a seminal thinker, but his personal history. Of upper class origin, exceptionally sensitive and extremely conscientious about everything he undertook, he experienced the whole range of social differences fairly rapidly, from the shanty towns on the outskirts of Paris to the scientific study of Colombian society. After an attempt at active political work, he finally escaped in effect, by committing suicide. There is something guilt-ridden about everything he did.

His desire to serve, his feeling of responsibility and also the impossible gap existing between his yearning for the absolute and the mediocrity of the actual prospects, probably come out clearly in his 'Message to the Students'. 'The students are a privileged group in all under-developed countries . . . What is

more, the university student ... is doubly privileged at the
same time: he is able to advance socially ... and to be non-
conformist and give expression to his rebelliousness without
this preventing his advancement. These advantages have
turned the students into a decisive factor in the Latin American
revolution ... I personally believe that we are rapidly approaching zero hour in the Colombian revolution. But only the workers
and peasants can announce it with sufficient force. If the
students, without being patronising, link themselves with the
people, in a spirit of learning rather than didacticism, they will,
at the historic moment, be able to judge objectively.'

When, after the relative failure of his United Front movement which finally, in competition with the already established
organisations, brought together only a handful of dissidents
and fringe elements, and after he had realised that the attention
paid him was due only to his being an ex-priest, he decided
to turn to guerrilla warfare; this decision seems to relate more
to his own internal feelings than to represent a rational political
choice.

Several attempts had been made by urban political groups
to create some effective political force out of the wreck of the
numerous combat movements. In other words, the Communist
Party and fragments of the extreme left that would not accept
the overlordship of the PCC tried to find a place for the survivors
of the period of violence and repression in the struggle for the
reform of the country.

Thus, on the one hand there was the National Liberation
Army (ELN), operating in the province of Santander, in liaison
with Castroite groups, and, on the other, the FARC (Revolutionary Armed Forces of Colombia), controlled by the Communist Party and active in the South as well as in several zones
of the Central Cordillera. The increasingly heavy blows struck
by the army forced the guerrillas to keep on the move continually. The time for the organisation of zones of self-defence
was over.

Even though their geographical remoteness from each other
prevented anything in the way of problems of co-ordination or

disputes arising between the two guerrilla movements, there was nevertheless a difference between PCC and Castroite ideas. While the PCC stuck to its contention that 'armed struggle was neither the only nor the ultimate way', the ELN publicly denounced the equivocal attitude of the Communist leaders.

The latter retaliated by criticising the ELN's taste for publicity and its purely propagandistic operations, especially the March 1967 train attack, with photographs taken by a Mexican journalist, which got world coverage but which provoked immediate and very costly reprisals.

It must be remembered that the Colombian 'guerrilla groups' contain a high percentage of peasants besides the student volunteers. Fabio Vásquez Castaño's and Víctor Medina's ELN was originally a student movement. The FARC, under the command of Manuel Marulanda, known as *Tiro Fijo*, sprang from the peasant leagues. Since the loss of the 'Republic' of Marquetalia and the banishment of the guerrillas to the wilderness, clashes have been less frequent.[3] In fact the guerrilla war is not as extensive as the *maquis*' public relations and the distortions of the European and Latin American press would lead one to believe. Paradoxically, in present conditions, the guerrillas can only fulfil their rôle if other political forces take advantage of their threatening presence to demand economic and social reforms.

13

Guatemala. Between Theory and Maquis

ONE SHOULD remember that Guatemala has a population of a little over four million, nearly two-thirds of which is Indian, and that the greater part of this population, sunk in illiteracy and poverty, is by tradition cut off from the life of the capital and even from the market economy; the political battles that take place are irrelevant to it. There is little precise, even limited, information on the country: we know something of the strength and influence of the United Fruit Co., of the army's preponderance and the power of the great landowning families. A number of fairly recent events should also be born in mind: the fall of the dictator Ubico, in 1944; the period of democratisation of institutions under pressure from the universities, young intellectuals and sections of the lower middle class; and then, after a period of relative modernisation during the presidency of Juan José Arévalo, the return in force of the coalition of vested interests, US firms, old-style officers, conservative groups, all seeking to get rid of Colonel Arbenz's government, which was accused of taking social reform too far and flirting with the Soviet Union in a time of cold war.

Subsequently the pendulum continued to swing between the forces of order and change, between the strong man Castillo Armas and General Ydígoras, Colonel Enrique Peralta and Professor Julio César Méndez Montenegro. One factor that is helping to change old Guatemala is the continual and rapid growth of population, the rise of suburbs where the Indians are crowded in their masses.

Guerrilla activity must be seen against this background. It is always hard to estimate numbers, but there would seem to be approximately 200 to 250 *maquis* fighters. Three-quarters of them are students and lower or upper middle class youths, plus a few ex-soldiers. The rest come from the peasantry.

The guerrilla movement is military in its origins. On November 13, 1960 a group of officers attempted a coup aimed at overthrowing the ruling military junta. This took place at the Matamoros barracks and the leader of the rebellion was Colonel Rafaël Pereira. The movement got off to a good start and Puerto Barrios was taken. General Ydígoras hit back, bombed the rebels' positions and forced Colonel Pereira to flee. A hard core of soldiers took to the mountains and among these survivors were two officers who were to make a reputation for themselves, Lieutenant Yon Sosa and Sub-Lieutenant Luis A. Turcios.

For some months, this guerrilla band bothered little about politics. It led a secluded, undisturbed life and its leaders profited from the complicity of many officers.

The movement was to take shape as a result of a certain inter-action between groups of civilian opponents and activists 'in the mountains'. Conflicts of view began simultaneously to affect the leading circles, provoking or masking personal antagonisms.

Yon Sosa who, as the highest ranking officer, had become the head of MR 13 (Revolutionary Movement of November 13), remained in this position and was apparently influenced by various Trotskyite groups. Luis Turcios withdrew and set up the FAR (Revolutionary Armed Forces). He collaborated with the Guatemalan Communist Party (PGT, Guatemalan Party of Labour), which had an organisation in the capital and in several other places, and which tried to capitalise on the anxieties and grievances of the student youth. A small peasant area was in effect occupied which, if it was of little economic or strategic importance, did act as a good base for operations.

Turcios brought off more and more brilliant feats of arms, made use of his connections, held wealthy bourgeois up to ransom, thrashed patrols of guards, profiting from the sympathy of the new generation which did not know what to do with its energy in a country where the power cliques and wealthy families controlled everything.

But the movement did not take root among the poor peasants and had scarcely any effect on the Indian population. The FAR, in spite of their para-Marxist terminology and Castroite arguments, controlled the town alone.

The long-drawn out controversy between Yon Sosa and Luis Turcios on the best tactics to be employed—permanent revolution under the leadership of the proletariat or an anti-imperialist alliance between workers, peasants and national bourgeoisie— was only marginally relevant to the Guatemalan situation. Texts coming from Mexico or Buenos Aires provided ammunition for the debates which proceeded to the delight of those 'talmudic' scholars that cluster so thickly in extreme left-wing intellectual circles.

When Turcios was killed at the wheel of his car, things began to go wrong. The guerrillas lost heavily. The 'commandant', as a former colleague of theirs, had been able to rely on the tolerance or complicity of the young officers; this advantage disappeared with him. The first 'Green Berets' landed from Panama and started combing the 'affected' areas. Extreme rightist leagues sprang up dedicated to purging the city and its outskirts of real or supposedly revolutionary elements. Betrayals began to corrode guerrilla confidence. Finally, the army got under way and penetrated the Sierra de las Minas that had lent its name to a political manifesto in 1965.

The PGT, which has always shown great flexibility in adapting itself to circumstances (it had supported a restoration of democracy in 1955 and armed struggle in 1961) but which does its utmost to keep the legal channels of action open; Yon Sosa's MR 13, of limited importance but up till now less affected by repression than the FAR; and finally the FAR, now under the command of César Montes, make up the three fronts of the guerrilla war,[1] three retreating fronts, in spite of the theory and in spite of three million impoverished Indians who are utterly indifferent to theory.

The agreement between the FAR and MR 13, published at the beginning of 1968, was not an alliance between victors, but a pact between forces on the retreat. It also marked the final break between the guerrillas and the communist political leadership.

The FAR declaration, published in *Granma*, on February 25, 1968, concludes with a constat: 'Let us see what the results are, after four years of struggle: 300 revolutionaries fallen in battle and 3000 of the common people murdered by the régime of Julio César Méndez Montenegro. The PGT (its ruling camarilla) contributed the ideas and the FAR, the dead.'

14

Bolivia. The Army Confounded

FOR NEARLY twenty years, conflicts between parties and political groups in Bolivia have often been decided by force. Originally, miners and armed peasants had fought to secure the acceptance of the electoral victory of the MNR (Nationalist Revolutionary Movement) and the nomination of Victor Paz Estenssoro as President, and had prevailed over the 'rosca', the feudal mining system, the landowners and the army. In 1952, a real wave of popular feeling swept aside the tradition of pronunciamentos, struggles between military groups, and governments imposed on the people. Agrarian reform was initiated by the crowd, spontaneously and inexorably, and it was up to the political leaders to impose some legal form on it and justify it subsequently in terms of law. Nationalisation of the mining industry was decreed from June, while the workers were setting up defence battalions in the mining centres.

The victory of the revolutionaries did not put an end to violence. The leaders of the MNR, a movement that for a number of years had given voice to the basic, socialising, nationalist demands, carved out fiefs for themselves from which to make their bid for power. The armed forces were virtually dissolved. Units of armed men, some regular, others less so, sprang up to defend local and regional interests in the social sphere, or occasionally to back a political leader.

There was, in short, the mining region, represented but also controlled by the Trade Union Federation and by Lechín's MNR group, with a dozen trends and internal pressure groups;

the quite distinct and geographically well-situated peasant region of Cochabamba, which has supplied the central government with many of its politicians (even today this peasant population remains the firmest basis of support for President Barrientos), and lastly La Paz, with its departments and official bodies, where everyone who counts for anything in Bolivia (though not necessarily Bolivian) comes to bargain and negotiate.

Probably one of the factors behind the revolutionary movement was the onset of a fall in the price of tin, following on the end of the Korean war. In the free-for-all international market in raw materials, liberalism or principles of planning are interchangeable, depending on the temporary interests of the large consortia of buyers. When prices fall, liberalism is sworn by; when a rise makes it look as though producers are going to profit, international solidarity and demands for the regularisation of prices come into play. This time, the new Bolivian leaders reacted above all nationalistically; the country's major source of wealth had to become the property of the nation, but there was still the problem of refining the raw materials, selling them abroad and the dependence on international prices.

One can easily imagine what such an imbroglio might hatch in the way of political combinations, economic intrigue, and unofficial trafficking. The United States, which was very important in the area since the elimination of Anglo-Dutch interests, behaved with apparent generosity as regards credits, gifts and advances, technicians and advisers. It indulged in no counter-revolutionary activity in the sense of supporting the former owners or helping the partisans of the fallen régime. But when it came to the main question, that is the price of tin, this generosity vanished; the strategic reserves of metal built up in the United States as a result of recent wars, enabled her to make the Bolivian producers, even where the state was the owner, dance to its tune.

Nevertheless, negotiations with Washington and the big American companies might perhaps have produced better results if a firm, well-defined and consistent policy had been followed by a united national government. The feudalist world of Bolivian politics could produce no common strategy. There was neither a revolutionary working class, nor a peasantry bent on modernisation, nor a coherent ruling party with a burning vision of the future. There was only a succession of rough and ready compromises that did more to keep the evils alive than to eradicate them.

With the dissolution of the MNR into competing factions, the gradual desertion to the opposition of groups that had formerly been linked, the increasing intransigence of rival parties, the refusal of economic sectors or peripheral regions to collaborate, the temptation to arbitrate all increased. It was the army, reconstituted as an instrument of the central power, a tool in the hands of the official MNR, that became master of the situation at the end of 1965. Supported initially by a large section of the opposition, which was determined to take advantage of Paz Estenssoro's removal to secure for itself a share in government, a military Junta was set up. In August 1966, General René Barrientos Ortuño, former Vice-President, former MNR militant, was nominated President, following elections that were mani-pulated in a way different from earlier ones.

A number of resistance movements sprang up in the mining areas, when it was learnt that Barrientos was not going to seek the support of the workers. They were suppressed and the army now had a footing in those areas that had always represented a threat to La Paz. Nevertheless, the hardest blow was struck later, in June 1967, when troops attacked miners celebrating the feast of St John. Two interpretations of this event were advanced. The first was that of the trade union organisations which claim that the workers had gathered for the celebrations, that they were taken by surprise and that only then, in self-defence, did they use dynamite. The other was put forward by General Ovando Candia, Commander-in-Chief of the Armed Forces: 'An attempt to storm the barracks was mounted in the mining region, an attempt we were able to frustrate through our intervention. . . . ' In his statements to the press, General

Ovando also accused Che Guevara of having been the instigator of this plan of attack.

And indeed, by late June, the Nancahuazú guerrilla war had become a central feature of the country's political life. For the present one can only speculate on whether the army leaders used the southeastern guerrilla war as a pretext for the action taken against the miners, or whether they decided to pre-empt any possible co-operation between the two bases by snuffing out the incipient movement of resistance in the mining region.

As the guerrilla war continued, a large number of questions were posed. Firstly, what were the intentions of the organisers of the Nancahuazú camp? Was this camp, dating from August 1966, a Bolivian-based training centre but with 'students' not necessarily being prepared for the Bolivian guerrilla war or was it, indeed, a spring-board for the revolutionary conquest of the country?

When a patrol was sent through the gorges of the Nancahuazú River, in early April, to check up on reports of a trader who boasted of selling a lot of provisions to a group of men living in this inhospitable region, it was much surprised to fall victim of an ambush. Another stronger patrol, sent out two days later, was also caught in a trap. Up till then, it had been assumed that the unknown jungle-dwellers were engaged in illicit activities, such as drug-peddling, gold-prospecting or smuggling.

Now there was no doubt about their constituting an armed band, and with some organisation and a code of behaviour at that; soldiers taken prisoner were fed, while all the officers received were lectured on the wretched social rôle they played. They were returned minus some articles of clothing and their boots, but otherwise in good condition. The wounded had been treated by a *guerrillero* doctor. The first journalist to travel with the detachment of the 1st battalion and to visit the camp, Murray Sayle of the London *Times*, reported the astonishment of the Bolivian military men at the efficient arrangement of the site: separate holes for those with automatic weapons, entry and exit tracks to observation points, field kitchen, oven for bread, and equipped infirmary, etc.

The camp was discovered by chance and not as a result of the activity of guerrilla fighters. The initial aim of the organisers had probably not been subversion in Bolivia but the establishment of a training base for a number of other countries.

The zone selected has the merit of being close to Argentina (it is even conceivable that the attempt made, in 1964, in the northwestern Argentine, on the Bolivian border, was part of the same plan), Paraguay and Brazil. On the other hand, the locality has few advantages and many disadvantages as a starting point for the conquest of Bolivia. The advantages are simply its isolation, the natural cover provided by the tropical vegetation and the relative proximity of the frontiers. The disadvantages are more serious: to march on Cochabamba and La Paz, it is necessary to cross the Andes, real natural barriers, and to climb to the high valleys and the *altiplano*. Moreover, there is no poor peasantry to ally with against the central government or the landowners. They are just simple farmers, without any great resources, but for whom the question of land is irrelevant. So while it was possible to find support there, it was not based on social causes. Finally, the only important centres were controlled by departments of the YPFB, the national petroleum company, with the help of numerous foreign technicians. From the international point of view, the closeness of Brazil might not just provide a means of withdrawal; it might invite the intervention of the Brazilian army which would not be unwelcome in certain military circles of the large neighbouring republic, a real possibility not apparently envisaged by the guerrillas.

Another mystery concerned the numerical strength and composition of the guerrilla band or bands. Captain Silva of the Bolivian army, in his interview with Argentine journalists (*La Razón*, April 13), estimated 80 to 100 'campers'. Major Rubén Sánchez, who was taken prisoner in the first ambush and then released, claimed (*La Razón*, April 14) that 'there are a number of Bolivians, but also many foreigners, especially Cubans, Argentines, Dominicans and Paraguayans among the guerrilleros'. He also said he had seen 'a number of Blacks with long beards'! One of the leaders of the Bolivian Communist Party (PCB), Jorge Kuello Cueta, in secret interviews, explained that the guerrillas had no difficulty in finding recruits among 'the unemployed, men expelled from the mines, opponents of Barrientos and Ovando' (*L'Unità*, Rome, May 30), but this leading communist did not seem to be much better informed than the journalist, nor even to be in touch with the armed movement. A journalist who supported the guerrillas and who had followed events closely revealed (*Marcha*, Montevideo, August 26) that 'the members of the guerrilla forces are young people, mostly university educated, from middle-class families, and converted, of course, to socialism; but there does not appear to be any uniform revolutionary criterion. A number of *guerrilleros* have studied in Europe, especially in the Federal German Republic. At least two leaders have been trained in the best existing school of guerrilla warfare, Vietnam.' This writer naturally does not reveal his sources. His information is rendered more credible by the fact that the first guerrilla prisoner taken was Jorge Vásquez Viana, who was captured in the vicinity of Camiri with a bullet wound. He was a student, the son of a well-known historian. He was to escape from the hospital a few days later.

Journalistic sources provided as little information as military communiqués. Nevertheless one can draw a few logical conclusions from the limited number of known facts. Basically the tactical superiority of the guerrilla group over the Bolivian armed forces, at least in the first phase of the struggle, May, June and July, indicated an experienced command, the presence of seasoned veterans.

After the two first battles, the group split up and dispersed. The military command jumped to the conclusion that it was a rout. This seemed so self-evident that the aviation units returned to base on the *altiplano*! The guerrilla fighters, however, were merely carrying out their basic elementary tactic, which was to melt away in order to avoid contact with superior forces, to avoid any head-on clash.

Thinking in terms of classical warfare, the Bolivian command tried to create a front. Without a front there was no enemy. Their mistake was to be revealed a little while later when the group, which had meanwhile re-formed, surrounded and took a village 'guarded' by an army detachment, to re-stock with food and pharmaceutical products.

The mobility of small guerrilla groups on the Santa Cruz road and on various secondary roads, was to worry the regular military command even more. The *guerrilleros* displayed a lack of constraint, which indicated that their leaders were conscious of their technical advantage.

On the basis of the fragmentary evidence available, one can assume that the guerrilla force was officered by non-Bolivian veterans from then on and that the body of men was composed of various national elements, partly students or militants of the revolutionary groups, partly refugees from the mining areas. Later on the exact numbers involved became known: 51 guerrillas at the most. In March 1967 there were 41 fighters, 18 of them Cubans, 20 Bolivians, 3 Peruvians.[2]

Che Guevara's presence, in so far as it might point to a certain technique, international connections and might lend the whole affair a symbolic character, was also the subject of discussion. In the welter of false and contrived reports, of 'revelations' immediately disclaimed, one must exercise extreme caution. Apart from the very firm statements of the Bolivian military command, which might perhaps have been politically dictated, there was only indirect evidence of the existence and rôle of the Argentine guerrilla leader.

On July 9, *Presencia,* a La Paz daily paper, published the statement of Carlos Alberto Bustos held at the same time as Régis Debray, and the Anglo-Chilean journalist, George Roth. 'He claims to have spoken twice with this character [Guevara]. In addition, he says that "el Che" is chief commander of the *guerrilleros* and that his word goes in everything.'

Bustos' Argentine lawyer was to confirm his client's statements with regard to Che's presence in the camp, in the Argentine weekly, *Así,* on August 22.

An anonymous report in the Buenos Aires magazine, *Juan*, on August 16, had given the same version.

And, on August 18, *La Prensa* published a report from United Press International (an agency closely linked, in Latin America, with the Buenos Aires daily), which was supposed to be the transcript of a tape of Régis Debray's press conference: '*Reporter:* M. Debray, can you tell us whether you personally saw and talked with Che Guevara? *Debray:* Of course! I saw him personally. *Reporter:* Approximately when? *Debray:* At the end of March.'

Since then the Bolivian army has stopped issuing over-simplified statements and, with the help of US experts or in spite of them, has tried to develop methods of fighting adapted to the character of the enemy and the terrain. It is significant that the first successful initiative of an army patrol was taken by soldiers coming from the Beni, a wooded region where *rastreo*, or 'beating' the forest for game is practised. Up till then, it had been men from the high plateaux, physiologically unused to the tropical region and who had had only three months in uniform, who were used for these operations.

How did the activities of a group of guerrilla fighters in the southeast effect Bolivia? Above all, in the mobilisation of about three thousand men to encircle the threatened area and round up the enemy. Financially, this effort was a considerable strain on the national budget. On the other hand, the danger provided the military régime with a *raison d'être*, some excuse for appealing to neighbouring authoritarian governments for aid, and an argument for obtaining firmer backing from the United States.

In spite of the bitter and grave problems that permanently affect the country, in spite of the political vacuum created by the collapse of the MNR and dispersal of the left-wing groups, and in spite of the fact that recent events have been marked by violence, it is unlikely that the guerrilla war can serve a more important rôle than that of providing the various Bolivian aspirants to power with ammunition for propaganda.

When the news of Che's death was announced, all sections

of the press and all observers went wild. 'Marxists', as well as the partisans of order, lost their sense of proportion and surrendered to the forces of irrationality. The position was painfully clear and the moral of it stood out.

With or without Ernesto Guevara, the guerrilla force in south-eastern Bolivia did not have the slightest chance of victory. With or without 'el Che', the guerrilla nucleus was encircled, split, at bay. With or without the leader, there was no longer any future in the enterprise, and this at a time when, on the continent as a whole, revolutionary bases were few and becoming fewer.

Among the propagandist magazines and news-sheets, and also among many journalists who had systematically exaggerated the guerrilla movement, there was panic fear lest not enough were left to keep even the illusion alive, and this led to a general flight into the world of mythology.

First of all, Che's death was denied. Then, it was declared that dead he was more alive than ever before, as his legendary example would rouse new generations of guerrilla fighters.

Opponents claimed that Che had died two years before, some saying that he had been assassinated and others that he had succumbed to an attack of asthma.

Thousands of words of testimony were taped by agencies trying to determine whether Che or his double had been killed outright, or whether he had died two hours or five hours after having been taken prisoner. People went so far as to deny the fact that the guerrilla chief had been killed. In the supposedly revolutionary circles he was the subject of a dispute between the boy scout and desperado elements.

But all this was just a side show compared with the display put on by statesmen. Opening it, Fidel Castro in Havana gave his personal assurance that it really was Che who had been killed, whether this was based on graphological or photographic evidence, or perhaps on the Bertillonage system.

There was at once an impassioned message from the CPSU, tears from the Chilean CP and condolences from the Italian PC. As the communist party secretaries put it so well, Ernesto

Guevara became a legend. One can be certain that Fidel Castro, on the one hand, and the old pre- and post-Stalinist apparatuses, on the other, will make sure that he remains so, because for Fidel, Che is less of a nuisance dead than alive, and for the CPS, the significance of wreaths is that the deceased has to be buried.

There had been no room in Havana any longer for the Argentine doctor. Guevara and the communist machine had been incompatible.

The Bolivian Inti Peredo, who survived Che Guevara's last battle and is familiar with the *altiplano* and the mining regions, and whose whole life as a militant has been bound up with the workers and peasants, tried to rekindle the flame. He appealed for the struggle to be taken up again. However, he could not remain totally silent about the recent past and condemned the defeatist behaviour of both pro-Soviet and pro-Chinese Communists. He could not hope for better facilities than Che had: a little money—no doubt much less—a few weapons, and some minor connections abroad. From now on he was dealing with an opponent who could not easily be put off: the ruling military apparatus, whoever its nominal or real leader was—Barrientos, Ovando or some inexperienced young colonel.

The government crises, the waves of discontent, the vicissitudes of parties and political opposition groups throughout 1968 indicated that the stability of the military régime was far from assured. These shocks, however, made it clear that the military had become a crucial factor in the situation and that the problem of government could not be solved without the intervention of the armed forces.

Inti Peredo, or any other militant, or a revolutionary group, would have therefore, even while using Che's name, to think up new tactics and try out methods that owed nothing to the theoretical or practical *contribution* of the guerrilla bands.

'The Bolivian guerrilla war is not dead.' *Tricontinental*, Prague, July 1968.

15

Brazil. The Army in Power

IN BRAZILIAN naval circles, there is a saying that affords the
officers of the admiralty little pleasure: 'The army makes the
revolution and the *Sorbonne* seizes power.' This means that the
armed forces intervene when they feel that the politicians are
leading the nation along the path of ruin or disorder, but that
it is the Staff College that then takes over direction of a régime
born of a *coup d'état* called revolution.

Now the Staff College actually possesses a doctrine, or at
least a system of ideas that can pass for one. One of its theoreticians, General Golbery do Couto e Silva,[1] has given clear
expression to this doctrine, which he calls the National Policy.
This National Policy implies a National Strategy, which in
its turn calls for subordinate military, economic, political and
psycho-social strategies. For our present purpose, the main
things to remember about this 'revolutionary policy' are that
it gives the armed forces the job of 'upholding' or guaranteeing
the national interests, both internally and on an international
scale, and that, in general, it implies alliance with the Western
block whose recognised head is the United States.

The armed forces regard it as their function, their essential
mission to further the growth of Brazilian power. Golbery,
still using geo-political terms, has determined, for instance, the
form internal colonisation should take: 'To propel the colonising
forces northeastwards, starting from the central platform, so
that the west-central wedge might be integrated into the
Brazilian sum of parts'. The initiative must necessarily come

from the government, 'The tragic truth of our confused times is that there is no salvation outside government.'

These few quotations are given to illustrate how it is the will of the armed forces that operates in this situation. It is not a case of an instrument manipulated by an oligarchy or capitalistic interest group, but of a separate force with a will of its own. We are not here concerned with the merits, value or practicability of the doctrine put forward by the armed forces, but with showing how little this type of army has in common with, for example, Batista's.

As far as Brazil is concerned, the establishment of a counter-government, through guerrilla action, seems especially difficult from now on. In reality, even if one can find instances in recent history where violence has sprung from social causes, from the *cangaceiros* at the end of the last century up to the recent armed groups of peasant rebels degenerating into bandits through a series of socio-religious movements associated with various visionary personalities, there is nothing that can be identified with guerrilla warfare as defined by its present exponents. Even the period when peasant leagues sprang up and developed in the Northeast and when groups of students from the towns tried to affect a union with the restless rural classes did not see the birth of any kind of guerrilla movement.

After the military *coup d'état* of March 1964, there were many instances of armed 'bases' in the Matto Grosso or Rio Grande do Sul. It seems clear that the significance of various incidents or of the very sporadic attacks was exaggerated as much by the police and propaganda departments of the military régime as by the groups of opponents in exile. Both sides obviously had a vested interest in blowing up out of all proportions what was subsequently revealed to be just so much material for the miscellany columns.

A handful of activists survived from the mutinous movement of naval corporals and petty officers that had come into being at a time when President Goulart was trying to whip up the maximum of popular support to prevent his collapse, and a number of these gathered some revolutionary groups around them and tried to establish insurrectionary bases. Most of these *grumetes*, with little experience of underground life, were arrested.

A training centre started operating in the Serra do Caparão, in the State of Minas Gerais, but the police and military detachments very rapidly put a stop to its activities. In the same way, some members of the Communist Party of Brazil (a pro-Chinese splinter section of the CP) tried to establish terrorist cells and to get what was subsequently called the 'Uberlândia Movement' going, in the mining triangle. If one is to believe the Brazilian press and official statements, this movement, taking over some of its groups, had followed on the *Rede* combat network created by the ex-congressman Lionel Brizzola when the latter was among those political leaders supporting João Goulart's régime.

The bill of indictment drawn up by the military court refers to twenty-five individuals, subversive activity dating from 1964 and including courses in guerrilla warfare, sabotage and terrorism, the acquisition of arms and material, technical training with a view to an assassination attempt on President Costa e Silva and the attack on a mail-train. In other words, guerrilla warfare had limited itself to a multitude of projects.

Be that as it may, the pro-Chinese CP of Brazil was not represented at the OLAS meeting in Havana.

16

Paraguay. The CP v. the Guerrillas

SINCE 1954, General Stroessner, armed with very extensive powers based on Article 52 of the 1940 constitution, has been governing Paraguay. He has the right, and makes use of it, to declare a state of emergency for reasons of internal or external security. His twin basis of support is the army and the Colorado Party.

The opposition consists basically of: the Liberal Party and its various factions, with the exception of the so-called Leviral group, named after its leader, Dr Carlos Levi Ruffinelli, who has played the part of official opposition and been rewarded for it; the socialising Febrerista Party that sprang up immediately after the Chaco war (1932–35); various Christian-inspired movements; a dissident section of the Colorado Party, the MOPOCO (Movimiento Popular Colorado), which stands for direct action; and finally the Communist Party with its mutually antagonistic tendencies.

Up to recently, public political life has been very restricted and the régime has operated on the basis of a single party and dictatorial methods. The trade unions were 're-organised' and became mere cog-wheels in the state administrative machine. The student associations were purged and reduced to miserable corporate sub-branches of a university, itself brought to heel. The arrest of political militants, various types of censorship, prohibition of propaganda, innumerable impediments to any kind of agitation, merciless repression and, last but not least, measures giving submissive labourers the advantage over oppositionists in getting jobs, produced an atmosphere of fear and hopelessness throughout the country.

Conditions for the emergence of underground resistance and armed action had therefore existed for several years up to 1963 when the dictator relaxed his grip and a number of liberalising measures were taken.

The history of the numerous attempted risings, the invasions by groups of exiles from the Argentine and Brazilian frontier regions, the military rebellions, could be reconstructed only on the basis of the testimony of surviving participants, many of whom are still in prison. All these forms of violent opposition were suppressed with extreme severity. There are still a few dozen survivors of the May 1960 and 1964 conspiracies remaining in the penitentiaries.

Even though there have been numerous attempts to overthrow General Stroessner by force, one cannot really talk of guerrilla wars as such, either during the period of active struggle or in the present period. The most usual technique employed by the various opposition groups has been that of the 'coup', assassination, or invasion, especially from the Argentine side of the border.

In contrast and since the time when the opposition groups, taking advantage of a certain relaxation and greater tolerance on the part of the politico-military authorities, have been principally involved in re-organising themselves, the controversy over the merits or demerits of the armed course has been at the centre of the internal life of the Paraguayan Communist Party (PCP). At the beginning of 1960, the PCP had supported the 'frontal revolution', at least for the purpose of overthrowing the régime. Since 1963 its secretary, Oscar Creydt, has been advocating the creation of a 'Democratic Front of National Liberation' which was supposed to unite the entire opposition, including the bourgeoisie and progressive officers. In late 1964, proclamations called on the students and workers to prepare for armed action against Stroessner, but still insisted on 'combining the peaceful struggle of legal organisations' with 'popular guerrilla warfare'.

Nevertheless, when Creydt tried to participate in the organisation of the armed struggle, a split occurred in the CP and this schism seems to have been intentional on the part of the international communist leadership, since Creydt's main rival, Miguel Ángel Soler, was supported by the *New International Review*, which had always kept faithfully to the Moscow line. This controversy is made even harder to follow in that the PCP operates, in effect, from exile in Montevideo, Buenos Aires, or São Paulo.

A page in the Chilean CP organ, *El Siglo*, on May 28, 1967, was devoted to a National Conference of the PCP, with delegates from the Uruguayan, Argentine and Chilean CPs. This pre-Congress Conference demanded the expulsion of the 'agents provocateurs', Oscar Creydt, Arturo López and Raúl Ramírez.

17

Peru. Suicidal Insurrection

AT HIS CAMP at Illarec Ch'aska,[1] Luis de la Puente sent many
letters, to inform, instruct and exhort militant revolutionaries
of Latin America. These letters are similar in tone and content.
On August 15, 1965, he sent one to the Argentine, Adolfo
Gilly, who received it only in December, after the death of its
author.

Our Movement comprises five guerrilla bands spread out along the
Cordillera. The Túpac Amaru group,[2] which started operations
in the central zone, is one of them. Our efficient propaganda network spread the news of the beginning of MIR guerrilla activities in
the South, thereby provoking repression, and subsequently we
attacked in the Central zone. The Atahuallpa[3] and César Vallejo
groups[4] are located in the north and the Manco Inca[5] and Pachacútec groups[6] in the Southern Sierra. These guerrilla bands will go
into action one after the other, as agreed . . .

This description makes it look as though there is a military
apparatus, and armed forces ready to give battle. One should
perhaps remember that the sum total of fighters, split up among
five different bases, must have been in the region of 100 to 150
men. At the time, Henry Raymont of the *New York Times*
estimated the total number of guerrillas at 100 (*New York Times*,
September 28, 1965). Was this small force the spearhead of a
large-scale popular movement?

. . . During this period, various acts of terrorism and sabotage in
the towns disturbed the rulers. Most of these actions were the work

of groups, cut off from the other parties, that did not want to stand aside from the historical process the MIR had set in motion; but as they were the product of improvisation and despair, and gave evidence of inadequate leadership and experience, they led to considerable losses being sustained. Anyhow, the movement is irreversibly under way and all the left-wing groups and parties will have to play their part if they do not want to miss the boat of history.

Are there at least any grounds for supposing that the MIR is a strong organisation?

It cannot be said that the MIR is a true party in the Leninist sense and still less that it is a party that controls the masses in the country, but even so we believe we were right to give priority to the tasks of armed struggle. The year we were establishing guerrilla zones, along the Cordillera of the Andes, we built the party up on the basis of the provisioning, information, liaison, propaganda, co-ordination and other services. Cells were created in town and *campo*, by means of practical work which satisfies the age-long aspirations of the exploited masses.

Thus, for over a year, little by little, Luis de la Puente and a handful of militants mounted a guerrilla operation—and one can imagine the difficulties they encountered. If the leader and his lieutenants were aware of the limitation of the available means and the weakness of the organisations that supported them, what did they hope to achieve?

. . . We think that our insurrection, beginning with guerrilla action, will, in a short space of time, transform itself into an agrarian revolution in the mountains and rural areas, and that the masses, backed up by armed groups and led by the revolutionary party, will occupy the estates of the great landowners in force, as they already once did spontaneously in 1963 throughout the area. Soon afterwards, the outer suburbs of the coastal towns, with their peasants who have left the Sierra and are living in sub-human conditions, in poverty, unemployed and full of resentment, will explode like a time bomb. . . . Another factor is that of the students. Of the sixteen universities in Peru, twelve are under left-wing control, and in countries like ours the student youth, in universities as much as in secondary schools, is very radical and has a highly developed fighting spirit.

Let us stop there. This letter, like most of the political documents of the MIR and the other revolutionary groups, makes it clear that the decision to go into battle was not the result of the pressure of popular forces which would have required minimal encouragement to make themselves felt, but of a series of assumptions and calculations with regard to the attitude these forces would take once a revolutionary vanguard has shown them the way.

However, conditions for the launching of a rebellion or the establishment of guerrilla bands could hardly have been worse. The millions of Indian peasants, who only yesterday have lived quite apart from the rest of the nation and who, furthermore, did not have homogeneous interests as a mass, but whose aspirations varied according to the different regions, had only recently shown that they did not think in terms of revolution. The experience of the Convención Valley, with which Hugo Blanco had been intimately connected (in the eyes of Lima and the foreign journalists, he was the central participant) had clearly shown that Indian self-consciousness was bound up with specific, concrete problems and did not result from the propaganda work of the intellectual parties. The peasants were on the move, but with their own objectives in view and not as the instrument of the Lima extremists.

In fact these vagabonds from the mountains and valleys were the real revolutionaries, in that it was their cautious, hesitant but inexorable pressure that transformed Peruvian society which, for the first time, they were penetrating. The guerrilla bands might take the names of Túpac Amaru, Pachacútec or Atahuallpa, but they remained the creation of townsmen, their sights were set on the government in Lima, and they formed part and parcel of the general political game, even if revolutionaries, referring to Marx or Lenin, were trying to modify this game in some way. Even when they settled in the heart of peasant territory, these pure products of the intelligentsia of San Marcos University and *enfants terribles* of the urban middle class could not surmount the barrier between themselves and the little Quechua-speaking men.

On what were expectations of a rising of the *barriadas*[7] based, if not the same reflexes that the caudillos and traditional demagogues exploited with far greater skill? That is to say, with promises, the offer of total security and evocative watchwords. But the poverty-stricken masses stagnating in the suburbs dreamed of penetrating the town and settling down in it, not taking it over.

These speculations were more in order when it came to the students. The guerrilla agitators, organisers, cadres were mostly university-educated, and the first shots would bring volunteers from the colleges and schools streaming into the *maquis*. Nevertheless, the phenomenon had a class character, or, if one prefers it, a social function. Whether making their way through official channels, political, administrative or commercial, or by means of the more rapid seizure of power, the students, who were the natural heirs to the leading rôles in society, felt a solidarity of interests. The logical destiny of many extreme left-wing university activists was to sit in government departments and on boards of directors, whether in private or state service.

Socio-political conditions in 1965 gave guerrilla voluntarists little grounds for hope. The great mass of the people was organised and controlled by well-established parties like APRA. President Belaúnde's popularity was not at the time entirely used up and there was still a reserve of confidence in his agrarian, housing and social reform programme. Finally, the public conscience on the coast and in the urban centres was still preoccupied with the ups and downs of the struggles between president, parliamentary opposition and economic pressure groups. It is in connection with these struggles that the guerrillas were immediately condemned, interpreted and exploited.

On a purely technical level, that is to say in the field, it goes without saying that the military apparatus and its command would not hesitate when it came to stamping out the insurrectionary bases.

The organisers of guerrilla action could not be unaware of all this, so that one may well ask what reasons other than those directly relevant to the Peruvian situation influenced their decision.

It is conceivable that it was precisely the realisation of the difficulties in the way of a classical revolutionary attempt (with organisation and conflict in trade union, political and university spheres) and the poor results that could be expected of it, that led to the decision to embark on such a desperate enterprise. The attempt at a rising, whatever its outcome, was designed to break the hold of political conformism over public opinion, dramatically to demonstrate a number of real problems, to show that there were other possible solutions to those cooked up by the 'system'. Finally, it allowed the combatants to bring their behaviour into line with their radically non-conformist statements, whereas in town their words were contradicted by their personal lives which, as a rule, fitted very well into the ordinary social set-up.

To return to Luis de la Puente's letter, his manner of indicating his whereabouts was more than just a *façon de parler*: 'From one of the MIR guerrilla encampments, in the Cordillera of the Andes, at night, under police siege . . . ' Evasive phraseology of this kind is met with in many of the notes written by *guerrilleros*. In the same letter, as in many others from resistance fighters, the notion that even failure, even suicide are useful sacrifices, crops up. For the struggle is not confined to one country: 'We believe that there will be no second Cuba in America. Latin America in its entirety will follow Cuba. Some countries will make more progress than others in this struggle, but the final outcome will be on a continental scale.' The conception is of a revolutionary community, where some fall and others triumph, but where the death of some and success of others are part and parcel of the same thing. Is this optimism or an attempt at self-consolation?

18

Elsewhere. Men, Words and Methods

HERE WE must bring to an end our brief and cursory examination of the events and situations that come under the heading of guerrilla warfare in Latin America. The movement is everywhere in retreat. No new base has been established since the one in south-eastern Bolivia. Most probably, there will be no further attempts to put Che Guevara's theory into practice.

Of course this does not mean that the question of guerrilla warfare will no longer form the subject of discussions. On the contrary, we can be certain that the survivors and their memoirs will figure *ad nauseam* in theoretical works, whether militant or commercial. But words will take the place of men.

The Castroite style has caught well in Chile. A centre of the Organisation of Latin American Solidarity was even established at Santiago, causing a lengthy and very lively discussion in the press and parliament. There are a number of political organisations that defend the method of guerrilla warfare. There is even a magazine devoted to expounding the Castroite point of view on revolutionary tactics. Nevertheless, as soon as one gets to the men behind all these words and all this paper, one is forced to entertain serious doubts about their revolutionary potential.

Salvador Allende, former presidential candidate and currently President of the Senate, is a supporter of the OLAS and the Cuban Revolution, so that he has, at the same time, to see that the Chilean Constitution is respected and to encourage subversion. Another man, who expresses himself in far more militant terms, is Carlos Altamirano of the Socialist Party: 'Are not revolutionary policies those that aim at maintaining or re-establishing hypothetical individual guarantees within the democratic representative forces?' This forthright individual is a senator. Nor should one forget the Communist leader, Volodia Teitelboim, a member of the Chilean delegation to the OLAS conference, where he made flamboyant, forty-eightish speeches which nevertheless adhered strictly to the party line, that is to say supported the electoral conquest of power.

In contrast there are countries where the social struggle against national privileges or foreign companies takes a violent form, but where the forces of repression are so well organised that any attempt to establish embryonic armed groups leads only to massacres. Nicaragua is one of these.

Mexico is a different case altogether. There are fairly frequent announcements about the uncovering of revolutionary plots and conspiracies for the establishment of insurrectionist bases. Manifestations of political or social discontent sometimes take on a violent character in the outlying states of the country. These signs reveal the extent and seriousness of problems about which official propaganda is silent, or which it plays down. However, they are not indicative of any basic ground swell, nor is it really conceivable even that they should be a prelude to the organisation of guerrilla warfare, as the dominant party system functions efficiently and the régime is extremely hard on all those that try to circumvent its law.

The most serious obstacle to guerrilla warfare, in a country at least as well suited to it both geographically and socially as anywhere else, is the very considerable possibilities of social advancement open to the young intellectuals. The steady absorption of new generations emerging from the university into the party, the state, its civil service and enterprises, channels off nearly all the energy that might otherwise go into criticising, waxing indignant, making demands and insisting on a juster world.

Since his death, Ernesto Guevara has become the enormously

popular symbol of open resistance to the exploitation of society and North American imperialism. Pictures of Che are to be seen in most university centres, from Berlin to Berkeley and from Paris to Tokyo.

The fact that he has become a legend does not mean that the Argentinian leader's theories have been adopted and that his admirers are trying to put them into practice. It is the image of the fighter-martyr that obsesses so many young intellectuals. They have not taken over his ideas.

Without dwelling on the industralised countries, where Guevara's technique of guerrilla warfare is excluded by definition, one may usefully observe that no armed action in Latin America actually corresponds to the theoretical scheme. The attempts at subversion were much more a case of classical political pressure, despair or adventurism, than of the application of the theories of the counter-state. This applied equally to Mexico, where student demonstrations and protests (unconnected with the peasants and which stimulate rather than express the latter's aspirations) only marginally and temporarily transcended the rules of the internal game played by the Institutional Revolutionary Party; to Argentina where, in the Tucuman area, groups of young neo-Peronists from the towns again tried to set up a rebel base that was immediately eliminated; and to Uruguay where most of the 'Tupamaros' —Movement of National Liberation—were arrested after a few months of activity involving bank raids, spectacular robberies, the establishment of arms depots and sporadic skirmishes with the police.

Part III

Documents

The following document was found on one of the guerrillas who was killed fighting in the northwest of Argentina. He was 'Captain' Hermés, who commanded a detachment of the EGP, the People's Guerrilla Army.

The original contains much slang—probably Cuban—and the spelling is eccentric. We have tried to preserve the style and language in the translation.

This curious 'diary' is a chronicle of insignificant events, an account of endless reconnaissance marches, searches for food, meetings with other groups nearby.

There is only one indication of a military operation and nothing about propaganda, but there are two executions of *guerrilleros* at the hands of the group itself. Failing to make an impression on the enemy, the counter-state turns on itself.

'War Diary' of the EGP

'CAPTAIN' HERMES

June 21, 1963: At 22 hours we were sworn in as members of the EGP and we entered the country. On the morning of the 22nd, some people we at first believed were police turned up; that day we walked till two o'clock, pitched camp and reconnoitred to find out where we were. The 23rd, we passed the Toldo River and took the path running along the top of a sugar-cane field; we ate, then went on, and at about one o'clock, I lost a blank cartridge, out of those I had in my grenades; higher up we buried part of the bedding, and a bit further on we halted and made a soup and two slices of salmon each. The 24th at dawn we left without a drop of water; about ten in the morning we shared a tin of milk, sweetened, between the five of us; then we found a very dense thicket, with the ground falling away on either side; after this we found some sour oranges, we ate and I went off to explore; I discovered an animal track, which climbed to a height of over 4000 metres.

157

When I got back, we decided to descend as far as the stream which was on our right; when we reached it, it was already late, we drank some water and camped there after some soup and a bar of chocolate each. The 25th, at dawn we went upstream again and got as far as the Palo encampment and from there Federico and I went off to reconnoitre; when we got back it was late and we slept. The 26th, we left the Palo encampment to return downstream; that day we walked in the water till about noon, and at noon we went off to reconnoitre, the doctor and I, and a few hours later we returned with the news that it was impossible to continue along the river. We went back to the Palo encampment to sleep and there we had some soup and a bar of chocolate. The 27th, Federico and I left to reconnoitre downstream; when we got back it was late to be leaving, and we bedded down in the Palo encampment again. The 28th, we left and set up camp on the Toldo, near the spot where the map shows a small house, which does not exist, but we found a large quantity of oranges and that same day Federico and I went off on another reconnaissance. The 29th, Federico, Lauriano and I left for Toldo, which according to our information was about 4 kilometres away, but we got lost and came out at Bermejo, opposite the Casa del Inglés. There, Lauriano tried to cross the river and nearly got himself drowned, but he managed to get back to us and we sent him to the Casa del Inglés where they told him where he could buy food; he bought food and at 5.45 he got back to us with some hard-boiled eggs, some rolls with pâté and milk; Lauriano and I ate and slept there, and Segundo went to the Casa to return with us on July 2nd; the 30th, Lauriano and I went back to Federico and the doctor who had gone off to reconnoitre on the 29th, had got lost and had come out at the Palo encampment; Lauriano and I brought them bread, milk, pâté and condensed milk; the 30th, we moved off a little as people had turned up at the place where they were. The 2nd, Federico and I left to reconnoitre and found the spot where we were to meet Segundo; we advanced a little with the others during the day and the same day I plunged into the Bermejo which carried me along a little; at seven in the evening we joined Segundo and Don Sinforoso; we took a jeep and left the country and returned before nightfall; Segundo had brought food already prepared; a little later, as we did not know where we were, we settled down to sleep near the trail and slept there on a slope almost in a horizontal position. The 3rd, Federico left for Toldo and Lauriano in search of a shop for food. Federico returned very late and we stayed at this camp, opposite the school. The 4th, Federico and Lauriano left to buy horses and returned at night with the horses; at dawn we left for Toldo where we arrived in the afternoon and Lauriano and the doctor went off to get a horse shod, and they stayed there five hours; Segundo, Federico and I had a plan to take the Toldo police; at 9 o'clock the lads arrived, Segundo discharged them and we left at night with the permission of the police who had given us the authority to do so. The 5th, we slept near the mill, on the Toldo road, and the next morning Lauriano and I left on horseback to reconnoitre. We returned after a little while without any information and then the doctor left for base at the Casa del Inglés to ask Don Sinforoso to come and fetch us at one in the morning; Federico and Lauriano stayed with the horses. The 6th, at eight in the morning, Lauriano and Federico went to base and on July 7 it was the elections. The 8th, we went to Bermejo to pick up Federico who was leaving for Resistencia. The 9th, we returned to base and on our arrival the doctor and Lauriano told us the news that Illía was the new President. The 10th, the doctor left for Resistencia and Lauriano for La Paz and we started building the House of the Rebels. The 11th, we sent for Lauriano who was still in Tarija. The 12th, Lauriano arrived at base. The 13th, Lauriano left for Resistencia with the letter from the rebels to get it published throughout the country and we stayed at base till the 23rd, waiting for those who were supposed to be coming. The 23rd, the first group joined us; when we reached a place where one had to cross, we found a newly-made road with lorries passing, about one every half hour, and we wondered whether this was the police patrolling. The 24th, the

2nd group joined us; before they got to us, the Correntino[1] and I had had a scout round without finding out anything definite and the same night we set off without knowing if there was an ambush ahead, till we reached a nearby stream where we bedded down. The 25th, at dawn, the Correntino and I went off to reconnoitre and returned several hours later without any information, then we followed the river; about 11.30, Alberto, who was out of training, felt tired and we had to continue very slowly; a half hour later we pitched camp and while I was preparing the food, Federico and Pirincho reconnoitred along one stream, and Lauriano and El Pupi along another; on their return, we took the path Lauriano had reconnoitred and at 18 hours we settled down near a stream. The 26th, we had some chocolate and milk and set off. Towards 11 hours we halted and the Correntino and I left on a reconnaissance. When we got back, it was already too late to continue; we prepared some food and bedded down at that place; the 27th, we breakfasted very early as on the previous day, and we left, climbed up to a track and climbed down again towards the Illesco River where we slept. The 28th, the Correntino and I went off on reconnaissance after breakfast and when we got back it was too late to set off again and we slept in the same encampment where we had had soup one day and rice and sardines the next. The 29th, at dawn, after breakfast (we had chocolate with milk every day then) we left and marched about 10 kilometres. The Correntino climbed up the hill, and we bedded down about three kilometres from the track; that day we had soup and early the same day the Correntino and I went off to reconnoitre without finding anything. The 30th, at dawn we went off to wait for the Correntino on the banks of an unnamed river, beyond the Pescao River, because we thought that the Correntino had left it at the Solasuti; at night, we slept on a path where we made cod soup; when we reached this track the Cordovan[2] and I went off to reconnoitre and we reached a spot where we found four little houses. We returned thinking we were on the banks of the Pescao River. The 1st, we set off without eating as we had no water and descended to a stream which was dried up, but following it we finally found water, which was very bad; we had to put iodine into it just to make it drinkable; an hour later we climbed up to a path that we followed and we reached the Bate encampment; we stayed at this camp the 1st, 2nd, 3rd, and on the 4th at about midday we left. The 1st, Federico and I went off to reconnoitre and we ended up near Gil Tadeo's farm and on our return we told them in the camp that we thought we were on the Naranjal estate; at 15 hours the Cordovan and Lauriano went to wait for the Correntino. The two of them came back without him and with the news that he was at the Solasuti, 12 kilometres away. Immediately afterwards the Cordovan left for Orán where, on the morning of the 3rd, he met the Correntino who had come from Salta; the same day Lauriano and Alberto waited for them on the road and in the afternoon they arrived at the Bate encampment with a large quantity of food supplies, this after one plate of soup a day since the 1st; the 3rd, Federico and I went off on reconnaissance and I lost the FAL[3] depot which we found again later, and that day Federico and I got back completely worn out. October 4th, in the Bate camp, the Cordovan took the oath, and the Correntino also; towards midday we set off but we did not walk long because water was quite far away and we did not know if we could reach the other river, the track being so bad.

The 5th, in the morning, we left and round about two o'clock the Correntino and I left to explore; we got back when it was already dark, and the others had some food ready for us, a large stock of tins of jam and fruit and chocolate we had shared out to lighten the load; and that day we finished off the water even though we had been very careful with it. The 6th, we continued through the virgin forest where we made about one kilometre's progress an hour, making countless détours, because the compasses were not functioning and the sun was hidden. That day we bedded down right there in the forest, without water. At dawn on the 7th we set off with the sun beating down, through the same forest, with the dust rising and parching our throats; our clothes soaked in sweat, we reached a spot where Segundo ordered the column to stop so that we could reconnaissance; this task fell to Alberto and El Pupi and I went as a volunteer; Segundo did not want me to go, but I wanted to, to give them cover; after about thirty metres or so we found a path; next we crossed the road which was about 50 metres away; we came back along the road to get an idea of where the lorries were going to and how many there were; it was already 11.30 and the sun was very hot and the people in the trucks must have been having a bite as hardly any vehicles passed us; when we reached the road, which one could see down for two or three kilometres, I told my companions that water was at least four kilometres away and that we would follow the road to fetch some; we set off, and at a quarter to one we reached the river and I drank at least three litres of hot water; a bit more and I felt sick and had to wait a bit before I could walk; coming back I counted my steps to where our comrades were; it was five kilometres; and when we got there we were informed that we had to leave immediately because a peasant had seen the column. We gave our comrades some water, then set off; we covered a bit of ground then we sat down because it was too hot to walk; then I told them what I had seen: we decided to wait for nightfall and to follow the road as far as the Solasuti; there we all had a drink and went on to a spot where we had an adequate meal of rice and sardines.

At dawn on the 8th, we set off with our bellies full and towards two o'clock we were already out of water; Segundo ordered the column to stop because we were near the Pescao River; the Cordovan and I set off to look for the Pescao, but we had been told to strike southwards so that we walked on a parallel course to the river and did not find it that day; the Cordovan was dropping with fatigue for lack of water and on our return it was the Correntino and Pirincho who set off; that night we lay down without water; during the night we heard the sound of the Pescao and at dawn the Cordovan and I went off to look for it; we went in a west by south-westerly direction and after 27 minutes of walking we reached the banks of the broad Pescao; around midday on the 9th, Pirincho and the Correntino returned with twelve litres of water; they had slept at Orán; we waited for nightfall and set off along the path running alongside the YPF (*Yacimientos Petrolíferos Fiscales*) pipe-lines; we walked for about an hour and stopped to sleep right on the river bank. On the morning of the 10th the Correntino set off for Orán to buy goods, and in the afternoon Federico and the Cordovan went to YPF to buy a chicken, some bread and hard-boiled eggs; we cooked the chicken and then waited for the Correntino, Alberto and El Pupi to come back to eat it; all of a sudden a gale blew up and started uprooting trees, one of which fell right on to the Correntino's and Albert's hammocks; they might have been killed had they been there; a branch off another tree crashed down on Segundo's hammock.

At dawn on the 11th, I went out looking for the Correntino, Alberto and El Pupi; I found them shortly and we returned to the camp where we spent the day; El Pupi and I went off on a night reconnaissance and passed the Pescao. The Cordovan who was looking for the ford fell into the mud. When we got near the YPF, El Pupi began to play the fool and we had to disarm him; we carried on along the bank and Segundo fell and gave himself a hard blow on the ankle; shortly afterwards we slept on a rock near a path; next morning we found the trail about twenty metres away; Lauriano and I set off, and when we got back, a safe enough camping spot had been found for the Correntino and Pirincho to establish contact with Grillo whom we had waited for at Salta; we stayed at that camp from the 12th to the night of the 17th. On the 16th, at night, we crossed the Pescao at two points; El Pupi fell at the second crossing of the river, and we bedded down at the entry to the Anta Muerta ravine. On the 18th, during the day, Federico and I went off to scout around, in mufti, and about six kilometres away we found an encampment (Fernández's) and Porfirio and Don Guitiérrez' house, which we reached at night. In the morning, Federico and I had bought some meat from Porfirio. When we arrived in the evening, Porfirio invited us to eat and sleep at his place; during the night Pirincho went to tend some sick people in the camp. On the 19th we reached San Ignacio, near the old source of the Irulia. On the 20th, Pirincho and I left on reconnaissance, in mufti, and we came back after we had bought bread . . . maté, sugar and oranges at Nino Salva's.

The 21st, we crossed the San Ignacio valley and at five in the morning we pitched camp near Rivera's house; the Correntino set off for Orán to get food; Federico and I went off at midday to scout; we found a river and in the afternoon we moved camp; that night we slept near the river and in the morning Segundo, Pirincho and I went one way and the rest the other, on reconnaissance; we got back about two o'clock and the others at about noon, except for the Cordovan who had stayed at the camp because he was leaving that day, the 22nd, to establish contact with his brother Emilio; the same day, a little before the Cordovan's departure, we moved camp. The 22nd, at night, El Pupi and Lauriano went to wait for the Correntino; we never found out what happened to him. We stayed at this camp till the 25th, when we moved early in the afternoon. A little later the Cordovan and his brother arrived; Alberto and El Pupi had missed him. The 27th, Emilio left with the Cordovan to have a toe nail removed. We waited for them at the camp until November 7; Emilio returned on the 4th at four in the morning. The 5th, the Cordovan went out with the new arrivals, and we executed El Pupi.

The 7th, we set off in the jeep and reached the San Andrés River. The 8th, the Cordovan and I went off to scout and we found a river Federico said was the Santa Cruz, but I did not agree with Federico, and Segundo sent the Cordovan and me to find the Santa Cruz; just before reaching the Santa Cruz we came across Emilio and Canelo who had not been able to cross the river because Canelo had been frightened to stay there; we continued reconnoitring and a little higher we found an empty house, and a *criollo*[4] told us about a '*colla*'[5] who lived lower down, warning us not to call on his house because the '*collas*' are bad, and when you are dealing with a '*colla*' you have to say: give me this or that and only ask how much afterwards, because otherwise they simply will not sell. Afterwards we reached a '*colla's*' house and asked him if he had fruit or anything else to sell and he sold us ripe bananas; on the way back, after about 2 km, it started raining and we had to bed down beside the San Andrés. At dawn on the 9th we set off again and got near the spot where the Santa Cruz and Naranjal join up. From there the Cordovan and Jorge went off to reconnoitre, lost their way and only got back on the 10th at night; at dawn, we set off again and started cutting across fields; we got to a point above a crossroads where we slept; that afternoon, Pirincho and the Cordovan had gone to Pereyra's house; coming back, they lost their way and had to sleep beside the river in the terrible cold. The 11th, Federico went off with another group to collect the goods that had remained near the river. He returned at night time, and the following day, that is the 12th, we set off very early; we walked for about an hour and a half and Lauriano, the Cordovan and I returned to get some goods; on our return they had already dug a hole to bury the things in; afterwards we proceeded along the dry bed of the Agua Blanca River when we thought we were in a tributary of the Santa Cruz; later on we left the river and proceeded through the woods; shortly afterwards we crossed a road leading to Agua Negra; we stopped almost at once and I went ahead four kilometres with Henry; it was late when we got back and we encamped there for the night.

At dawn on the 13th we set off again: we crossed the Santa Cruz River and cut through the woods till we reached a deserted house where we ate some limes; from there we proceeded along the Sausal River and met a '*colla*' Indian who after a few minutes talk asked us to join him in some grapefruit; we ate grapefruit and stayed there talking for over two hours. Afterwards we continued till we reached the house of an old widow who gave us coffee, tortillas and corn off the cob; that day we slept near the widow Gimédes' house.

At dawn on the 14th, we followed the road to Yjinio Gimódes Guenseslao's house, where we were told how to get to the

Mesada Hills. That day we were not able to climb to the Mesada; after three hours march Lauriano went off to reconnoitre, lost his way and did not get back till the next morning. The 15th, the Cordovan and I went off to reconnoitre and we reached the Playa Ancha River. We returned and on the 16th in the morning we set off again for the Playa Ancha River, and the Cordovan and Pirincho cut through the Humahuaca gorge in order to make contact with Emilio. The 17th, Federico returned, he had gone with the Cordovan and Pirincho. The 18th, we arrived at Don Manuel's and Don Pedro Gimédes' house, we stayed there two days then we left to meet the couriers. While we were proceeding along the Santa Maria we met a lad who was going to pick up the traps on our way; a fox had got caught in one of these traps, we went on a bit and then stopped to sleep. The 20th, in the morning, Federico set off to find a place to camp; he got back early and a little later we set off for this camping spot to wait for the couriers, and goods which arrived on the 20th at night. The 21st, we stayed in this camp and a few of us went off to reconnoitre; we returned in the afternoon. The 22nd, towards noon, when the sun was scorching, we went off to meet some newcomers who arrived with packs on their backs. We stayed in this camp from the 22nd till after the 'Trampolín' operation.[6] The 22nd, Grillo and Canelo arrived and the 23rd we returned to camp. The 24th, the fat Emilio, Canelo, Pirincho and Deferico left. The 28th, Pirincho and El Papi arrived with the mail; the 30th, El Papi and Pirincho left to join up with Federico and put operation 'Trampolín' into effect. Meanwhile we trained the newcomers in the camp. The 4th, I left with Enrique and Grillo to meet Emilio and Canelo. They arrived on the 5th. The 6th, I returned to camp and it was Enrique, Alberto and Grillo who went to fetch the rest of the goods. The 7th, Alberto, Enrique and Grillo went to wait for the men in operation 'Trampolín'. The 10th, the whole group engaged in this operation returned, so the 'Trampolín' mission was accomplished. The 11th, the group went on leave. The 13th, a section of the group left for Manuel's house to get some food. The same day Lauriano and Emilio went off to work in town. When those who had gone to get food returned and were told that the next day we were off on a reconnaissance, Pirincho said he was too tired. The 15th, Segundo and I with a section of the men went off to reconnoitre, looking for a path that would lead us to the Colorado River. The 16th, we returned without any information; Segundo did not feel so well at that time, due to parasites we had all picked up. We stayed in the camp till the 20th; that day I went off with Papi and Enrique to reconnoitre in the direction of the Colorado, and we came out at the Seco River and Devil River; passing through the settlement of Santa Rosa, where we arrived on December 24, we said we were going fishing, and the driver of a car who took us as far as the settlement told us that to fish one had to go up the River San Francisco and the Bermejo; fine, we'll do that then!; but at 9.30 we arrived at the camp with brioches and nougat to round off the comrades' dinner which that day had consisted of a *doble-ancha*, that is a little wheatmeal boiled in sugared water (in other words, paste).

The 25th, we stayed in the camp. The 26th, Federico, Henry and Jorge set off to look for the Colorado and returned on the 27th without having found it; on returning from this reconnaissance Henry blew up a depot of 45-calibre machine-guns; the following day Henry, Enrique and Mamerto set out to look for the dépôt; we waited at the camp; we could not all set off in a body because of the arms and munitions that were stored there and because we were awaiting newcomers who were due.

The 29th, Canelo returned with a large quantity of food. There were eight men to carry the food, plus one who had just joined up with us and we ate fit to burst, as for several days we had been reduced to polenta with sugar at midday, and with salt in the evening. The Cordovan had said that he would come that evening, and he arrived at 11 p.m. on the 30th. We made a soup out of wheatmeal, just with water, salt and meal, and as we could not cook it, when the water was boiling we threw the flour in and made little balls like gnocchi. The 31st, we started constructing a path, the first path made by

167

the EGP, to move camp to a new spot the next few days; this job took us two days to complete.

The 2nd, we stayed in the camp till the afternoon; the Cordovan and Pirincho were on the path when, around two o'clock, I felt like a walk and I joined them and set to work. Suddenly I came across a plant like a 'malanga'. I said to the Cordovan: 'Look at this plant, just like the Cuban "malanga"; here, take a sniff, exactly like the yellow "malanga".' The Cordovan tasted it: 'It's good. Have a taste too, like that we'll both cop it if it's poisonous.' I began to chew and said: 'It's a bit sharp, yes it's a bit on the sharp side.' And with the piece in my mouth, I picked up my water-bottle and took a swig. The water had hardly gone down before I suddenly felt sick. I started vomiting and so did the Cordovan soon after. We really had poisoned ourselves and the effects of it, for me anyway, and even though I said I was alright, lasted nearly a week, with heartburn and nausea especially. The 3rd, we stayed at the camp. The 4th, we went as far as Manuel's and Guenceslao's house at Aguas Negras. The 5th, we returned to the camp and after we had passed on the results of our expedition, a party set off to establish a new camp, and a few of us stayed behind to keep watch over the arms depot. Two days after, Segundo sent me a message asking for men and food as he intended carrying out an exercise.

The 8th, Segundo and the others returned to camp. The 9th, the Cordovan left to establish contact near the River Santa María, but this could not be done till the 11th; he had got to the middle of the ford but had not been able to continue. As for Carlos, who was coming for this purpose, he had an attack of epilepsy when he reached the Vado Hondo and he had to be left there, at the Vado Hondo; Lauriano, Pirincho and Grillo, who had been bitten by a spider and could not walk, stayed too. Pancho it was who came as representative of the party group, for discussions and work with the EGP. After three days he left full of enthusiasm to work in Córdoba and rejoin the representatives of the party groups of the different provinces; in his capacity as representative of the EGP, he undertook, with

the fat guy, to see to the organisation at Córdoba. When
Pancho left for Córdoba, Carlos left with him bound for
Bolivia, and was taken as far as Agua Blanca. The 17th, the
Cordovan, Jorge, Oscar, Nardo and I left to reconnoitre a new
route to the Colorado. The 20th, we returned to camp after
we had seen tracks leading to the Colorado and investigated
another river that was on our maps; the 21st, we rested; the
next day, Federico and the Cordovan set off with a part of the
group to get goods at the Colorado; the fat chap was supposed
to rejoin us at the camp and the rest of the men to continue as
far as one of the rivers we had investigated. The 23rd, in the
afternoon, the fat chap arrived in camp, with me waiting for
him near the waterfalls which he had already left from . . . he
had found the pack and had taken another route to ask for the
pack to be fetched. The 24th, the fat guy was promoted to
lieutenant and the same day he left with Lauriano for Córdoba.
The 27th, Federico arrived with part of the group. That day
they rested and the 28th they set off with some of the stored
weapons. The 29th, I returned to the camp with another
part of the group. The 30th, we left again, Segundo, Pirincho,
the Cordovan and I with the rest of the group. The 29th, it
was decided I would leave at 7 o'clock; but Segundo had got
behind and according to the Cordovan they moved slowly
because they had overtired themselves in the foot-hills and
when they reached the river they were dead beat and we
caught up with them. Then Segundo made a scene and told me
that if we wanted to play at seeing who was the toughest or
who would get there first we could leave the column and go
our own way; that they were not taking it easy at all and that
I was killing the men; I replied that I did not know what was
going on as I had not travelled with them; the argument lasted
a full five minutes and he concluded by saying that from now
on I should be under the strictest orders; I replied that, for
my part, I would obey willingly; what also came up in the
argument was that the leader ought to help his men; later on,
referring to Nardo, he said that he had been the cause of this
upset, that when he stopped it was better to leave him alone

and not worry him too much because otherwise he would go on doing the same thing. The 31st, we stayed in the camp, without Jorge and Enrique who had been bitten by a spider and were in Salta. We stayed there till the 2nd. That day, Canelo, Jorge and Alberto returned, and Enrique set off for Orán with Papi. The 3rd, Papi and Enrique returned and the next day Papi set off again for Orán as he had not been able to meet his contact; he returned without him. The 7th, Lauriano arrived with something to eat. We left to make contact and stayed on the banks of the Colorado; two days later I sent a messenger to the camp where Segundo was to let him know that the place was unsafe; we stayed in this camp till the 13th; that day the Cordovan was promoted to lieutenant and Alberto, Enrique and Henry combatants. I stayed till the 20th. The 18th, Nardo had been tried and condemned to death and he was executed on the 19th; I was chairman of the tribunal. The 20th, four of the comrades—with me it made five—went out on an expedition along the Picada stream as far as the Valle Morado River, and got lost on the way back. We spent a day lost in a maze of rivers and the 25th, when we got back to camp where Henry and Marco had remained, there was hardly any food left; the 26th, Henry and Marco left to find food, carrying with them the results, in writing, of the reconnaissance. Segundo had not come with us because he had to wait for a contact; he had to have an interview and people were supposed to come. During the course of this reconnaissance we were to find some trails that were very important to us as regards food provisions and security (up to 26–2).

The following pages are taken from a publication issued by the Peruvian Ministry of War, in 1966.

Besides chapters on 'the antecedents of subversion', Hugo Blanco's movement and the propagation of guerrilla movements, the book contains the report on the military operations here translated.

Four sketch maps of the operational zones, aerial photos of the sites of battle, photographs of groups of guerrilla fighters and of recovered war material complete this document, which is entitled 'Las guerrillas en el Perú y su represión'.

The Guerrilla War in Peru and its Repression

CHAPTER VI: INTERVENTION OF THE ARMY

Trusting in the good will of the citizens and in harmonious and patriotic collaboration with the other military organisations and auxiliary forces, the army, conscious of the historical moment the country was living through, was getting ready to intervene.

The 2nd military region (SRM) received instructions from the Army High Command to plan, co-ordinate and carry out operations within the Púcuta-Satipo zone.

The FAP Command gave orders that a suitable number of fighter planes should be kept on the alert, ready to operate from the Jauja base. During the six months of the struggle these were constantly in action, pin-pointing guerrilla installations, dropping supplies, transporting troops to danger spots, evacuating the wounded, etc.

The Naval Command determined that the river forces, based on Iquitos, should control the region of the Alto Ucayali, through their vigilance and patrolling activities preventing the reds extending their tentacles into these rich and important zones of virgin forest; and that they should also co-operate with the army in patrolling and carrying out operations on the Tambo, Perene and Ene Rivers.

Concurrently with these preparations, the armed forces waged an intensive propaganda and premonitory campaign, broadcasting messages in local dialects over loudspeakers installed in planes or helicopters, dropping thousands of leaflets so that the peasants of these regions, whether they could read or not, should refrain from collaborating, out of fear or ignorance, with the *guerrilleros*.

In order to facilitate the task of clearing the area between the San Fernando, Mántaro, Ene and Sonomoro Rivers and restoring order there, the inhabitants were urged to avoid any contact with strangers or suspicious individuals or at least to try to reduce them to a state of helplessness and deliver them up to the authorities. They were informed that attempts to resist the forces of order charged with defending the national sovereignty would encourage subversive activities. They were warned that the possession of arms or explosives, without permission from the Ministry of the Interior, was regarded as an offence, as was the hiding of spies or native or foreign agents.

As the known tactics of the extremists when in flight is to make use of the local inhabitants as guides or hostages, they were warned that those who collaborated would be arrested and punished as accomplices.

Finally, in order to avoid the shedding of innocent blood in the troubled area, women and children were asked to keep away from any suspect.

Having duly carried out these preventive measures in the troubled area, in the centre of the country, the armed forces, pursuing the mission entrusted them by the government, embarked on counter-guerrilla operations for the restoration of order.

To this end, the SRM Command co-ordinated and made preparations for the action of those units that were to take part in the operations, carefully positioning them as required, so that the cunning and agile enemy should not slip out of the net.

Given the size of the zone where this was going on, it was decided that the Second Light Division (DL) together with combat troops from Cerro de Pasco and Huancayo, should proceed to the elimination of the guerrilla bands that had been located. To this force was added a company of Republican Guards (GR) specially equipped for these operations, and under its command were placed the Civil Guard and Police and Political Police (PIP) forces, which were to go into action in the area right from the start of operations.

Operational Command (2nd DL) readjusted the initial disposition and placed the auxiliary forces in the built-up areas and on main peripheral points of the troubled zone in order to isolate the guerrillas and prevent their making contact with Huancayo, Cuzco, Cerro de Pasco and Lima.

On June 19th, 1965, it ordered Loma and Zorro companies, the latter belonging to the GR, to be transported respectively to the road termini of Chilifruta and Shihua. At Chilifruta, army troops constructed a heliport to facilitate joint army-airforce operations.

The Command Post (PC) of the 2nd DL and its supporting forces were situated in Huancayo, while the remaining combat units in this Combined Force remained in Carmen Chico (Cerro de Pasco) and Huancayo. Two transport planes were kept at Jauja, the FAP operational base, and two helicopters at Chilifruta, so as to carry out the reconnaissance and logistical support operations required by the 2nd DL.

Loma and Zorro companies reached the base camps selected by the Command, Huancayo and Balcón respectively, on foot. Progress was very slow in view of the extremely awkward terrain and the need to keep to the peasant plots in order to avoid mines placed along the narrow sunken paths, as well as the rock falls prepared in advance.

Some guerrilla fighters and collaborators were captured, and information concerning the existence of guerrilla camps at Púcuta, Intihallamuy, Ajospampa, Jatunhuasi and Yugurpampa, in the mountain zone, was confirmed by them.

As soon as Loma and Zorro companies reached their base

camps, the advance on Púcuta and Intihallamuy, where the most important guerrilla encampments had been reported, was begun. Loma was to advance on Púcuta along the Huancamayo-Lima road in order to take the *guerrilleros* of this zone by surprise and occupy the encampments in a locality the latter regarded as inaccessible. From Balcón, Zorro was to strike out towards Lihuiña and capture Intihallamuy, preventing the extremists from escaping towards the Sonomoro and Alto Anapati valleys, and thereby helping to wipe out those guerrillas which might have slipped through the Loma net.

During this phase, extra precautions were taken as the terrain was harder and there was a permanent danger of ambush. The troops surmounted the harrowing worries of the situation and advanced keeping a sharp watch out, continually on the alert, but concentrating on the mission in hand.

On July 30, the first clash took place between Zorro company and the extremists who attacked with small arms, home-made bombs and dynamite. They were beaten off, leaving four of their numbers dead on the field.

In view of the insurmountable hardships due to the nature of the terrain, Zorro's marching orders were altered and the company moved on Púcuta to carry out a pincer movement together with Loma. This operation was to be covered by two FAP planes. The battle for Púcuta broke out on August 1 and 2 after bombardments and several rounds of aerial machine-gunning, and the place was taken after a stubborn resistance.

On August 1, near Púcuta, an Army patrol found the bodies of guards Diógenes Valderrama and Eusebio Silvera (who had been captured shortly before the Vaguarina ambush) mutilated in a way that suggested they had been slowly and barbarously martyred with a sadism so refined that it was unequalled by even the most savage and superstitious tribes of the last century.

After the capture of Púcuta, the reds fell back on Intihallamuy leaving eight dead behind them. The companies occupied themselves in dismantling the base, clearing the area and carrying out reconnaissance missions up until the 3rd, when the Intihallamuy operation was resumed. On starting down into the Santa Rosa gorge, there was another clash in which three guerrilla fighters were killed, while Zorro lost six men: three killed and three wounded. The wounded were picked up and evacuated by FAP helicopters operating from the Chilifruta heliport.

Once the reinforcment of the Púcuta base had been completed, the troops advanced on Intihallamuy, which they found abandoned; they proceeded to destroy the dépôts and emplacements prepared by the guerrillas: trenches, tunnels and other defence works.

Sufficient troops were left behind in Púcuta and Intihallamuy to carry out operations in the mountains and it was decided to send part of Loma against Ajospampa, part of Zorro against Jatunhuasi and a section of the GR to Yugurpampa, all of which places were occupied without any resistance being met, except at an escarpment near Yugurpampa where two GR soldiers were slightly wounded.

After these successes and knowing, without there being confirmation yet, that the combatants of the 'Túpac Amaru' guerrilla band had abandoned the mountain region (subsequently it was confirmed that they had taken to the forest zone of the Sonomoro and Anapati Rivers), it became essential to restore the confidence and calm of the inhabitants of the region, as well as the agricultural and commercial activities that had been paralysed since the beginning of the acts of violence. In addition it was necessary to intensify the search for information on the location of bases and areas of guerrilla activity and to continue hunting down the guerrillas.

To this end, Civil Guard and PIP units were stationed in posts on the periphery of the zone and two detachments of 40 men each at Jatunhuasi and Kubantia respectively, to keep a watch and maintain control. At the same time, mobile units of Loma, Zorro and Huaco companies (the latter transferred from Cerro de Pasco) were formed, charged with carrying out a permanent and intensive patrolling action, leading to the arrest of guerrillas who might still be in the area, and in order to reassure the inhabitants that the communist bands would not be back to terrorise them.

Owing to the difficult topography and the size of the zone, these apparently straightforward operations made great demands on the troops, both in terms of sheer effort and time. They also called for intense activity on the part of the FAP to meet the requirements for troop transportation, supplies and evacuations. In most cases, the aerial missions were carried out in conditions of minimum security, which confirms the indisputable skill and spirit of self-sacrifice of our pilots and crews. Thus it was that, thanks to the sustained effort and devotion to duty of the united forces of order, the mountain region returned to normal.

While the mountain area was being cleared and consolidated, as described above, the *guerrilleros* launched a violent attack in the forest.

The Kubantia massacre

A police detachment was installed in Kiatari and Kubantia, situated on the Sonomoro River, to keep the peace, enable agricultural activities to proceed and keep watch over the roads connecting these places with the Púcuta-Jatunhuasi region.

On August 9, violence broke out: a police patrol carrying out a liaison mission by van between Kiatari and Kubantia was ambushed by a group of guerrillas and Campas Indians.

GC Sub-Lieutenant Guillermo Alcántara Mena, Sergeant José del Carmen Huamán and engineer Ismael Castillo, administrator of the Kiatari Hacienda, were wounded and treacherously murdered, and two Campas workers from the same estate who were with them were left severely wounded.

This, together with information received through intelligence units that had already taken up positions in the forest, confirmed the presence of *guerrilleros* in the area and the existence of one of their bases in the Bustamante Indian camp, south of Kubantia. At the same time we received alarming and contradictory information regarding the presence of 'bearded ones' near the Mazamri and Perene Rivers, or the imminence of an attack at Satipo. All these pieces of news came in rapidly one after the other, swathed in mystery.

In view of this situation, Operational Command altered arrangements, organising a variable number of small detachments out of troops returning from the mountains, that were placed at different points such as Púcuta, Ajospampa, La Boca, Yugurpampa, Alegría, etc., with orders to prevent all contact between the guerrillas and their mountain liaison units, and to assist in the counter-guerrilla operations in the forests.

The 50-man Huaca detachment was made up of soldiers from Huancayo and was transferred to Satipo. To the same place was flown the Puma commando detachment, which, in two days forced march, was to reach Kubantia. Finally, the 80-man León commando detachment, which for 40 days had been carrying out raids, day and night reconnaissance missions and other exacting tasks in patrolling the area between Teresita (River Apurimac) and San Noce de Secce (Huanta Province), with the object of preventing the guerrillas from escaping towards Mesa Pelada and normalising the situation at Ayacucho, was transferred, on foot, through virgin forest to Missión and Puerto Rico (both on the Ene River).

Once the units had been deployed according to the new dispostion, the order was immediately given for the guerrillas to be pursued and the Puma detachment was used for this purpose, intensively and painstakingly patrolling the whole of the valley of the Sonomoro River, including its tributaries, between Mazamari and Kubantia. In an attack on the Bustamante camp, two Campas, collaborating with the guerrillas, were captured and told us of the flight of the latter towards Mazaronquiari. The attacks were intensified without a break, even though, at the outset of the operation, we could not rely on the Campas guides who, as has already been mentioned in connection with the origins of the guerrilla movement, had been won over to the guerrilla cause after a long period of infiltration and indoctrination. But the *guerrilleros*, forewarned, kept on avoiding a direct confrontation with Puma. The encampments and other small villages were totally deserted because of the alarm caused by the presence of guerrilla fighters. The schools were empty and many children were ill and inadequately fed. In addition to their main task, the commandos carried out the humanitarian one that fell to their lot: they repaired and fitted out the Mazamari mixed school, treated and fed the children, making over a portion of their field rations to them; they held frequent talks with the natives, showing them the error of their ways and urging them to resume their normal occupations. This produced a chain reaction that greatly benefited the forces of order. The Campas began collaborating openly and loyally with the Army.

Meanwhile, the *guerrilleros*, who were beginning to feel the effects of their gradual loss of support, who were living from day to day continually on the retreat, and who felt their strength ebbing away in the face of the efficiency and zeal of the armed forces, realised they were in a desperate plight and determined to recapture the initiative by carrying out a daring attack on the garrison at Púcuta, a fort held by only 30 army soldiers. The extremists did not attain their objective and were repulsed leaving three dead behind them. The section of the Marte company which garrisoned Púcuta also lost three men. After the failure of this attempt to regain certain positions they retired to the Shuenti encampment where the two 'Túpac Amaru' guerrilla groups apparently linked up.

Operations at Shuenti

Operational Command decided on a rapid action against the Shuenti 'Guerrilla Base', a camp situated at an altitude of about 3000 metres above sea level, near the sources of the Anapati River, difficult to reach, surrounded by dense vegetation and on very rough ground.

The operation took the form of a pincer movement on the part of the Loma detachment and a section of the León detachment, consisting of 35 men from the town of Puerto Rico. The first group, which was two days march away, was to advance, over half a day, in the direction of La Boca and

Shuenti, and stop there to seal off the Alto Anapati, while the León section, which was 130 kilometres off, was to reach the camp, keeping to the paths and fields in order to maintain secrecy, and destroy the enemy.

The *guerrilleros*, informed of the movement of the two detachments, sent a strong group under Lobatón against Loma, which was closest to them, with the object of laying an ambush and destroying the detachment. But the encounter never took place as Loma had reached its destination, half a day's march away, without incident and without being observed.

Leaving aside the details of the raid carried out by the two units, here are a few outstanding examples of courage, determination, stamina and initiative. The León commando unit, under a major, receiving its orders to march on Shuenti and destroy the guerrilla base, left Puerto Rico on September 27, with sufficient rations for two days; supplies were to be dropped, on demand, by helicopter. On the 28th, the commandos carried out a surprise attack on the Alto Sumabeni camp, capturing the first *guerrillero* scout. There, they secured the assistance of two Campas who attached themselves to the force. On the 29th, they reached Alto Tincabeni and captured the second look-out man and one Campa offered to collaborate. On the 30th, they carried out another attack and captured the third look-out man. That same night they made a raid on the Shenquiari camp and established their first 'meeting zone'.

On October 1, they continued their advance through the forest and established the second 'meeting zone', near the target area.

Only five days had passed and the gallant commandos had covered 130 kilometres of forest, over rough and very precipitous ground, that is to say an average of 26 kilometres a day, or more than the regular day's march over normal ground, which is 24 kilometres. They carried out four surprise attacks and two raids and reached the target area without being seen. They arrived with virtually nothing left but their weapons, their uniforms in shreds, and bootless, having made their two-days rations last for six, as the leader of the detachment consciously and deliberately silenced the radio transmitter and did not call for supplies, so that the helicopters should not give away their presence.

On October 2, a surprise attack was launched, at dawn, on the Shuenti camp and another look-out man was captured. Three Campas supplied our information on the position of the guerrilla camp and the departure of sixteen *guerrilleros* in the direction of Mazaronquiari to lay an ambush for the Loma detachment. It was 16·00 hours when the last look-out man was captured. At 16.30 hours the Shuenti camp was in sight. The leader of the detachment took all useful steps to surround the base and charged forward, followed by the entire leading patrol. The guerrillas reacted swiftly and opened fire, wounding the major and two sergeants who continued fighting until the camp was taken. Eleven guerrillas were killed (Lobatón, Velando and Herrera were not in the group) and 17 were captured, these subsequently being evacuated. The weapons, bombs and equipment were taken and then the base was destroyed. Much of the recovered material belonged to the Civil Guard and among other objects was a ring inscribed 'Horacio-Hilda', a memento of a marital union tragically shattered at Yaguarina, on June 27, 1965.

With the operation completed, Shuenti was kept under surveillance, in anticipation of the return of the group that had set off to lay an ambush for the Loma detachment. This never took place as the guerrillas under Lobatón were fleeing towards the Sonomoro River.

The final chase

Throughout October, the troops continued their rounding-up operations along the Sonomoro, expelling the remaining guerrillas from those areas where they could still hope for some support from the Campas.

At the same time, the army was beginning to reap the rewards of its rapprochement with the Campas, rapidly gaining the support of these people who began to see things in their true light and to realise how they had been duped.

November arrived and very encouraging news was received. Under continual troop pressure, the guerrillas were abandoning their last Sonomoro refuge, in a desperate attempt to leave the operations zone, and were making for the Gran Pajonal, crossing the Perene River. They had probably determined on this course with the object of reaching the Brazilian frontier, assisted by local Campas; the attitude of the latter towards guerrillas however had completely changed, thanks to the public relations work carried out by the army which could now count on the collaboration of the majority of them.

In view of their alarming situation, the reds sent Máximo Velando Gálvez, 'Mamani', to Puerto Bermúdez to make arrangements for the group's escape; but he was stopped by the Campas who delivered him to the garrison in that place and from there was evacuated to Satipo; there he made a suicide attempt, inflicting wounds on himself that proved fatal, despite all attempts to save him. He died on December 7, 1965, just as he was about to be evacuated to Huancayo.

In this final period, operations followed each other more rapidly and smoothly; seven small combat squads, carried by aeroplane and helicopter, replaced the detachments based on platoons. The Amazon river force, for its part, intensified its supervision of the ports and wharves of the region, as well as its patrolling of the Alto Ucayali and its navigable tributaries, so as to cut off all escape routes for the guerrillas.

The guerrillas went from one base to another, always on the run. They left Mapishiviari on November 25 and made for the Hacienda Shumahuani and subsequently for Oventeni, a village where they remained during the 28th and 29th, returning afterwards to Shumahuani again and thence to Mapishiviari and Nevate.

The Rayo combat squad, previously installed at Shumahuani moved rapidly on Nevate and on December 9 captured the enemy watch and surprised the guerrillas, eight of whom were killed. The remainder of the extremists, including the leader of the 'Túpac Amaru' guerrilla band, tried to reach the Perene River again on their way to Villa Rica.

On December 12, the reds were located at Miritiari, on the 13th at the Piñango camp and, on the 14th, at Shimpeni, where they were surprised by the Flecha squad; the outcome, however, was not conclusive as some of them, including Lobatón, succeeded in getting away.

With all lines of escape cut off, the extremists fled in despair and tried to find a way out over the mountains, where they were to remain in hiding and where there was to be another clash, on December 22, at Kuatsiriqui, in which Florian Herrera Mendoza (Jaime Martínez) met his death. The troops went on tightening the noose until January 7, 1966, when Guillermo Lobatón and the few who were with him fell in an encounter with one of the combat squads near the Sotziqui River.

The 'Túpac Amaru' guerrilla band was thus destroyed and peace restored in the area.

The guerrilla bands at 'Mesa Pelada'

The activities of the 'Túpac Amaru' guerrilla band in June and July, in the mountains of Central Peru, had repercussions in Convención province where they encouraged local extremists in their incitement of the peasant mass to rebellion and violence. Meanwhile, the main revolutionary force, the 'Pachacútec' guerrilla band, was completing its training at the Mesa Pelada base, and was about ready to sow violence and terror throughout this valley. The military intelligence service was able to determine the attitude and the probable actions of the guerrilla group based on Mesa Pelada. The government took the evidence seriously and was aware of the danger threatening the southeast; it issued the Supreme Decree of August 13, 1965, which called on the army to organise and conduct joint operations in Convención province, using the procedures prescribed for the Andamarca-Satipo zone; the objective of the Mesa Pelada operations was to surround, capture and, if necessary, destroy the entire guerrilla force in the area.

The Army Command gave orders for the 4th Military Region (CRM) to draw up the plans and carry out the anti-subversive operations.

To this end, the Region established a huge zone of vigilance, with GC and PIP forces, in order to seal off all escape routes and keep watch over the Lares, Vilcanota, Quillabamba, Occobamba, Santa María and Vilcabamba valleys. A control area was established, bounded by the valleys around Mesa Pelada, with small groups of army men placed at the various points that the plan of operations required to be held. Finally, the counter-guerrilla zone, in which various detachments responsible for the main action against Mesa Pelada were to operate, was plotted out.

The FAP was to support the operations from the beginning, with two transport planes and two helicopters, and to keep, moreover, a sufficient number of fighter planes on the alert to carry out other supporting missions when circumstances demanded.

Just as in the central Sierra, before action commenced, a propaganda campaign calling for alertness was mounted among the inhabitants, who were urged, by means of pamphlets and broadcasts in the Quechua language, to keep away from the zone of operations and to refuse the guerrillas any type of support. It is essential to avoid the loss of innocent people and to prove to people that they have been duped by the anti-patriotic forces.

The operations began on the night of August 29, 1965, with a swift and sudden troop movement towards Cuzco-Amparaes-Colca-Occobamba, and towards Cuzco-Urubamba-Ollantay-tambo-Chaullay.

The disposition of the troops was as follows:

Occobamba Sector, Leopardo and Tigre detachments.

Chaullay Sector, Cóndor, Águila, Lince detachments and the Cernícalo section of the GC.

The presence of troops in these zones had a good effect on the population which, impressed by the way it was treated and the propaganda campaign immediately mounted by the respective commando units, in turn offered effective help.

Once the circle had been closed, the first operational phase began; this consisted in land and air reconnaissance missions to find the paths, remove the mines laid along them, pin-point the camps that were clearly there and, more important, to determine the size and movements of the 'Pachacútec' guerrilla band.

On September 9 occurred the first clash with the guerrillas, who were laying an ambush for a patrol of the Condor detachment; five of the rebels were killed and two members of the patrol were wounded by a mine laid by the extremists.

Towards the summit

On September 20, 1965 there began a converging movement of five army detachments on the summit of Mesa Pelada. The same day, the Cóndor detachment made an assault on camp no. 6, during which two guerrilla fighters were killed. The commander of this camp and his principal lieutenants fled. The troops proceeded to destroy the camp and recover the weapons, ammunition, provisions and other equipment stored there.

Águila detachment reached its objective without meeting much resistance. Nevertheless, we suffered the loss of three men through the intense cold during this action.

On the 24th and 25th, Leopardo detachment made a daring suprise attack on camps nos. 3 and 4, located in the Occobamba Sector. On the afternoon of the 25th, the extremists attempted a surprise raid to recover no. 4 camp. Three guerrilla fighters were killed in this attempt and the others fled.

Also on the 25th, in the Chaullay Sector, Lince detachment faced a strong assault from another armed band, killing three guerrilla fighters and taking a few prisoners.

The intensity of the campaign was maintained so that the bands would not be able to re-organise, and in order to capture and destroy their remaining bases. Simultaneously, the air force carried out a number of day-time bombing raids, in order to neutralise and confuse the rebels. Heavy 120 mm. mortar fire harassed them at night, forcing them to stay awake and keeping them in a state of disarray. These actions were made possible by the depopulated nature of the heights of Mesa

Pelada. The troops were exposed to continual skirmishes, and a number of our men were lightly wounded by snipers. Surveillance over and control of all the access routes tightened as the troops got used to the terrain.

Every day, extremists descending from the summit in an attempt to reach the valleys and find food or make preparations for the flight of their leaders, were captured.

In mid-October, things had reached a point where confrontation with the Pachacútec guerrilla band was becoming imminent. They could not avoid a battle for much longer; the circle had tightened and ten of their camps had been destroyed, which limited their possibilities.

In these circumstances, the *guerrilleros* tried something desperate; on October 23, they turned up at a saw-mill near the Hacienda Amaybamba and demanded help. The peasants refused point-blank and three of them were murdered by means of fire-arms and home-made bombs. The explosions were heard by the garrison situated at Amaybamba, and its commander immediately sent a combat squad out against the guerrillas who were annihilated. Luis de la Puente Uceda, Raúl Escobar and Rubén Tupayachí were identified among the dead. The patrol lost three men.

This last battle completed the destruction of the MIR leadership and the Pachacútec guerrilla force.

The guerrilla bands at La Mar-Vilcabamba

On September 25, 1965, the 'Javier Heraud' guerrilla band, under the command of the extremist Héctor Béjar, began its campaign of armed violence in the Hacienda Chapi, in a treacherous, cowardly and blood-thirsty manner, killing in their sleep EP (R) Major Gonzalo Carrillo Rocha and his nephew Miguel Carrillo Cazorla, owners of the farm, as well as a young man living there. They seized a large sum of money, distributed the animals, provisions and goods among the peasants and incited the latter to take possession of the farm.

They then issued a declaration stating that the National Liberation Army, to which the 'Javier Heraud' detachment belonged, had begun its fight. At the same time, peasant agitation increased in La Mar province and especially in Chungui, San Miguel and Ayna, where one noted the presence of students from San Cristóbal National University at Ayacucho. The fear of the neighbouring landowners and local inhabitants reached a climax.

On the basis of information received, it could be deduced that the subversive operations were originating in La Mar province (Ayacucho department) and more precisely in a rectangular area marked out by the Torobamba, Pampas and Apurímac Rivers.

The 4th Military Region, which had just successfully completed its Mesa Pelada mission, was entrusted with the handling of anti-subversive operations in this area.

Operations began on November 25, 1965. The army detachment Sota and the GC section Potro were placed between Teresita and the junction of the Apurímac and Pampas Rivers, with the job of bringing pressure to bear on the extremists of the East and West, in the general direction of the Torobamba River, and following the northern course of the Pampa River.

On December 6, after a secret land and air transfer of the main part of the force, a gigantic circle was formed by the following detachments, made up of light combat units of the CRM, veterans of Mesa Pelada:

Torpedo and Roso at Luisiana and San Miguel respectively.
Rodillo at Occobamba (Andahuaylas).
Rombo and Topo at the junction of the Pampas and Apurímac Rivers.

The FAP played an important part in this operation contributing to the effects of surprise and speed.

Between December 6 and 15, the troops advanced simultaneously, carrying out essential reconnaissance missions, tightening the steel circle. They foiled a number of attempts at ambush made by the extremists near the gorges leading to the inhospitable summits of Chungui, Anko and Punquí. On December 17, opposite Osambre, the first clash occurred between a Potro patrol and a group of *guerrilleros* who were trying to open a path northwards. Juan Zapato Bodero and Ricardo León, lieutenants of Héctor Béjar, were killed there.

On December 19, during Sota's advance, there was a clash, at the Chapi Hacienda, with a group of guerrillas who had carried out a surprise attack. Two extremists were killed and five others captured.

The Rodillo detachment advanced rapidly and seized the bases at Socos and Moyoc. The extremists offered resistance and three of them were killed.

On December 24, 25 and 26, there were successive clashes in the sectors where the Rodillo and Ronco patrols were operating. Five extremists were killed and several others taken prisoner. In the forces of order, only one recruit was wounded.

The final battles took place at the beginning of January. A large number of guerrilla fighters were taken, and they bitterly confirmed the desertion and flight of their leader Héctor Béjar Rivera, together with one of his lieutenants, after he had tricked them into taking part in a desperate enterprise, letting his comrades die in a senseless cause, while he himself was able to get hold of large sums of money.

These districts returned to normal, thanks to the intervention of the armed forces, as in the central Sierra and Convención, and, under the protection of the law, the population got over its apprehensions and resumed work. On their arrival, the troops were received with joy by the inhabitants, whose open and disinterested collaboration, had, it must be admitted, enabled the 'Javier Heraud' guerrilla band to be routed in a matter of 30 days, despite the size and difficulties of the area.

The guerrilla movement in Ayabaca and Huancabamba

The capture of six *guerrilleros*, between October 18 and November 5, 1965, brought confirmation of the fact that the 'Manco Cápac' guerrilla band had settled at Ayabaca and made it possible to estimate the extent of the subversive operations being planned and about to be carried out, this being on an international scale, as there was, in addition, to be intervention on the part of a number of subversive elements from the country's northern neighbour (Ecuador).

This new and dangerous guerrilla base had to be eliminated before it had a chance even to begin its nefarious activities. To accomplish this, contingency plans for the zone, which came under the 1st Military Region, were put into operation by the 1st Cavalry Division, a special force made up of Pacaso, Lagarto and Iguana army detachments, and sections of the Civil Guard to keep the area under surveillance.

The counter-guerrilla force was disposed in the following manner:

Pacaso at Huancabamba
Lagarto at Ayabaca
Iguana at Ayabaca.

On December 11, 1965, the three units began to move, converging on Cerro Negro, which was supposed to be the principal guerrilla base, under the command of Gonzalo Fernández Gasco.

As they advanced, they took in the San Sebastián, Pato Piedra, El Indio and San Pedro camps where they found provisions, ammunition and equipment in large quantities. In spite of intensive patrolling activities carried out up to December 30, 1965, the *guerrilleros* were not located; according to information received, they had fled towards Ecuador, where they should now be under assumed names.

General results

'Mission accomplished'. This is the usual military way of referring to a successful operation. Mission accomplished, we told the government and the Peruvian people, at the end of an anti-guerrilla campaign that has had the following concrete results.

The 'Pachacútec', 'Túpac Amaru', 'Javier Heraud' and 'Manco Cápac' guerrilla bands which, at the beginning of the struggle, had wanted to plunge the country into a bloody conflict, have been broken up and destroyed one after another.

Weapons, ammunition, explosives, provisions, material and

other equipment, built up by the communists over a period of more than three years for their own use and for the development of the armed struggle, have been confiscated.

It has been proven to the extremists and other elements won over by the forces of subversion that there are no areas in the country inaccessible to a well-trained army.

It has been made clear that the Peruvian people rejects communism and will not assist it in its nefarious plan to deliver the country into the hands of foreign powers.

Below is the full text of the report drawn up in 1965 by a Commission of Inquiry on the functioning of the 1st Military District (DM) corresponding to the federal district of Caracas.

The document circulated only among the leading cadres of the MIR and the Communist Party of Venezuela. It sheds light on the size of the combat network, its structure and problems.

Differences between activities from the brigades and detachments and leaders of the political apparatuses show themselves, even though this is only the beginning of 1965, well before the break between the FALN and PCV.

The Smolen affair, which is frequently alluded to, concerns the kidnapping of a North American officer. It led to numerous police operations that wore down the terrorist position.

Report of the Commission of Inquiry of the Armed Forces of National Liberation in the Federal District

In accordance with the resolution of the Political Bureau to set up a Commission of Inquiry of the FALN of the 1st Military District, this Commission was duly formed, with the participation of all the comrades who were appointed to it. The Commission proceeded to draw up a plan of action and to arrange for investigatory meetings and discussions to be held with the district brigades, detachments, units and administrations. In addition, individual discussions took place with a few comrades who were special cases or whose opinions and remarks were of special interest. A number of documents were collected from the various organs and the Commission discussed the problems raised at the meetings or in the documents. On the basis of these meetings, discussions, individual conversations and documents, as well as of the problems discussed, we have drawn up the following report.

The Commission has gone over its own work; it admits to having made many mistakes regarding the time it would take to carry out the work required in certain circumstances or the importance that should be attached to different problems; it is aware that it has worked very slowly and subject to long delays. Furthermore, if there are perhaps attenuating circumstances, in that certain cadres selected to take part were simultaneously involved in the daily work required of them by the Party and that there were difficulties to be overcome in maintaining security and collecting opinions and information from the largest possible number of bodies and individual comrades, the Commission has not aways been equal to the task set it by the Political Bureau; hence the unjustifiable delay in completing the work.

OBSERVATIONS

The Commission considered the manner of its appointment and came to the following conclusions:

(*a*) Leaving aside the fact that all the members are completely in agreement on the need for an inquiry into and reorganisation of the FALN, 1st Military District, we regard the method used by the Political Bureau in appointing the Commission to be incorrect, in that the 1st Military District is a body under the guidance and supervision of the Regional Committee of the Federal Department and that it was, therefore, in this Regional Committee's competence to appoint the Commission and conduct the inquiry. This does not mean that the Political Bureau should not have discussed the situation of the Military District, but the proper method would have been to recommend or order the Regional Committee of the Federal Department to carry out a series of inquiries or to appoint a Commission for this purpose, in view of the aforesaid situation.

The actual method used looked like intervention, even if we know that that was not the intention of the Political Bureau. We make this comment in the certainty that the possible ill consequences flowing from such a procedure will not escape the Political Bureau.

(*b*) The appointment of the Commission with powers extending 'as far as the right to disband', amounted, in effect, to a dismantling of the command and left the FALN without leadership in the district, an anomalous situation from which certain consequences must flow.

MORALE AND THE STATE OF THE ORANISATION AS ASCERTAINED BY THE COMMISSION

1. *Morale*

At the time of its meetings with organs and members of the FALN, the Commission was able to ascertain that:

(*a*) The morale of the combatants and the organs was extensively affected by the uncertainty resulting from the misuse of the truce and despondency at the failure of the last plan of operations and at the political state of the organisation as revealed on that occasion.

(*b*) We found, in the organs and among the militants, a large measure of confidence in the leadership of the Party, as regards its ability to correct the mistakes, faults and defects revealed by the inquiry. This confidence is expressed in the enthusiasm with which the announcement of the Party's decision was greeted and is confirmed by the advice offered and spirit of co-operation that was revealed when the inquiry got under way. We find, therefore, a will to work in the organs, which explains how the organic structure was preserved and various tasks fulfilled in spite of all the mistakes and difficulties.

2. *State of the organisation*

At the time of the inquiry, we found the state of the organisation to be as follows:

1. District: not functioning normally as an integral body.

2. Brigades: B. 1. Brigade command dispersed as a result of conditions created by the Smolen case.

Toribio García detachment: command integrated and functioning somewhat irregularly.

Ángel Linares detachment: detachment command not

functioning normally. Two UTCS (Technical Combat Units) operating.

The rest dispersed for security reasons.

César A. Ríos detachment: detachment command disintegrated. Only one UTC operating at all normally. One other dispersed. The remainder of the combatants dispersed or withdrawing. The extant UTC has been assigned to the Ángel Linares detachment.

This brigade constituted the political department.

Livia Gouverner detachment: destroyed for known reasons. The four comrades unknown to the police have been integrated into other detachments.

B. 2. Brigade command: functions more or less normally.

Juan Cárdenas S. detachment: the command functions more or less normally.

Luis González detachment: normal functioning of command. Three UTCS are operating. Another one has difficulties and is dispersed.

Felipe Fermoso detachment: the command functions normally. The head of the EM brigade is responsible for this, the commander having abandoned his post. Three UTCS. Two of them dissolved after the business with the commander, who had not transferred them.

This brigade consisted of a Political Department and the Operation, Production and Solidarity Departments.

B. 3. Brigade command: functions normally.

Manuel Ramón Oyón detachment: command functioning normally, very diffuse organisation given the character of the bridge: thirty-five comrades in five groups.

Isidro Espinoza detachment: command irregular, fourteen combatants dispersed.

Br. Thirty people under orders, but no definite organisational character.

B. 4. In process of formation, six units ready.

INT: Functions normally but under independent control, and without any Front command organ.

INS: Functions, but at present independent of District control.

SUMMARY OF THE PROBLEMS IDENTIFIED AND
CONCLUSIONS ARRIVED AT BY THE COMMISSION

The results of the Commission's work, discussions held with
the brigades, detachments, UTC sections and district members,
meetings and conversations with individual combatants, documents and reports of meetings, can be summarised as follows:

1. The establishment of fundamental bases for an Urban
Army, which has shown itself, in practice, able to withstand
persecution, to maintain its organisation in the face of assault,
to train numerous military cadres, to generate the proper
military and organisational spirit, can be considered an un-
doubted success and significant in the present context.

We feel it necessary to stress the positive aspect as above, to
guard against the danger of seeing only the bad side of things,
minimising the part played by the FALN in this district and of
underestimating the real successes achieved, once we have
identified and analysed the faults and errors committed by the
organisation, its cadres and combatants.

2. Before proceeding to the enumeration of the errors and
faults revealed in the organisation, the deficiencies that came
to light during the course of the inquiry, we wish to draw
attention to the causes, which, if they are not eliminated, will
continue, in our opinion, to be productive of new and more
serious problems.

(*a*) Inadequate ideological training of FALN cadres and
combatants and weakness of Party and District measures to
make good this deficiency.

(*b*) Inadequate evaluation of the political rôle of the
organisation and unsatisfactory level of political consciousness
of members, in view of the important tasks to be accomplished.

(*c*) Indifference to the question of the organisation's connection with the masses and the importance of this in the
development of the concept of popular war.

(*d*) Inferior technical level.

(*e*) Individual responsibility of cadres in their work, determined by each concrete case.

Without interrupting their activity or withdrawing from the fight, the Party and the FALN should systematically tackle these causes and others that are at the basis of the errors, faults and weaknesses.

3. The following is revealed by the inquiry into the basic faults, errors and deficiencies in the organs of command:

Absence of a properly planned training and educational policy, directed at improving and strengthening the theoretical, technical and practical levels of accomplishment.

Lack of political discussion at all levels and especially in the UTCS.

Absence of a policy of permanent, strategic, operational planning, irrespective of whether action has or has not commenced.

Militarism and authoritarianism.

Weakness of the spirit of self-criticism in the organs.

Little help for the UTC.

Irregularity in circulation of political news as well as in distribution of documents, newspapers and FALN and Party propaganda.

Irregularity in liaison, in the fulfilment of tasks assigned and in the control of organs.

Little interest in ideological and political difficulties of the combatants.

Absence of a definite policy as regards the control of personnel and lack of concern for individual difficulties.

Failure to make regular use of the UTC as a body organised for action.

Use of inadequately trained combatants.

Carrying out of operations without sufficient authority and without preliminary study of the relevant organs on the other side.

Carrying out of terrorist actions.

Orders to put operations into effect without there existing the organisational political conditions that would assure their success.

Putting into effect of operations without guarantee of the necessary technical means.

Violation of security norms and of the secret of the conspiracy.

Use of 'piratical' methods to resolve personnel problems,
thereby weakening discipline in the Party, Youth and FALN.

Neglect of the Party and Youth in arriving at a correct and
timely resolution of personnel problems.

Lack of control over combatants who have passed through
the Party and Youth, to such an extent that many militants
have now drifted away from both organisations.

Non-existence of a permanent internal effort with regard to
combatants who are prisoners or in a precarious position; this
fault should be made good by the Party, Youth and the FALN.

Indiscriminate officialisation of combatants, so that in order
to join the UTC it is practically obligatory to be an official.

Use of irregular means and methods to obtain resources.

Little attention given to the solution of logistic problems,
security measures, dépôts, hiding-places, transport, etc., and
absence of a team engaged in the systematic examination of
these problems.

Few lessons drawn from the accumulated experience of the
operations carried out.

Faulty methods used in the resolution of disciplinary
problems.

Incoherence of the plans and military work of the Party,
Youth and FALN, making joint or simultaneous actions impossible and forcing the organisations to work apart.

Little Party spirit in the FALN ranks.

The above points summarise the most important errors and
faults examined in the discussions with the brigades, detachments, UTCs, departments, etc. Other general but less serious
problems, as for example the specific problems of each corps,
have been dealt with at special meetings, in an effort to correct
and overcome them.

In this discussion, the weakness of the self-critical spirit in
the brigades, detachments and UTCs had been stressed. Attention

has been drawn to the marked tendency to see only the negative aspects of their respective superior organs, without any attempt being made on their part to judge their own activity objectively. In this respect, a number of problems have been resolved and more, although still not sufficient, self-criticism has been activated, in discussion with these organs: their own responsibility and mistakes have, at least, been made explicit.

THE TRUCE

A number of the questions raised here were discussed at the plenum that took place at the beginning of 64. The need to set in motion a process of self-criticism within the urban FALN was raised at this plenum. Unfortunately, this was not achieved and consequently the necessary measures were not applied with sufficient force to eliminate the faults. For this reason, when conditions made it possible to go into action again, the FALN displayed signs of inherent politico-military and technical weakness, and one is driven to the conclusion that the truce was not put to good use.

THE SMOLEN AFFAIR

(*a*) We have ascertained that the Smolen operation was submitted to the CR and approved by that organ.

(*b*) This operation was also brought to the notice of the Party's National Military Committee, for the information of the Political Bureau.

(*c*) As to the nature of the Smolen operation, the DM concluded that it came under urban operational norms and included it in the general politico-military plan of campaign, with another complex of operations, which, for various organisational reasons, was not fulfilled.

(*d*) As regards security measures, these were roughly defined by the DM, which especially stressed the organ in charge of the operation, but the measures were really inadequate, which shows that the repercussions and the repression that this operation would bring in its train had not been foreseen clearly enough. This factor, together with the liberal attitude running right through the organs (from the DM to the UTC), accounted for the flagrant violation of the rules of conspiracy; the enemy did not fail to take advantage of this to strike hard and effectively.

In general, it can be said that the concatenation of events accompanying the Smolen affair in a way revealed the difficulties and irregularities that had long existed in the organisation.

(*e*) The Commission analysed the behaviour, in the face of the machinery of repression, of members of the FALN who were taken prisoner, in consequence of the situation created by the Smolen case and after studying the relevant methods we arrived at the conclusions set out in detail in appendix A to the present document.

CHARACTERISTICS OF THE 1ST MILITARY DISTRICT AND GENERAL DIRECTION OF THE WORK

1. In a war of national liberation, the Military District is of great strategic and tactical importance. The DM is an economic, political and military centre, which means that it has an infinite number of objectives and that it can cause the government and its army serious difficulties in trying to implement them.

The DM constitutes the mass basis of the National Liberation Movement, by virtue of the density of its population, the extent of the latter's political and organisational consciousness and the military experience accumulated by the masses in their struggle with the enemy. In view of its nature, the DMI was called on to make a positive contribution to the revolutionary movement, to take advantage of insurrectional prospects that have long existed in our country, and to deal some shrewd blows which will influence the growing importance of the war of national liberation.

The DM is an important base of human and strategic resources in general, which exist as a positive factor in the development of the war on a national scale.

By virtue of their position inside the DM, the FALN general staffs constitute a fundamental source of information concerning the plans of action, mobilisation and the state of the enemy in the national context.

From all this, it follows that:

(*a*) The DM's military organisation must be able, through commando action, to hit the enemy's military apparatus (land, air, naval and FAC forces).

(*b*) The DM's military organisation must be able to guide the military organisation of the masses, to plan the battles effectively, and it must be capable of multiplying without losing its basic organisational character.

(*c*) The military organisation of the DM must be active and closely linked with the masses, not merely in principle, but concretely and in the densely populated centres. In these centres, the members of the military organisation must be in touch not only with the problems and political tasks of the moment, but also with the problems and demands relevant to the particular community with which they are to work, the object being to win over larger and larger bodies of the people and to draw them into the armed struggle.

(*d*) The military organisation of the DM must be able to guide and direct the penetration of the enemy's vital centres, so as to carry out actions of sabotage and, at the same time, to collect as much information as possible about his plans and movements, both nationally and locally.

2. The military planning and organisation of the District must be directed towards the effective implementation of previous decisions; this requires a harmonisation and unification of the political and military activities of the Party and the FALN. To this end, the DMI must be directed and guided by the Regional Committee of the Federal Department, the liaison machinery being developed to allow for more specific control, until the FLN in the district has been stabilised and the FALN

organically integrated. In these circumstances relations between the FLN and FALN will be established and the Party organisation in the FALN will develop, under the control of the Regional Committee.

3. To guarantee the success of the activities of the District, it is necessary:
(*a*) To raise the ideological, political and technical level.
(*b*) To work out a strategic plan within the context of the general strategy.
(*c*) To work out the plan of action and the tactics that will enable the strategic objective to be attained.
(*d*) To raise the organisational level, to increase the necessary human and material resources.

4. We believe that, in order to clarify the work of Brigades I and II, they must be given permanent objectives to be attained in common with the Party in town, by assigning their detachments to different Party districts, so that the operational plans and tactics for use in cases of popular upheaval, surprise attacks, etc., should be unified while at the same time helping the Party's military work with the masses; and so that the planning of insurrection should be developed and the procedures with regard to interdependence, personnel, etc., should be simplified. The norms to be applied are as follows:
(*a*) A command comprising the military leaders of the Party, the Youth and the head of the detachment assigned to the District shall be set up in each district to co-ordinate the specific military plans.
(*b*) The detachment will be responsible for the plans of operation in the physical sector covered by the District assigned it, and the actions, men to be mobilised, arms, etc., will be co-ordinated within the command organ with the Party and Youth, so that there should be continuous operational planning.
(*c*) The political commissar of the detachment will be integrated within the District. There he will co-ordinate everything relating to the part played by the detachment in the

Party's and militias' work of military training and everything connected with the FLN, solidarity, personnel, security, organisation of the rear-guard, etc. We believe that this will enable the Party to obtain a better understanding of the problems of the FALN at all levels, and to help in resolving them, in addition to providing the UTC with a permanent function.

The distribution of the detachments is laid down elsewhere. The same liaison mechanism must be established between Brigade 3 and the Party, but it must be closer because of the nature of its work. To this end, as well as in connection with the development of Brigade 4, the future DM will have to work out exact functional and work norms.

5. Special Command detachment. A special detachment will be formed for operations requiring specialised personnel which will be responsible for carrying out these operations and which will have recourse to all the means available; it will come directly under DM Command.

6. Intelligence. This service will be operational and also orientated towards the defence of the organisation.

FINAL CONCLUSIONS

1. The Commission, together with other members of the FALN, has established sub-commissions within its own framework, to examine problems of discipline, cadre policy and irregularities. These will report respectively in due course.

2. The authorised organs will take all the necessary decisions with regard to administrative machinery, establishment of a hierarchy of jobs, definitive structures and selection of cadre, etc.

3. In a special document, the Commission will present a report on the organisational work, transfers, questions of discipline, etc., which will have arisen since it began to function.

4. As well as the present material and a special plan regarding the solutions to be applied to specific problems raised by

different organisations and many militants, the Commission has also organised a series of 'summing-up and end of work' meetings. We shall also take note of the opinions expressed in the different bodies and transmit them to the leading organs.

This is a propaganda text and based on an incident in Colombia. It was published in numerous pro-Castroite magazines, it has nearly always been accompanied by photographs taken during the operation.

In his presentation of the facts, the reporter somewhat overreaches himself, viz. the remarkable discipline of the assault force, the respect for military conventions as between combatants and 'commander', the highly developed state of field communications.

The Attack on the Train[1]

On March 9, 1967, at a point between the Carare and Opón Rivers, a unit of the José Antonio Galán Front, under the command of Fabio Vásquez, attacked a train carrying a party of carabineros, a specialised repressive force used by the Colombian Government against the peasants.

The attack took place on a railway branch line running from the Atlantic coast into the interior of Colombia. The spot chosen was a small rocky gorge with ledges of earth, three metres apart, running along the sides.

In the middle of the ledge on the west side, Fabio Vásquez Castaño is in radio contact with the group that is to give advance warning of the convoy's approach: 'HK-1, HK-1, HK-1: when you change position, make contact, make contact... HK-1, HK-1, HK-1: when you change position and reach the target, make contact.' From the various strategic points, not many kilometres off and well covered by the vegetation, the rebel commandos keep in touch over the radio and report minute by minute on the situation prior to the ambush.

The mines have been laid between the rails the previous day. A *guerrillero* checks them and then clambers quickly up to Fabio Vásquez:

'Comrade Fabio, permission to speak ...'

The young *guerrillero* who has given up his studies at Cali to

join the ELN, salutes as he waits for the commander to reply.
'Granted.'

'The two mines are in position on the rails, with a detonator
and parallel circuit; all we are waiting for now is the train's
arrival and your orders ... '

'Right, comrade. The new positions must be shown, in
anticipation of the explosion: one of you see to the radio
contact and the other to the manœuvre.'

'Your orders will be carried out. With your permission,
I shall leave.'

'You may leave.'

The defile between the Carare and Opón Rivers is strategically
suited to an ambush, and the intelligence service of the 5th
Brigade, centred in Bucaramanga and under the command of
Colonel Valencia Tovar, had sent reinforcements there that it
subsequently withdrew, not believing that the ELN would dare
attack the train. Fabio Vásquez, however, had other ideas.

The ELN commander positioned his men. He sent his brother
Manuel and Víctor Medina Morón, with twenty-three other
guerrillas, to the east side of the gorge and kept an equal number
with himself. A young guerrilla of sixteen set off for the Macias
bridge, a short distance from the ambush point, with a transistor,
to warn ('HK-22') of the approach of the target. The whole day,
March 8, passed in this way. The train did not appear. The
guerrilleros retired to the mountains for the night and returned
early the next morning.

Even so, on March 9, the guerrilla patrol arrived too late
at the ambush point. The train, which was supposed to pass
between 9 and 10 a.m., had passed at 8. As this had been a
mail-train carrying at least 300,000 pesos, as well as the
weapons of the carabineros guarding it, the rebels regretted
missing it. All the same the patrol of about fifty men took up its
position to await the train's return which was scheduled for
noon.

While they were waiting anxiously, a messenger brought
encouraging news. This was a letter from Ricardo Lara

Parada, commander of the Camilo Torres Restrepo Front, informing them of a victorious action.

The letter handed to Fabio Vásquez was dated March 4, 1967 and read:

Comrade commander of the National Liberation Army, Fabio Vásquez Castaño:

The general staff of the Camilo Torres Restrepo guerrilla Front takes great pleasure in informing you that operation Alejandro, executed on February 27, has been successful on the politico-military level required by the people's war.

On the 26th, at 14.00 hours, we set off and reached the target area at 22.00 hours.

On the 27th, at 5 a.m., the assault group under the command of Mario and comrade Alejandro, with each member carrying small arms, went into action. The main force waited at a distance of 200 metres.

At 6.00 hours, when the first shot rang out, we hurled ourselves forward in two sections. When we got within range, it was all over already, as the assault group, where a grenade had exploded, was 99 per cent master of the situation.

We made an immediate appeal to the people, using these slogans: Long Live the National Liberation Army! Long live Camilo! Long live Fabio Vásquez! and others that I will leave to your imagination.

We managed to get about 200 people together in this way and I talked to them about our struggle for 40 minutes. They applauded and cheered our statements and our revolutionary slogans. We fired off volleys into the air both on entering and leaving, in order to frighten the civil defence.

We entered the village at 6.00 hours and left at 7.10.

I believe that it is a victory when a revolutionary guerrilla band takes a conservative village for the first time and destroys the conservative myth according to which the revolutionaries are the enemies.

Enemy losses: 5. On our side: none. Enemy wounded: 2. On our side: 1 (in the elbow). Weapons recovered: 4 unused M-1 rifles, with 24 cartridge clips; 300 M-1 rounds, a Colt 38 revolver; an Astra revolver and 9 shells, a dozen uniforms and other articles of little importance.

We completed our withdrawal at 5 o'clock on the following evening, just avoiding a clash with the army. We are now in a safe place. The messenger, comrade Gentil, will give you a more detailed account as he has been with us on all our adventures.

For security reasons, I am not writing at greater length. All the men send you greetings and embrace you in guerrilla fashion. I also embrace you, Andrés, Germán, Alberto, Juan and you other beloved *guerrilleros*.

Not a step backwards! Liberation or death!

Ricardo Lara Parada

All is silent in the defile bordering the railway line. The patriots merge with the thick vegetation, while the sunlight streams on to the rocks. Suddenly, over the radio: 'HK-22, HK-22, HK-22, target approaching; good luck . . . '

The military train tears along the rails of death. A *guerrillero* pushes the handle and there is an explosion; stones shoot up into the air, the locomotive, hurled off the line, is hidden in a cloud of dust. Bursts of fire from 'San Cristóbals', the Dominican automatic rifles used by the Colombian government's force of repression, come from the carriage. The bullets smash the ground near a group of guerrilla fighters.

Fabio Vásquez springs from his hiding place with a cat-like leap and opens fire with his M-1. From the other side of the gorge, Víctor Medina Morón cries: 'Long live the National Liberation Army', and his M-1 also begins its deadly work. 'Hernando', a dedicated doctor and one of the favourite disciples of the *guerrillero*-priest, shouts at the top of his voice: 'Long live Camilo Torres! Down with these mongols!' He cannot disguise his hatred. Like other veterans, he always remembers the face of his trampled on master, murdered by the soldiers of the military dictatorship. His rifle rains death on the carabineros.

Someone discovers civilians on board: 'Get out! Get out! We don't want to kill civilians!'

A carabinero leans out of a window and aims his gun at Fabio Vásquez, but even before he can pull the trigger, a bullet from Leonardo's M-1 gets him between the eyes.

The Attack on the Train

Manuel Vásquez notices one of the soldiers trying to take cover behind a carriage seat; he set his rifle for a burst and squeezes the trigger; the carabinero leaps up, mortally wounded; 'Gregorio's' Madsen sub-machine gun finishes him off.

The civilians try to get out, but a member of the repression corps threatens them and, in a cowardly manner, uses a woman as a shield; the poor creature desperately tries to free herself. Fabio Vásquez orders the revolutionary side to cease fire. Gregorio hurls himself forward to board the carriage and the carabinero, thinking he has the chance to kill him, momentarily lets go of the woman who takes the opportunity to escape. The *guerrilleros* immediately open fire to cover their comrade in danger. The carabinero is killed outright and hangs half out of the window, riddled with bullets.

Bursts from the Madsen are heard: Gregorio has just found a carabinero hiding near the door. The soldier also fires and the rebels edge along the gorge. Víctor Medina Morón falls down. The engine driver fires a revolver which had been hidden under some parcels and is killed by Silverio who catches sight of him in time. The civilians leave the carriage by the rear exit and a few *guerrilleros* immediately swing on board. There is a sharp burst of rifle fire: the last carabinero, up till then under cover of two bullet-torn seats, falls. Hernando, the guerrilla doctor, looks after a wounded woman, while two sections start collecting the weapons, ammunition, uniforms and soldiers' packs. Up above, on the earth platform, Fabio Vásquez and other rebels keep watch over the road. Vásquez shouts out a question as to whether there have been any losses on the rebel side. The reply is in the negative.

Fabio Vásquez gives the order to fall back along the railway track. Twenty-five minutes have passed since the train had been sighted by the sentry.

Operation Camilo Torres Restrepo has been a striking success: the seven carabineros have been killed; no one on the rebel side has been killed or wounded, apart from which six San Cristóbal automatic-rifles, a Madsen, five 38-calibre long-barrelled revolvers, one 38-calibre short-barrelled revolver, four 94-round clips for the Madsen, twelve San Cristóbal clips with 432 rounds; seventy-one 38-shells for long-barrelled revolvers and five 38-shells for short-barrelled ones, boots, uniforms, etc.

As they withdraw to their encampment, the *guerrilleros* sing the ELN anthem. Rubén's voice leads the others as they plunge into the depths of the forest.

In this declaration, the Political Bureau of the PCV denounces the activities of Douglas Bravo and of his followers, condemns the steps taken by this group to turn the FLN and the FALN into autonomous organisations, and expels Bravo. The document dates from the summer of 1966.

Declaration of the Political Bureau of the Communist Party

A so-called re-organisation of the FLN-FALN, recently communicated to comrade Fidel Castro in a letter that included the names of Douglas Bravo and Américo Martín—the latter, head of the MIR—shows that an important step has been taken to stimulate the divisive process within the revolutionary movement in general, and factionalism in our Party in particular.

Aware of the negative effects that a division in its ranks would have on the whole revolutionary movement, the Venezuelan Communist Party has been extremely patient in considering the question of comrade Douglas Bravo. We have gone to some lengths to convince this comrade that his factionalist activities can only harm the revolutionary cause. Nevertheless, making allowance for the initiative taken by comrade Douglas Bravo in appending his signature to a document that, in fact, deals with the question of the division in the revolutionary ranks, the Political Bureau of the PCV feels that it is necessary to bring the events leading up to the present situation to the attention of the whole Party and of the revolutionary movement in general, and to analyse them.

1. From October 1965, comrade Douglas Bravo initiated a series of clearly fissiparous activities: several comrades were approached in his name, with a view to creating 'a new leading nucleus'; several comrades undertook journeys in his

name, accused the Political Bureau before the Regional Committees of an alleged 'capitulation' and canvassed support for Douglas Bravo in his attempt to 'save' the Party's political line. One of the most significant episodes of this period was the elaboration in detail of a document that was sent to the Political Bureau by various Party leaders, to 'prove' the alleged capitulation. Without accusing anyone, it must be noted that this document was printed and distributed by a number of comrades who claimed to be representing Douglas Bravo.

2. Called before the Political Bureau, of which he was a member, Douglas Bravo denied his fissiparous activities. He even voted for sanctions to be applied against Comrade Alberto who appeared to be the driving force behind them.

3. Nevertheless, Douglas Bravo did not discontinue his fissiparous activities, but went on working towards the creation of an apparatus parallel to the Party's. Alberto also continued his party activities, organising meetings without the knowledge of the regular Party and FALN organisations, and allowing others access to documents exclusively reserved for the information of the Central Committee. This work of splitting was a preliminary to the 're-organisation' that Douglas Bravo had decided to carry out in the FLN and FALN, ignoring the military movements and political groups that comprised them and appointing himself Supreme Commander. This unilateral action, where Douglas Bravo, on his own authority, made use of the names of several *guerrillero* commanders who subsequently denied all knowledge of the manœuvre, was categorically rejected by the military movements that make up the FALN, by our Party and, at that time, by the MIR.

4. In the face of this full-scale 'onslaught', the leadership of the revolutionary organs of the Political Bureau once more summoned comrade Douglas Bravo, who continued to deny that his activities were in any way fissiparous. But, in view of the glaring evidence and his attitude, which was totally unselfcritical, the Political Bureau decided to suspend him as a member of the organ and to pass his case over to the Central Committee.

5. On this occasion, Douglas Bravo promised to respect the resolutions of the Political Bureau and to condemn every undertaking in his name directed against Party unity and the revolutionary movement. It goes without saying, as is borne out by the facts, that not only was this promise not kept but that the splitting work made further progress with the winning over of the MIR leader, Américo Martín.

6. We cannot consider this alliance, to which a prominent MIR leader belongs, as anything less than an act of aggression against our Party and against the whole revolutionary movement. Taking into account the way it was made public—the MIR at the time of the first FLN-FALN re-organisation, informed us that it disagreed with the step—there is no point in concealing the fact that it will have a negative effect on the Venezuelan revolutionary process. Furthermore, the factionalists must bear the very serious responsibility for the unilateral repudiation of the official report on the foundation of the FLN and for participation in the re-structuring of a new FLN, of which the most striking characteristic is a violent discrimination against the PCV as well as against other sectors and individuals.

And now, what reasons does Douglas Bravo give in justification of his fissiparous activity? Are they political? Basically, they are not. A perusal of the so-called Iracara Manifesto, the alleged platform of the factionalist group, reveals that, apart from a few disagreements with the political line of the party, and notably with the resolution of the 8th Plenum as regards current tactics, there are no significant differences. In fact all the time Douglas Bravo was a member of the Political Bureau he never gave evidence of disagreeing with the Democratic Peace policy.

The explanation lies, therefore, in a militaristic deviation that attempts to substitute its own opinions and personal attitudes for the opinions and resolutions of the Party leadership. In our view, this deviation consists, in part, of ideas and practices alien to Leninist organisational norms; and also of a spirit of self-sufficiency, springing from the misuse of a prestige won to a large extent as a result of the collective efforts of the whole Party.

As regards the MIR, even though this Party, with its somewhat leftist and impractical attitude, might frequently have expressed its disagreement with the tactics of our Party, no one, let alone honest revolutionaries, could be justified in taking up a position that sanctions division within the revolutionary movement and, what is more, the weakening of forces which, like our Party, are steadfastly resisting the offensive mounted by imperialism and its local agents.

We believe furthermore that the differences manifesting themselves in the revolutionary movement are of secondary importance when compared with the high degree of harmony that exists and in no way justify so negative a course as to split the revolutionary movement organically. We do not wish to pre-judge the subjective factors that might lie at the basis of this divisive activity (in any case, we shall leave the resolution of this question to History), but the least we can do is to point out that this split in the revolutionary movement *objectively* plays into the hands of our people's direst enemies and we do not hesitate to affirm, as from now, that it is doomed to failure.

If the divisionists were to put forward a policy that differed essentially from the PCV's, a platform that gave expression to their oppositionist charges of capitulation, maybe they could find some justification in history for their stand. Maybe, in this event, they could claim that a split was the lesser evil. But devoid of any political motivation, the divisionists can only play into the hands of those who regard the weakening of the PCV as the prime condition for the destruction of the whole revolutionary movement.

For our part, we begrudge no one the right to call himself revolutionary but we do believe that there are a number of historical models in our country by which one may judge the true revolutionaries. We do not believe that it is essential to militate inside the PCV to be a revolutionary, but it seems to us very doubtful if those who base their actions in the first place on the struggle against a Party that, right from the beginning,

placed itself decisively at the head of the revolutionary movement, that did not spare the lives of its own militants, that ran
every risk and made the greatest possible contribution to the
struggle against the imperialist enemy, are true revolutionaries.
This Party's policy has always served the best interests of the
Venezuelan revolution, and nothing, neither the internment of
nearly a thousand of its best cadres, nor the death of some of its
most prominent leaders and hundreds of its militants, has caused
it to deviate one iota from the line sketched out at the 3rd
Congress in 1961 and ratified since by successive plenums of its
Central Committee.

In Venezuela, where our people has learnt much from
experience and where the political position of the PCV throughout these years is a matter of record, those who have undertaken
to create a factionalist group inside the Party and have tried
to divide the revolutionary movement will have much to
answer for before the court of history.

We sincerely believe that the Cuban comrades published the
letter in all good faith, believing it to express the sentiments
of the whole Venezuelan revolutionary movement.

There was good reason for getting this letter published in
the pages of *Granma*; as the Cuban comrades are united in their
real concern for the future of the struggle of all the peoples of
the world, a factionalist group could treacherously use this
publication to give the impression that it had received international sanction, since comrade Fidel Castro and the Cuban
revolution enjoy a well-deserved reputation among the Venezuelan masses.

In the columns of *Granma*, the FALN 'restoration' carried out
without the knowledge of the great majority of the combatants
and the FLN, without the consent of the parties, sectors and
individuals that comprise it, the signatories of the letter forget
that Venezuelan revolutionary policy is worked out and
implemented in Venezuela.

The signatories of the letter addressed to comrade Fidel

Castro were trying to take advantage of a *de facto* situation: the fighting men, cadres and leaders of the FALN are, at present, going through a period of organisational re-structuring and improvement. Our party is playing an important part in the process and is keenly interested in its success. Therefore, the violation of this process, in opposition not only to the PCV but also to the interests of the FALN, can be explained only in terms of 'caudillism'. Let there be no mistake about it: our resistance to attempts to split the Party will lead to the strengthening of the FALN in their determination to overcome their problems and guarantee our people success in the accomplishment of their mission.

We solemnly declare that any initiative taken in support of the armed struggle, however radical the language used, amounts in fact, to sabotage of that very armed struggle, becomes an obstacle in the path of its further development, if it denies, depreciates or simply casts doubt on the steadfastness and perseverance of our Party.

Finally, the mutual esteem, fraternity and solidarity that have always governed the relationship between the Cuban Communist Party and ours allow us to expect that in future the splitters will not be able to make use of the pages of the official organ of the PCC, nor of any other Cuban publicity medium, to propagate their aims.

The Political Bureau of the PCV regrets and condemns categorically the splitting activities against the movement of liberation and our Party. The already serious problems that the revolutionary movement has to face will grow more serious and more extensive.

The Political Bureau makes no attempt to hide the seriousness of the crisis. At present there are a number of political and personal factors operating that make it possible for the divisionists temporarily to deceive a few revolutionary sectors, if our Party together with the whole progressive movement does not throw itself energetically and resolutely into defeating this attack on its unity and the unity of the movement of liberation.

The Political Bureau calls on all its Party militants to rally around its leadership and resolutely to oppose factionalism. The recent university elections are a good indication that the policy of our Party is right and that it enjoys the support of the masses. The voting in favour of the list, of which the Communist Youth was the main axis in the Central University, points back to the line established by our Party in its struggle against imperialism and its creole agents, as well as to the tactical line currently followed by our Party.

We affirm most solemnly that the factionalist rebellion will not make us deviate from the tasks undertaken by the Party on the various work fronts, and more particularly in the sphere of armed struggle, in its development and strengthening, and, as we have said, such insubordination to the Party, the FLN and FALN is provocative and inconsistent in the context of this armed struggle.

The difficulties existing in the revolutionary movement and our Party will not force us to retreat, but, on the contrary, our revolutionary spirit and determination to defend our Marxist-Leninist principles will make us persevere in the course we have mapped out for ourselves to bring the liberation of our people to a victorious conclusion and to stand up to the gorilla-Betancourtist terror.

Political Bureau of the Communist Party
of Venezuela

Douglas Bravo, leader of the José Leonardo Chirinos Guerrilla Front, in the mountains of the State of Falcón, was a member of the Political Bureau of the Venezuelan Communist Party (PCV), until, in agreement with most of the commanders of the Armed Forces of National Liberation, he began to re-organise the latter and was expelled from the Communist Party whose authority he no longer accepted.

The following pages are excerpts from statements made by Douglas Bravo to the Mexican magazine *Sucesos* which were taken up again by several publications supporting the guerrilla movements. These statements were taken down in the 'Iracara Mountains, Sierra de Falcón'. One searches in vain for 'Marxist' formulas in them.

Douglas Bravo's Thesis

The FALN, therefore, are the product of the whole resistance movement of the people in the towns, in the hills, in the mountains, on the plains and in the barracks, so that one can say they rest basically on four supports: the rural guerrilla fighters or mountain guerrilla fighters who form the centre or axis of the whole Venezuelan armed movement; the urban guerrilla fighters we call UTC (Unidades Técnicas de Combate), who make up tactical sabotage units; the patriot-officers in the barracks; and the suburban guerrilla movement.

As a result, the FALN belong to no political party, no sect, no social class. They are the military wing of the National Liberation Front, and the latter, in the present stage of the struggle, comprises the association of revolutionary classes opposing North American imperialism and native oligarchy. This movement does not reflect any rigid doctrine, but relates to the broad ideal of Venezuelan liberation. In its present stage, the liberation of Venezuela is simply the continuation and ultimate assertion of the liberation struggle begun by Bolívar in 1810.

The FALN are the revolutionary military organisation of the Venezuelan people, having the following aims; to achieve

216

national independence, liberty and democracy for the nation; to preserve the national heritage, integrity and wealth; to set up a revolutionary, nationalist and popular government; to see that revolutionary laws are applied and to support the authorities created by the Revolution; to protect the interests of the people, its property and its institutions; to establish a sovereign, independent government that represents all progressive sections of the country and that prevents power and all the instruments of power from falling into the hands of the native oligarchy and North American imperialism.

Once such a government has been established, we shall be able to carry out a policy of economic independence, to industrialise the country, recover the national heritage, integrity and wealth from the hands of foreign powers and, specifically, from North American imperialism. This industrialisation will return the national riches, oil and iron, to the control of Venezuelans. It is a fact that, with the production of oil and iron, the other productive sectors, to be more exact, the agricultural sectors, have noticeably weakened.

We intend to dismantle the old feudal structure through agrarian reform. At present, 71·6 per cent of farmers work only 2 per cent of the land, while 1·5 per cent of the land and livestock owners occupy 78 per cent. Over 70 per cent of Venezuelan land is being exploited by a minority (the oil companies currently own 6 million hectares), while the great majority of the Venezuelan people owns barely 2·5 per cent of this land.

The working population of the Venezuelan *campo* consists of about 900,000 peasants. Approximately half a million of them work the land in plots of three hectares on the average, whereas 3000 big landowners own 17·43 million hectares.

Another part of our programme concerns foreign policy. These anti-patriotic governments that have stifled freedom inside the country, that continually abuse the people, follow a foreign policy of submission to North American imperialism. They have not displayed the least bit of Venezuelan patriotism, but have perpetually bowed to the United States and even sunk as low as to censure the liberation movements in other countries. For years the Venezuelan government has taken an anti-patriotic stand as regards the Algerian revolution; in the case of the Vietnam revolution, the Venezuelan government has openly supported the United States government; in the case of British Guyanan independence, the Venezuelan government has adopted a lame and contemptible attitude in the face of North American monopolies. Foreign policy has, in general, been entirely dictated by Washington.

All who have taken up arms in the countryside and in the towns, in the barracks, in the universities and in the colleges are naturally inspired by the idea of liberating the country.

We have risen in rebellion, as the only alternative to slavery and national affront was the path of national liberation, inevitably requiring the use of arms.

In the case of the patriots of 1810, three hundred years of Spanish domination, of submissiveness, of the draining away of national wealth, forced the Venezuelan patriots to take up arms, to choose the path of insurrection, the path of armed combat, to raise the men of the fields and the plains in the struggle for the liberation of the country. Those patriots, like ourselves today, found themselves at the crossroads, forced to make a hard choice: either to serve the Spaniards and submit to them, like slaves of a foreign power, or to throw themselves into the fight for liberty.

The patriots of 1810 and the patriots of this decade opted resolutely for the second course of action: to take up arms resolutely in the fight for liberty and national independence. To take up arms against the oppressor is the basic characteristic of any revolutionary, it is the basic characteristic of men who hope to bring about great changes.

To create a world where there are neither oppressed nor oppressors, a world where the peasants, workers, students and the people in general can share in material benefits and advantages, requires war. This is not because the revolutionaries have so decreed it, but because the reactionaries, the rich and those who are bolstered by North American imperialism force the people and the revolution armies to wage this war and induce the people to take up arms.

We are pacifists, but understand us well, we are not the kind of pacifists you find here, like those who oppose the development of the armed struggle. We are fighters who want a peace that is in a sense broader and more profound: as fighters for and lovers of peace, as men striving for a new world, we take up arms.

The revolutionary, patriotic struggle goes through several stages: the present stage, which one might call tactical, requiring the use of armed force and during which conditions are created for the great changes to take place; this leads naturally into the second stage, the stage of peace and tranquillity. But it must be quite obvious—and everyone must be made objectively aware of this—that the conditions in which the semicolonial and colonial peoples dominated by North American imperialism and by powerful oligarchies live, make it materially impossible to achieve these changes through electoral means, through peaceful means.

The Venezuelan revolution is part of a chain of national liberation movements which, throughout the world, are struggling to be rid of imperialist domination. To be more concrete, the Venezuelan revolution is an integral part of the movement for Latin American independence. It is impossible to remove any one Latin American national revolution from the context of the struggle of the peoples of Latin America against North American imperialism.

Our revolution is clearly continental in character, even though it has certain specific features of its own, and the path chosen is determined both by these specific features and by the general context of Latin American republics.

The Venezuelan revolution is a spearhead turned against North American imperialism. As it grows strong, as it develops, as it gets closer to victory, it marks the beginning of the liberation one after the other of the peoples of Latin America.

In Venezuela, the United States has vaster investments than anywhere else in Latin America. In effect, when Washington invests a dollar in Latin America, sixty-six cents end up in Venezuela.

The North American investments in Venezuela give the United States considerable military and political advantages. The wars waged by the North Americans in other countries of the world, their wars of depredation and domination, the mobilisation of their own war machine, of their own economy, depend, to a large extent, on the way they exploit our country. It is from here the iron and petrol come, classed in the present epoch as key products, as the strategic products of the modern world.

If the North Americans begin to suffer, to get dislodged from other countries, they will try their utmost to entrench themselves in Venezuela, so as to be able to continue extracting the minerals and natural wealth that enable them to keep their war machine functioning. That is the reason why the Venezuelan revolution, which is part of the continental revolution to be made by the peoples of America, is crucial to the unleashing of a gigantic movement of liberation building up in the other sister republics.

The Political Bureau of the Central Committee of the Communist Party of Venezuela's denunciation of Fidel Castro's position is dated March 15, 1967. The stakes are now down and the break, not only between the PCV and the PCC, but also between the PC of Venezuela and a communist faction led by Douglas Bravo, is complete.

In his winding-up speech at the first OLAS Conference, held in Havana in August 1967, Fidel Castro had the audacity to read the declaration 'that has become the *raison d'être* for a whole mafia, a real mafia of detractors and slanderers of the Cuban Revolution'.

The CP of Venezuela Denounces Fidel Castro[1]

Fidel Castro, General Secretary of the ruling Communist Party of Cuba and Prime Minister of the Socialist Government of Cuba, from his easy vantage point, has attacked the Communist Party of Venezuela, a clandestine party, hundreds of whose militants are in prison, dozens fallen in the mountains and streets of this country, subjected to a daily, merciless persecution and, at the very moment when Fidel Castro was speaking, suffering new losses.

The same man who finds an excuse for his verbal extravagances in the fact that Cuba is in the forefront of the anti-imperialist struggle, ought to have the elementary decency to weigh his words carefully when referring to the Communist Party which is fighting in the Latin American country where yankee imperialist intervention is the most concentrated, and fighting under the most difficult circumstances.

With the eyes of the world upon him, aware of his prestige, Fidel Castro still has not hesitated to abuse a Communist Party which, because of the repression, has scarcely been able to reply.

For that reason, Fidel Castro's action is base, opportunistic, treacherous and totally lacking in that sense of honour and valour that has always characterised the Cuban revolution.

Fidel Castro has passed judgement negatively on the assassination of Iribarren Borges, insisting on his right to formulate an opinion about it. However, with astonishing impudence, he actually denies this same right to the PCV. Fidel Castro, apparently, does not wish the Communist Party of Venezuela, present and in Venezuela, to formulate an opinion and give its verdict on a Venezuelan political event that has taken place on Venezuelan soil and that, consequently, affects the life of the PCV very closely. He, on the other hand, from his base in Cuba, is entitled to give his opinion.

In his eyes, when we speak we are playing into the government's hands, whereas when he does, his is the voice of an intangible oracle of revolution. This strange way of reasoning testifies to an arrogance and irresponsible self-complacency that is unworthy of a chief of state.

As regards the event itself, the PCV said precisely the same thing as Fidel Castro, neither more nor less. On the other hand, we claim that it is speeches like Fidel Castro's, slanders like those he hurled at our Party, his attempt to split it, and events like the assassination of Iribarren Borges that really play into the hands of the reactionaries and of imperialism.

The PCV insists on its right to work out its own political line without interference from anyone. The fact that Cuba has honourably followed an arduous revolutionary path provides an example and inspiration for us, but we have never been, nor shall we ever be, Cuban agents in Venezuela, any more than we are agents of any other communist party in the world. We are Venezuelan communists and we accept the tutelage of no one, however great his revolutionary merits may be.

If there should be any revolutionary group in Venezuela that submits of its own free will to the tutelage and protection of Fidel Castro, that is its own affair. The PCV never shall. If Fidel Castro does not like it, so much the worse for him. Now why is Fidel Castro taking this action against the PCV precisely at this moment? Because the PCV has already begun, in practice and not just ideologically, to rout the anti-party movement of Douglas Bravo; because the Party and Communist Youth movements have enjoyed great success politically and organisationally in the application of their policy; because the successful recent escape of comrades Pompeyo, Guillermo and Teodoro has filled all communist militants in the country with enthusiasm and renewed energy; and finally because the anarchistic, adventuristic policy of the anti-party group has demonstrably failed completely and has helped enormously in clarifying the problems under discussion.

This is precisely why Fidel Castro has thrown the whole weight of his prestige behind an attack on the PCV in a desparate bid to help the anarchistic and adventuristic group protected and sponsored by him, in order to bring about a split in the PCV.

However our policy and our action every day show how meaningless are those epithets of 'unsteady', 'faint-hearted' and 'opportunistic', applied by Fidel Castro to the PCV leadership. And this is being proved here, in Venezuela, despite the outrageous tricks that Fidel Castro has played and will, no doubt, continue to play on us.

But let it be quite clear to him and to the whole PCV that we are not even discussing the sovereignty of the PCV.

Fidel Castro has called the PCV leadership cowardly in a further demonstration of his irritating tendency to regard himself as having a monopoly of valour and courage. We Venezuelan communists do not give way to that puerile exhibitionism that consists in proclaiming from the housetops one's qualities in this domain. But when Fidel Castro was still only a child, Gustavo Machado, that great patriarch of Venezuelan communism, was already attacking Curaçao and mounting an armed invasion of Venezuela. And from that moment the story of the PCV, which is political, is also the story of the men who resisted the terror of Gómez and Pérez Jiménez and who led the insurrection of January 23, 1958; it was thanks to their efforts that Fidel Castro received a plane-load of weapons when he was still in the Sierra Maestra; and if there is one thing they have not grudged these last eight years, it has been the sacrifice of their lives.

Here, Fidel Castro has the best demonstration of the character of the PCV. Accustomed to believing in his power as Grand Sachem of the revolution, he thought, no doubt, that his speech would overwhelm and confuse us. He was completely mistaken. And now Fidel Castro will see why yankee imperialism and its agents put so much effort into trying to liquidate the Communist Party of Venezuela.

In his speech, Fidel Castro tries once again to play the part of a kind of arbiter of the revolutionary destiny of Latin America and of a super-revolutionary who, in our place, would already have brought about the revolution.

We have already made one reference to the character of the Cuban struggle and the place where Fidel Castro would still be if it had occurred to him to unfurl the red flag in the Sierra Maestra. For the moment, we will limit ourselves to rejecting the rôle of 'daddy' of the revolutionaries that Fidel Castro has taken on himself.

We categorically reject his claim to be the one who alone decides what is and what is not revolutionary in Latin America. In Venezuela this question is a matter between the PCV and its people, and no one else. But we should like just to ask this Fidel Castro, supreme dispenser of revolutionary titles, who wonders what North Vietnam would say if Cuba traded with South Vietnam, if he ever gives a thought to what the Spanish people is saying about his trade with Franco and the Spanish oligarchy, or what the black people of Zimbabwe, of Rhodesia, and the patriots of Aden might be saying of his trade with imperialist England. Or does Fidel Castro regard as opportunism in others what in his case is bathed in the lustral waters of self-complacency?

This controversy is distasteful, giving great joy to the enemy, but clearly it can no longer be put off. Fidel Castro's speech has driven us beyond the limits of endurance. So be it. We shall argue it out. And just as we appeal to Simon Bolívar and the Fathers of our Land in our anti-imperialist struggle, so we assure Fidel Castro that the descendants of Simon Bolívar and Ezéquiel Zamora will tolerate from no one the kind of insolent and provocative language that he used in his speech of March 13.

The Venezuelan believes himself no better and no worse than anyone else; but if there is one thing that rouses his proud fighting spirit, it is abuse.

And this time Fidel Castro will begin to realise that he has come up against something different, that he has come up against Venezuelan communists.

We do not deny that such actions as Fidel Castro's make difficulties for us, but we do not despair. We have the calm conviction of the one who knows that right is on his side, and we are filled with revolutionary zeal to defend it.

March 15, 1967, the Political Bureau of the Central Committee of the Communist Party of Venezuela: Pompeyo Márquez, Guillermo García Ponce, Alonso Ojeda Olaechea, Pedro Ortega Díaz, Eduardo Gallegos Mancera, Teodoro Petkoff, Germán Lairet.

Ernesto Che Guevara's little book *La Guerra de Guerrillas*, has been circulating for a number of years, in several languages. Nevertheless, we are reprinting two passages that seem to us essential to an understanding of the counter-state thesis held by the late guerrilla leader.

Two Passages from Guevara's 'Guerrilla Warfare'

Beginning, Development and End of a Guerrilla War

We have now abundantly defined the nature of guerrilla warfare. Let us next describe the ideal development of such a war from its beginning as a rising by a single nucleus on favourable ground.

In other words, we are going to theorise once more on the basis of the Cuban experience. At the outset there is a more or less homogeneous group, with some arms, that devotes itself almost exclusively to hiding in the wildest and most inaccessible places, making little contact with the peasants. It strikes a fortunate blow and its fame grows. A few peasants, dispossessed of their land or engaged in a struggle to conserve it, and young idealists of other classes join the nucleus; it acquires greater audacity and starts to operate in inhabited places, making more contact with the people of the zone; it repeats attacks, always fleeing after making them; suddenly it engages in combat with some column or other and destroys its vanguard. Men continue to join it; it has increased in number, but its organisation remains exactly the same; its caution diminishes, and it ventures into more populous zones.

Later it sets up temporary camps for several days; it abandons these upon receiving news of the approach of the enemy army, or upon suffering bombardments, or simply upon becoming suspicious that such risks have arisen. The numbers in the guerrilla band increase as work among the masses operates to make of each peasant an enthusiast for the war of liberation. Finally, an inaccessible place is chosen, a settled life is initiated, and the first small industries begin to be established: a shoe factory, a cigar and cigarette factory, a clothing factory, an arms factory, bakery, hospitals, possibly a radio transmitter, a printing press, etc.

The guerrilla band now has an organisation, a new structure. It is the head of a large movement with all the characteristics of a small government. A court is established for the administration of justice, possibly laws are promulgated and the work of indoctrination of the peasant masses continues, extended also to workers if there are any near, to draw them to the cause. An enemy action is launched and defeated; the number of rifles increases; with these the number of men fighting with the guerrilla band increases. A moment arrives when its radius of action will not have increased in the same proportion as its personnel; at that moment a force of appropriate size is separated, a column or a platoon, perhaps, and this goes to another place of combat.

The work of this second group will begin with somewhat different characteristics because of the experience that it brings and because of the influence of the troops of liberation on the war zone. The original nucleus also continues to grow; it has now received substantial support in food, sometimes in guns, from various places; men continue to arrive; the administration of government, with the promulgation of laws, continues; schools are established, permitting the indoctrination and training of recruits. The leaders learn steadily as the war develops, and their capacity of command grows under the added responsibilities of the qualitative and quantitative increases in their forces.

If there are distant territories, a group departs for them at a certain moment, in order to confirm the advances that have been made and to continue the cycle.

But there will also exist an enemy territory, unfavourable for guerrilla warfare. There small groups begin to penetrate, assaulting the roads, destroying bridges, planting mines, sowing disquiet. With the ups and downs characteristic of warfare the movement continues to grow; by this time the extensive work among the masses makes easy movement of the forces possible in unfavourable territory and so opens the final stage, which is suburban guerrilla warfare.

Sabotage increases considerably in the whole zone. Life is paralysed; the zone is conquered. The guerrillas then go into other zones, where they fight with the enemy army along defined fronts; by now heavy arms have been captured, perhaps even some tanks; the fight is more equal. The enemy falls when the process of partial victories becomes transformed into final victories, that is to say, when the enemy is brought to accept battle in conditions imposed by the guerrilla band; there he is annihilated and his surrender compelled.

This is a sketch that describes what occurred in the different stages of the Cuban war of liberation; but it has a content approximating the universal. Nevertheless, it will not always be possible to count on the degree of intimacy with the people, the conditions, and the leadership that existed in our war. It is unnecessary to say that Fidel Castro possesses the high qualities of a fighter and statesman: our path, our struggle, and our triumph we owed to his vision. We cannot say that without him the victory of the people would not have been achieved; but that victory would certainly have cost much more and would have been less complete. . . .

Civil Organisation

In view of the importance of relations with the peasants, it is necessary to create organisations that make regulations for them, organisations that exist not only within the liberated area, but also have connections in the adjacent areas. Precisely through these connections it is possible to penetrate a zone for a future enlargement of the guerrilla front. The peasants will sow the seed with oral and written propaganda, with accounts of life in the other zone, of the laws that have already been issued for the protection of the small peasant, of the spirit of sacrifice of the rebel army; in a word, they are creating the necessary atmosphere for helping the rebel troops.

The peasant organisations should also have connections of some type that will permit the channelling and sale of crops by the rebel army agencies in enemy territory through intermediaries more or less benevolent, more or less friendly to the peasant class. Joined with a devotion to the cause which brings the merchant to defy dangers in such cases, there also exists the devotion to money that leads him to take advantage of the opportunity to gain profits.

We have already spoken, in connection with supply problems, of the importance of the department of road construction. When the guerrilla band has achieved a certain level of development, it no longer wanders about through diverse regions without an encampment; it has centres that are more or less fixed. Routes should be established varying from small paths permitting the passage of a mule to good roads for trucks. In all this, the capacity of the organisation of the rebel army must be kept in mind, as well as the offensive capacity of the enemy, who may destroy these constructions and even make use of roads built by his opponent to reach the encampments more easily. The fundamental rule should be that roads are for assisting supply in places where any other solution would be impossible; they should not be constructed except in circumstances where there is a virtual certainty that the position can be maintained against an attack by the adversary. Another exception would be roads built without great risk to facilitate communication between points that are not of vital importance.

Furthermore, other means of communication may be established. One of these that is extremely important is the telephone. This can be strung in the forest with the convenience that arises from using trees for posts. There is the advantage that they are not visible to the enemy from above. The telephone also presupposes a zone that the enemy cannot penetrate.

The council—or central department of justice, revolutionary laws, and administration—is one of the vital features of a guerrilla army fully constituted and with territory of its own. The council should be under the charge of an individual who knows the laws of the country; if he understands the necessities of the zone from a juridical point of view, this is better yet; he can proceed to prepare a series of decrees and regulations that help the peasant to normalise and institutionalise his life within the rebel zone.

For example, during our experience in the Cuban war we issued a penal code, a civil code, rules for supplying the peasantry and rules of the agrarian reform. Subsequently, the laws fixing qualifications of candidates in the elections that were to be held later throughout the country were established; also the Agrarian Reform Law of the Sierra Maestra. The council is likewise in charge of accounting operations for the guerrilla column or columns; it is responsible for handling money problems and at times intervenes directly in supply.

All these recommendations are flexible; they are based upon an experience in a certain place and are conditioned by its geography and history; they will be modified in different geographical, historical, and social situations.

In addition to the council, it is necessary to keep the general health of the zone in mind. This can be done by means of central military hospitals that should give the most complete assistance possible to the whole peasantry. Whether adequate medical treatment can be given will depend upon the stage reached by the revolution. Civil hospitals and civil health administration are united directly with the guerrilla army, and their functions are performed by officers and men of the army, who have the dual function of caring for the people and orienting them toward better health. The big problems among people in these conditions are rooted in their total ignorance of elementary principles of hygiene. This aggravates their already precarious situation.

The collection of taxes, as I have already said, is also a function of the general council.

Warehouses are very important. As soon as a place is taken that is to serve as a base for the guerrilla band, warehouses should be established in the most orderly fashion possible. These will serve to assure a minimum care of merchandise and, most important, will provide the control needed for equalising distribution and keeping it equitable at later times.

Functions are different on the external front both in quantity and in quality. For example, propaganda should be of a national, orienting type, explaining the victories obtained by the guerrilla band, calling workers and peasants to effective mass fights, and giving news, if there is any, of victories obtained on this front itself. Solicitation of funds is completely secret; it ought to be carried out with the greatest care possible, isolating small collectors in the chain completely from the treasurer of the organisation.

This organisation should be distributed in zones that complement each other in order to form a totality, zones that may be provinces, states, cities, villages, depending on the magnitude of the movement. In each of them there must be a finance commission that takes charge of the disposal of funds collected. It is possible to collect money by selling bonds or through direct donations. When the development of the struggle is more advanced taxes may be collected; when industries come to recognise the great force that the insurrectional army possesses, they will consent to pay. Supply procurement should be fitted to the necessities of the guerrilla bands; it will be organised in the form of a chain of merchandise in such a way that the more common articles are procured in nearby places, and the things that are really scarce or impossible to procure locally, in larger centres. The effort always is to keep the chain as limited as possible, known to the smallest number of men; it can thus perform its mission for a longer time.

Che Guevara's Farewell Letter to his Parents[1]

Dear Folks,

Once again I feel between my heels the ribs of Rosinante; once more I hit the road with my shield upon my arm.

Almost ten years ago today, I wrote you another letter of farewell. As I remember, I lamented at not being a better soldier and a better doctor. The latter no longer interests me; I'm not such a bad soldier.

Nothing has changed in essence, except that I am much more aware, my Marxism has taken root and become purified. I believe in the armed struggle as the only solution for those peoples who fight to free themselves, and I am consistent with my beliefs. Many will call me an adventurer—and that I am, only, one of a different sort—one of those who risks his skin to prove his platitudes.

It is possible that this may be the finish. I don't seek it, but it's within the logical realm of probabilities. If it should be so, I send you a last embrace.

I have loved you very much, only I haven't known how to express my fondness. I am extremely rigid in my actions, and I think that sometimes you didn't understand me. It hasn't been easy to understand me. Nevertheless, please just take me at my word today.

Now, a will which I have polished with delight is going to sustain some shaky legs and some weary lungs. I will do it.

Give a thought once in a while to this little soldier-of-fortune of the twentieth century. A kiss to Celia, to Roberto, Juan Martín and Pototín, to Beatriz, to everybody.

An *abrazo* for you from your obstinate and prodigal son.

Ernesto

Notes and References

PART I: CHEMISTRY AND ALCHEMY

1 Proclamations and Appeals

1. This document appeared in the Colombian newspapers, it was frequently reprinted and is translated here from the monthly *Cristianismo y Revolución*, Buenos Aires, September, 1966.
2. Jorge Eliécer Gaitán, a liberal leader whose assassination in 1948 unleashed a wave of popular violence in Bogotá, which has gone down in Colombian history under the name of *bogotazo*.
3. *Caudillismo*, a political movement linked to the person of a leader.
4. The Spanish *Sbires* refers pejoratively to mercenaries and the guardians of the official system.

2 Theoretical Difficulties

1. Comandante Ernesto Che Guevara: 'Guerra de Guerrillas, un método' published in *Cuba Socialista*, No. 25, Havana, September, 1963, and reissued as a pamphlet by Ediciones de la Liberación, Buenos Aires 1964.
2. Roberto Fernández Retamar, in the preface to the Cuban edition of *Revolución en la Revolución*, January, 1967, published in the *Cuadernos de la revista Casa de las Américas*, writes: 'After Cuba, Debray travelled in several countries of the continent, making close contact with revolutionaries, on some occasions sharing the life of the *guerrilleros*'. And further on: 'Of course Debray has not written a history of that process (the Cuban Revolution) but he has drawn fundamental military political conclusions from it, contrasting them with the personal experiences, the successes and mistakes of other guerrilla movements which he knew directly, or about which he was able to obtain fresh and reliable information'.
3. Among the books that were a source of military inspiration for Fidel Castro, Régis Debray quotes, for example, Hemingway's *For Whom the Bell Tolls*.

4. The extracts from *Revolution in the Revolution* are translated from the Spanish text published in Havana.
5. *The Long March;* 'El Castrismo: la larga marcha de América latina'. Published in French by *Les Temps Modernes*, translated many times in Latin America, especially in Chile.
6. The reference, 'A man on his own ...', is to the valley of La Convención, in the province of Cuzco.
7. 'Fidel Castro parle...', *Cahiers Libres*, Nos. 24–5, ed. François Maspero, Paris 1961.
8. 'La Revolución sin ideología', *Política*, Caracas, May, 1967.
9. Published in *Autocrítica de la Revolución Cubana*, Montevideo, 1962.
10. 'Organizaciones Revolucionarias Integradas': the name given to the attempt at a single organisation to bring together militants of the July 26 Movement and of the Cuban Communist Party.

3 Variations in the Cuban Government's Position

1. 'Algunos problemas de la unidad de acción en el movimiento revolucionario', in *Teoría y Práctica*, No. 38, Havana, July, 1967.
2. The excerpts are from the text published by *Granma*, Fr. ed., August 20, 1967.

4 Reservations of the Extreme Left

1. *Ruedo Ibérico*, No. 6, Paris, May, 1967.
2. *Vanguardia Revolucionaria*, an extreme left-wing publication, produced in Lima.
3. The initials, PIP and GC are those of the various Peruvian political police forces.

5 The USSR and China in Latin America

1. Carl Schmitt, *Theorie des Partisanen*, Duncker and Humblot, Berlin, 1965.
2. Carlos Marighella, *A crise brasileira*, 1966. The publisher and place of publication are not known. Since then Marighella has become a hard-liner and the Brazilian authorities regard him as one of the leaders of subversion.
3. *Entreguista* is a cheapjack who surrenders the national wealth to the foreigner, and one who has no national feeling.
4. Hart's speech at a plenary session. This extract is from the French edition of *Granma* (organ of the Cuban PC) August 13, 1967.
5. There is an excellent bibliography on the arguments of both sides in Alain Joxe's work, published in duplicated form by the Parisian *Centre d'Etudes de Politique Internationale*, and, in Spanish in his small book: *El conflicto chino-soviético en América Latina*, Arca, Montevideo, 1967.

Notes and References

Another useful work, issued by the Center of International Studies of the Massachusetts Institute of Technology, is by Ernst Halperin, *The Sino-Cuban and the Chilean Communist Road to Power*, February, 1963.
6. 'The Bolivian guerrilla movement is not dead', *Tri-continental*, suplemento especial, July, 1968.

6 Origins of the Guerrilla Fighters

1. Orlando Albornoz, *Aportes*, No. 5, Paris, July, 1967.
2. Humberto Cuenca, *Revolutionary University and Army*, Caracas, 1964.
3. Humberto Cuenca, *University and Revolution*, Buenos Aires, 1962.
4. Text of an interview recorded by Mario Menéndez Rodríguez, Mexican journalist, attached to the magazine *Sucesos*, and reissued by *Punto Final*, Santiago de Chile second half of July, 1967.
5. When, in May 1962, Alejandro Gil Bustillos was arrested in Caracas after an exchange of fire with a police patrol, he behaved exactly as a conspirator should. He knew nothing, except that he obeyed the orders of a cell leader who had been killed at his side, and that he slept in a truck in the university precincts. He knew no one. He had taken part in no attack. He acknowledged only one item concerning himself, and that went back to 1952. The interrogation records his plea: 'In 1952, I took part in an armed raid on a tax office, together with Alfredo Alvarado, the "king of the Joropo" and Vicente Garrido. It brought us 2000 bolivares, which we shared out equally. For this crime, I was sentenced to two years solitary confinement with hard labour.'

7 Military Methods

1. Alberto Bayo, *Mi aporte a la Revolucíon cubana*.
2. Alberto Bayo, *op. cit.*
3. Alberto Bayo, *150 preguntas a un guerillero*, 1960. Place of publication not indicated, probably Havana.
4. *Relatos de la guerra revolucionaria*, Editora Nueve 64, Buenos Aires 1965.
5. Ernesto Guevara's talk to *Nuestro Tiempo*, January 27, 1959.
6. Ernesto Guevara, *La guerra de guerrillas: un método*, Education Department of MINFAR (Ministry of the Armed Forces), Cuba.
7. Camilo Cienfuegos, Report of the Commander, Fidel Castro, on the march of the Antonio Maceo column from Oriente province to Las Villas province.
8. Camilo Cienfuegos, *op. cit.*
9. Ernesto Guevara, *op. cit.*
10. Ernesto Guevara, *op. cit.*

8 Theories and Techniques of Counter-Guerrilla Warfare

1. Mao Tse-tung, *Guerrilla warfare*, Manuales Huemul, Buenos Aires 1966.

Guerrillas in Latin America

2. James Eliot Gross, *Luta de Guerrillas, Natureza e Política*, ed. GRD, Rio de Janeiro 1965.
3. Peruvian Ministry of War, *Las guerrillas en el Perú y su represión*, 1966, out of print.
4. Robert P. Case in *Aportes*, No. 6, October, 1967.

9 Guerrillas within the Political System

1. The term 'gorilla' was used by the opposition to refer to partisans of government by military strong-men. (Translator's note.)
2. *El Movimento Izquierda Revolucionaria y la Realidad Venezolana*, Caracas and Montevideo, January, 1961.
3. Régis Debray, *La gran marcha de América Latina*.
4. 'Le Président Belaúnde à mi-course', Note and Documentary Studies, *La Documentation Française*, No. 3383, April, 1967.
5. The *altiplano* is the high inland plateau of the Andean countries. (Translator's note.)
6. Paz Estenssoro, *Il Giorno*, Milan, September 14, 1967.
7. Paz Estenssoro, *Marcha*, Montevideo, August 26, 1967.
8. Orlando Fals Borda, *La Subversión en Colombia, El Cambio social en la historia*, ed. Tercer Mundo, Bogotá 1967.

PART II: THE NATIONAL SITUATIONS

10 Venezuela. The Long Way Back to Legality

1. Letter from a group leader, PCV militant, in the eastern zone, August 19, 1965.

11 Argentina. A Trial Run

1. 'The CIA intervenes in Argentina', *Pólitica Internacional*, Buenos Aires, July, 1967.
2. John William Cooke in 'Definiciones', *Cristianismo y Revolución*, Buenos Aires, October, 1966.

12 Colombia. Putting Violence to Some Use

1. *La Violencia en Colombia*, Vol. II, ed. Tercer Mundo, Bogotá 1964.
2. The meaning of *vereda* is defined in another article: 'What is meant by *vereda* or vicinity is the portion of the population that gets its stocks of meat from the same slaughter-house.'
3. The toll of the anti-guerrilla struggle between January 1, 1966 and March 31, 1967 is as follows: 154 members of the armed forces, 29 guerrilla fighters, 384 people belonging neither to the guerrillas nor

236

the forces of repression, killed; 541 people arrested. (Figures supplied by government authorities.)

13 Guatemala. Between Theory and Maquis

1. The latest report on César Montes' detachment, published in *Marcha*, Montevideo, September 2, 1967, and which was prepared by the journalist Eduardo Galeano, sums up the situation as follows: 'The large-scale military campaign to wipe out the guerrillas has not succeeded. That the guerrilla fighters should have lost geographical control of certain zones does not matter provided they retain the absolute sympathy of the local inhabitants. Even though it has been expelled from its habitual territories, the guerrilla force is unbroken, it has warded off the blow. Mobility is becoming essential.'

14 Bolivia. The Army Confounded

1. *The Complete Diaries of Che Guevara and other Captured Documents*, Stein and Day, New York 1968, p. 323.

15 Brazil. The Army in Power

1. General Golbery do Couto e Silva, *Planejamento Estratégico*, Biblioteca do Exército Editora, Rio de Janeiro 1955. Also by the same author, *Geopolítica do Brasil*, Rio de Janeiro 1967.

17 Peru. Suicidal Insurrection

1. *Illarec Ch'aska* means 'morning star'.
2. The Túpac Amaru group were named after the last of the Inca line who was executed by the Spanish viceroy in 1571 and also after the leader of the great Indian Rebellion of 1780.
3. The Atahualpa group was named after the last Inca emperor.
4. The César Vallejo group was named after the great leftist poet of modern Peru.
5. The Manco Inca group was named after an Inca.
6. The Pachacútec group was named after an Inca.
7. *Barriadas* are urban slums.

PART III: DOCUMENTS

'War Diary' of the EGP

1. The Corrento, in Spanish, refers to the city of Corrientes in Argentina. (Translator's note.)
2. The Cordovan, in Spanish, refers to the city of Córdoba in Argentina. (Translator's note.)

3. The abbreviation FAL probably refers to the Argentine Liberation Front.
4. A *criollo* is an Argentine of pure European extraction. (Translator's note.)
5. *Colla* is Argentine slang for an Aymará-speaking Indian. (Translator's note.)
6. The 'Trampolín' operation: a gendarme report states on this subject: 'Between November 1963 and February 1964, a main base is established on the banks of the Playa Ancha River, from where operation "Trampolín", provision of war material and food from Bolivia, will be launched.'

The Attack on the Train

1. The Attack on the Train: this extract was published in *Punto Final*, supplement, No. 34, Santiago de Chile, August, 1967.

The CP of Venezuela Denounces Fidel Castro

1. The CP of Venezuela Denounces Fidel Castro: this extract was published in *Granma*, Fr. ed., August 20, 1967.

Che Guevara's Farewell Letter to his Parents

1. Che Guevara's farewell letter: this was reproduced together with a photocopy of the original letter in *Siete Dias*, Argentina, May 23, 1967. The letter was written in mid-1965 and is translated here by Lee Lockwood.

Index

Index

(1966), 132; national petroleum company (YPF), 134; political groups, 95–96; rebellion of miners, 34, 56, 95–8, 130, 132–3; Revolutionary Workers' Party (POR), 50; Trade Union Federation, 130; trade with USA, 131
Borges, Iribarren, 222
Bourricaud, François, 94
Boyaca region (Colombia), 120
Bravo, Douglas, 90–1, 112–14, 209–11, 222; expelled from PCV, 210, 216; thesis of, 216–20
Brazil, 40, 45, 58, 63, 71, 88, 93, 134; army in power, 140–2; Communist Party, 142; military *coup d'état*, 140–1; 'National Policy', 140; role of guerrillas in, 61, 80
Brizzola, Lionel, 142
Bucaramanga (Colombia), 204
Buenos Aires, 115, 117, 128, 137, 145; Economic Council meets at, 41; university, 70
Bustamante camp, 176–7
Bustos, Carlos Alberto, 136

Caldas region (Colombia), 120
Caldera, Rafael, 105
Camagüey province (Cuba), 77
Camiri, 135
Campas Indians, 176–81
Carare river, 203–4
Cárdenas, Juan, 193
Carrillo Cazorla, Miguel, 185
Carrillo Rocha, Major Gonzalo, 185
Carupano, rebellion at, 71, 107
Castillo, Ismael, 176
Castro, Fidel, 38, 40–3, 53–4, 76, 114, 209, 213–14, 228; attitude to China, 44–5, 51–2; attitude to Soviet Union, 44–5, 48, 51; breaks with Betancourt, 105; confirms Guevara's death, 138–9; denounced by PCV, 221–5; speaks on: Cuban CP, at first OLAS conference, 45–8; on democracy (in New York), 41; on 'organising the party', 43; on public loans to Cuba, 41–2; speech at Tricontinental Conference (1966), 51
'Castroite theory', 73

Catavi, 15
Cauca region (Colombia), 120
Caudillismo, 12
Cauto region (Cuba), 77
Cerdas, 15
Cerro de Pasco (Peru), 173, 175
Céspedes, Carlos Manuel de, President of Cuba, 74
Chaco war, 143
Chile, 34, 51, 138, 151–2; Communist Party, 145; role of carabinieri, 40
Chilifruta heliport, 173, 175
China, 44, 51, 55; policy and position in Latin America, 57–8, 62–6, 96, 139, 142
Christian Democratic Movement, *see* COPEI
Cienfuegos, Camilo, 77–8
Clausewitz: *Vom Kriege*, 84
Coccioli, Carlo, 97
Cochamba, 131, 134
Colombia, 23, 38, 52, 80, 118–25; Church in, 123; Communist Party (PCC), 120, 124–5; guerrilla propaganda in, 11–13, 27–8; laws and regulations, 121–2; Liberals and Conservatives, breach between, 118–20; National Liberation Army, *see* ELN; regions and armed groups, 120–1; Soviet support for, 44; train attack (1967), 125, 203–8; United Front movement, 12–13, 124; violence and chaos in, 118–21
Colorado Party (Paraguay), 143
Colorado river, 167, 169–70
'Colorados', 49
Communist parties in Latin America, 59–61, 63, 66, 70, 138–9; Declaration expelling Douglas Bravo, 209–15 (*see also under each country*)
Convención, 52, 55, 148, 182
Cooke, John William, 117
COPEI (Social Christian Party, Venezuela), 90–2, 105
Córdoba, 115–16, 168–9
Cordova Claure, Ted, 97
Costa e Silva, President of Brazil, 142
Costa Rica, Liberación Nacional, 49
Creydt, Oscar, 144–5

Index

on, 50–3, 56; policy in Venezuela, 110–14; put down by army in Peru, 171–89; techniques of, 73–80; trial and execution by the group, 115, 164, 170

Guerrilla Warfare (Guevara's manual), 53–4, 76–9, 226–31

Guerrilla Warfare (Mao Tse-tung's *Yu Chi Chan*), 81

Guevara, Ernesto Che, 4, 7, 45, 66, 113, 133; death of, 42, 137–9; *Diaries* and other writings, 29–36, 42; farewell letter to his parents, 232; popularity of, 152–3; reported to be in Bolivia, 136–7; theory of guerrilla warfare, 50–1, 76–9, 151, 153, 226–31; writes on Bolivia, 34; on civil organisation under guerrillas, 228–31; on contributions of Cuban revolution, 29, 42; on first period or war, 75–6, 90; on peasantry, 35, 228–9; on role of force, 30–3

Guevara, Moisés, 66

Gutiérrez, Don, 163

Guyana, 218

Guzmán Campos, Germán, 120

Hart, Armando, 62

Havana, 41–2, 48, 51, 138–9; OLAS Conference, *q.v.*; Tricontinental Conference, 44

Havana Declaration, Second, 29–30

Heraud, Javier, 53, 185–8

Hermés, Captain, 116; Diary of, 115, 157–70

Herrera Mendoza, Florian, 180, 182

House of the Rebels, 159

Hsinhua news agency, 63

Huancabamba, 187–8

Huancayo, 173, 177, 181

Huanta province, 177

Huila region, 120

Humanité, L', 45

Illarec Ch'aska, camp at, 146

Illesco river, 160

Illía, President, 159

Indians (South American), 84–5, 93, 126–9, 148, 164–5 (*see also* Campas Indians)

Inter-American Defence Junta, 88

International Petroleum Co., 25–6

International Police Academy (Washington), 86

Intihallamuy camp, 173–5

Iquitos (Peru), 171

Iracara Manifesto, 90, 211, 216

Irulia river, 164

Isauro, *alias* Lister, Yon, 121

Jauja (Peru), 52, 54, 171, 173

Juan magazine, 137

Jujuy province (Argentina), 115

July 26 Movement, 33, 39, 42, 73–4

Khrushchev, Nikita, 104

Korean war, 131

Kubantia massacre, 176–8

Kuello Cueta, Jorge, 135

La Boca (Peru), 177–8

La Coronilla, 14

La Mar-Vilcabamba, 185–7

La Paz, 15, 131–2, 134, 136

Lara, Guillermo, 50

Lara Parada, Ricardo, 204–6

Lares (Peru), 52, 54

Larrazabal, Admiral Wolfgang, 105

La Toma, 115

Laws of the Plain, 121–2

Lechín, Juan, 34, 130

Lenin, 5, 33, 39, 62, 84, 148

León, Ricardo, 187

Leoni, President of Venezuela, 108, 111

Le Tourneau Co., 26

Levi Ruffinelli, Dr Carlos, 143

Leviral group, 143

Lima, 70, 97, 148, 173

Linares, Angel, 192–3

Lister, *see* Isauro

Lleras, Camargo, 120

Lobatón, Guillermo, 17, 53, 66, 179–80, 182

Long March, The, 37, 39, 67

López, Arturo, 145

Lunar Márquez, Gregorio, 112

Machado, Gustavo, 74, 223

Manchurucuto, 113

Index

244

Index